THE SLAYING OF THE DRAGON WITHIN

A Question of Educational/Psychological Diseases of School Children

JOEL MACHT, Ph. D.
University of Denver

JEM Publishing Company
Littleton, Colorado 80161

The Great Tragedy of Science . . . .
The slaying of a beautiful hypothesis
By an ugly fact . . . .

-Thomas Henry Huxley [*1825-1895*]

There are, in Effect, Two Things,
to know and to believe one knows;
To Know is Science,
To Believe One Knows is Ignorance . . . .

-Hippocrates [*c460-360 B.C.*]
The Law

Library of Congress Cataloging in Publication Data:

Macht, Joel, 1938-
The Slaying of the Dragon Within

Bibliography: p.
1. Special Education 2. Children—Education
3. Child Psychology 4. Philosophy of Education

ISBN 0-938030-00-0

Printed in the United States of America

10 9 8 7 6 5 4 3 2 1

Dedication

To: David Gottesfeld . . .

Who, throughout his young life, with the unending support and love from his mom and dad, and countless others whom he touched, faced the Damn Dragons, looked them square in the eye, fought them . . . and won!

Carrie and Roy Fronczyk . . .

Who experienced the most difficult Dragons of all, and accomplished what few people in the world would consider possible.

Randy, Jobi, Kim, and David . . .

Who will never be touched by the irrefutable ones.

Other Books by the Author

Teaching Our Children
(A Book for Parents)

Teacher/Teachim: The toughest game in town
(A Book for Teachers)

Table of Contents

PART ONE: THE CHILD

Etiology: The Elusive Ghost 3
For the Children: An Alternative 6
The Acceptance of Differences and the Question of Expectations 12
The Meaning of Differences
Historical Precedent
The Blue Flag
Perspective
Educational and Psychological Diseases: Their Prevalence 23
Facts
Problems from Within, Problems from Without: A First Look
The Suspicious Signal: Behavior The Critical Question: "Why?" 30
Behavior: The Signal
"Why?" The Critical Question
The Adjective Versus the Noun
Circular
Safe and Irrefutable
Sick
The Accountable "Why?"

PART TWO: THE DRAGONS

Out From the Darkness 39
Circa: 102,000 B.C.
Circa: 5,000 B.C.
Circa: 20th Century A.D.
Dragons - The Metaphor 65
Birth of the Dragons
The Irrefutable Dragon — The Suspicious One
First: The Behavior Column
Second: The "Why?" Column
Third: The Treatment Column
Fourth: The Outcome and Conclusion Columns
M.I.A.H.I. + A.A. = B.H.D.

Medicine's Germs: The Precursors to the Irrefutable Dragons of Psychology and Education 83
Early Medicine's Demons, Devils, and Dung
The Microscope
The "Germ" Theory of Physical Illness
Accurate Prediction of the Underlying "Germ"
Psychology's "Germs": The Case of the Wandering Uterus 94
Some Early Dragons and Their Treatment
New Differences But Same Logic
The New Dragons — The Breed that Lives Within Us All
The Balloon
A Few Explorers and Their Unique Discoveries
Education's Dysentery: Dyslexia, Dysgraphia, Dyscalculia 126
The End of Conformance, The Death of Silence
Educational Diseases of School Children
Exceptionality
The Answers for the Difference
The List
The Assignment
My Students' Reaction
A Closer Look
Learning Disabilities
Emotional Disturbance

PART THREE: ALTERNATIVES
The Complexity of Causes 157
The Alternative Explanations
The Educational Environment: Another Choice
Flow Chart Overview
Step One: The Individual Child
Genetic Predispositions
Physiological Parameters
Interests and Values
Experience
Step Two: The Individual Teacher
Step Three: The "Inner-Person"
Step Four: End Product
Step Five: Evaluation
Step Six: The "OK" Category
Step Six-B: The Deviation Category

Step Seven: "Why?"
Step Eight-A & Eight-B: The Child, The Teacher
Step Nine-A & Nine-B: Treatment

The Method: The Tool for the Non-Categorical Approach 183

Programming for Differences
Partnership for Success
Goals
Present Performance and Developmental Levels
Academic PPL'S
Language PPL'S
Interest/Values PPL'S
Sequential Learning
Trials to Success

The Pin The Tail On the Donkey Game 193

The Absence of Behavior and the Question "Why?"

THE CHILD

Etiology: the Elusive Ghost

"I just don't understand," Mother said, bewildered. Her face flushed. There were no tears for the disbelief prevented her emotions from having their full impact. The tears, however, would come later. "We never gave any thought to the possibility that a problem existed. Should we have been able to tell . . . to see a sign . . . a clue?" She asked. The authority did not respond. Best to keep quiet at a time like this. "If we had only known . . . ." The Mother's voice trailed off. She was beginning to accept the reality the authority was presenting. The first tear swelled. It rested tentatively until her closing eye sent it spilling down her cheek. The rapid stroke that brushed it away reflected the anger she felt for not recognizing earlier that something was wrong with her child. For a moment, thoughts of "problem," "something wrong," "handicapped," "special child," raced through her mind. She remembered her neighbor's child. The one in the wheel chair. The one who would never walk. She remembered how often she had requested that her own children be nice to him, talk to him, play with him. "But he can't play," her son had responded. "He can't do anything," her child had said. It was a child's evaluation, she had told herself.

For the first time in years, her thoughts reminded her of the nine-year-old who had lived down the block. The nine-year-old with the long, flowing blonde hair. The one who looked so normal. Dressed so normal. The one who would come to the house, ring the doorbell, and say "Hi" when the door would open, but say nothing else. The one who played only with the two and three-year-olds. The one who found herself alone most of the time. The one who went to some special school, on a special bus, with the other special children. Her mind, that now seemed to be operating independently of her body, reminded her of the private relief she had felt when the family, and the nine-year-old, had moved away. Suddenly, a new emotion overwhelmed her, and her tears flowed freely.

She fought to bring herself from the past and back to the present. There were things she had to find out. Her voice wavered as she asked,

"Can you tell me *why* my child is having his problems? Can you tell me what I am supposed to do?"

The teacher's reply was not immediate. She already knew what she was going to say, but she wanted to wait for the right moment. As it was, no moment would have been any more right than another. When you are about to tell a parent that there is something wrong with her child, now or later becomes irrelevant. The effect will be the same. Hurt, despair, fear . . .

* * * * *

The scenario must end as it did. There is no way to know how it will continue. We can't be certain how the authority will answer the parent's question, "Why is my child having his problems?" Any number of answers are possible. What suggestions will be made to help the youngster is, again, a mystery, for there are a host of possible choices. Thus the ending of the scenario is only the beginning of a sequence of events that will have a tremendous impact on both the child and the child's parents. Along with all the possible answers and possible suggestions for treatment, there is one additional possibility that must be considered. The entire experience may have been *unnecessary* for both the child and the parent — for there may have been absolutely *nothing wrong* with the child! Indeed, the authority may have made a crucial mistake.

I recognize the seriousness of the assertion of a possible authoritative-error. The ramifications of such an error are immense. But it happens and it happens frequently. It will continue to happen until the authority's credibility is challenged, rather than assumed.

The story you are about to read will hopefully convince you that some questions need to be asked. It is a story that will allow us to explore one of the most pressing problems faced by educators and psychologists who work with young children. It is a problem also faced by an increasing number of parents. The problem deals with the word "etiology." The term is of Greek origin. "Etio" means cause. "Etiology" means the study of causes. For our purposes, the term represents what we believe to be responsible for the various actions and inactions of many school aged children. The implications and importance of this term has concerned man for no less than 100,000 years. It is as topical today as it was when an inquisitive mortal first asked the question "Why?" The answer to that question is often as elusive today as it was those many centuries ago.

The power of the term "etiology" is enormous. It sets the stage for many of our therapeutic endeavors. It can result in the alteration of plans and programs that are initiated in behalf of children. It can produce the justification for professionals to prescribe medication for school children that can modify both their brain and body chemistry. It can result in children being removed from a particular classroom and being placed in another one that may be worlds apart from the former one. It can be used as evidence to convince parents that their children are in need of long term, often unfamiliar, often frightening interventions. Indeed, this seemingly simple word of Greek origin can literally alter the course of a life. It can do so even though the proposed alteration will be of no benefit to the child.

For the Children: An Alternative

It was a bright Spring day when David readied himself for school. His large brown eyes sparkled as he anticipated another fun day with his classmates and teacher. After finishing breakfast he told his mom and dad what he was certain his preschool teacher had planned for the day. There would be music and crayons and some new words to practice and a chance to play "duck, duck, goose." For a four-and-a-half year old, the day couldn't be better.

The May sun was already warm as he walked the two blocks to the small preschool that was located in the sunlit lower level of the church building. As he approached the front door of the school he was greeted by several of his classmates and together they enjoyed the brief moment of free, unsupervised socialization that had become a part of the morning routine. Moments later, after light jackets and sweaters were hung on the tree-like coat rack, the teacher welcomed each child with a warm smile and a gentle touch. For her, the children were a spark of life that made Mondays a welcomed day. Her enthusiasm was evident and infectious.

Although unplanned, one of the children had brought a large stuffed birthday bear to class and asked if it would be all right to tell her classmates the animal's name. Permission was granted and the new, temporary classmate was introduced and briefly shared. David quickly calculated that his birthday couldn't be more than a whisper away. As he held the bear in his small hands he knew, without question, what his number one priority would be. Reluctantly, he gave the animal to Steven who was sitting to his left. His eyes, however, never left the black and white fuzzy with the neatly tied red ribbon.

Most of the early morning was spent with singing and drawing pictures. Occasionally, the teacher would produce large cards with several letters printed on them. After introducing the new words, she would incorporate their sounds and meanings into a song and the children would practice them. The children were excited to know that they were "reading" and most of the youngsters eagerly awaited the chance to share the new words with their parents.

Milk and cookies were quickly followed by a fifteen minute recess period and the teacher agreed that it was warm enough to forego the cumbersome jackets and sweaters. Once the games were finished the children returned to the classroom. When they were settled and quiet hands were observed, the teacher looked at the children and asked, "How many of you are going to the big school down the block after Summer vacation is over?" (The big school was the public school. It was expected that several children would go there for Kindergarten.) David's older sister was already there and he knew he would join her in the Fall. Excitedly, he waved his hand, as did Steven and one other youngster.

"That's wonderful," the teacher replied, acknowledging the three waving arms. "We will be sorry to see you go but I know you will do very well at the big school." The three children nodded their agreement. "Now," the teacher continued, "there is something that we must do." She stopped for a moment and passed out crayons and paper to the children who were not going to the big school. After giving them some suggestions, she returned her attention to the three other children. "We must learn to write our names correctly," she began. "We want the big school down the block to know that we at the little school do good work. So we will show them how good we can write our names." With that, she gave the three lined paper and a big red pencil.

"That's easy!" Steven answered immediately. "I can do that real well."

"Me too!" Kelly said after taking the pencil into her hand.

"Me too!" David echoed. "No sense in being *different*," he thought to himself. "If Steven and Kelly can do it, I can do it too," he added.

"Take your time," the teacher suggested. "We want it to be just right."

Without further hesitation, Steven took his pencil and comfortably held it as his mother and father had taught him. He leaned slightly towards the paper. While resting his hand on the paper, he meticulously produced what the teacher had requested.

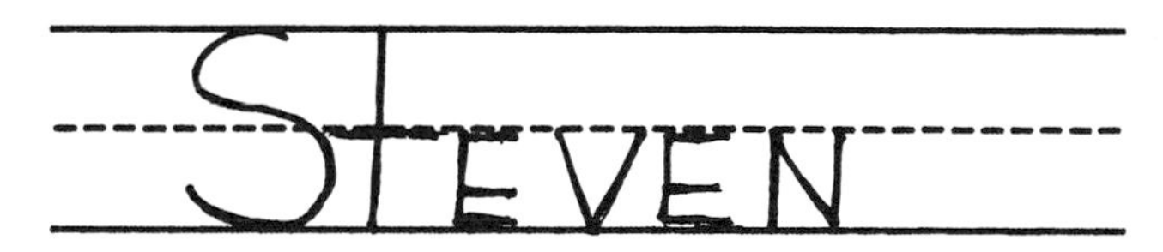

Steven placed his pencil on the table and waited for the teacher to inspect his effort. He knew she would be pleased. His own pride was evident. The many hours of practice and the hundreds of previous attempts were, as his parents had suggested, worthwhile.

Kelly's approach was slightly different although the results were reasonably similar to Steven's. Her nose almost touched the paper as she carefully produced her letters. While her right arm rested on the table, her right hand glided an inch or two above the paper. When she finished, she, too, was pleased.

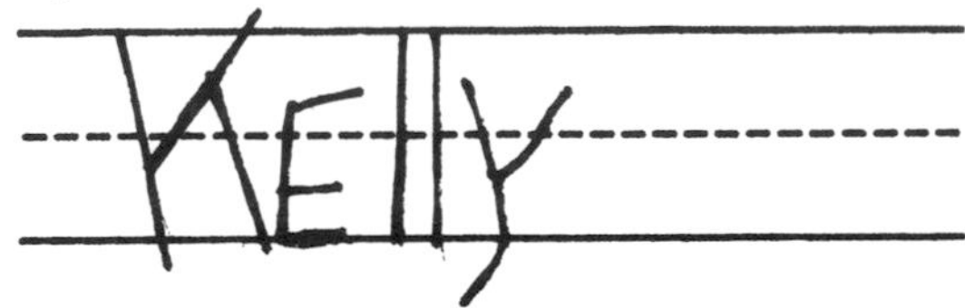

David watched his two friends while they worked. His pencil was still on the table. When the two finished they looked toward David and the three of them smiled at one another. David's eyes gave neither a hint of congratulations nor envy. They simply had a beautifully naive sparkle that made his entire face radiate. His two friends sort of shook their heads as if to prod him into action. His subtle shrug of his narrow shoulders indicated that he realized it was his turn. He looked toward the teacher who was still with the other children on the opposite side of the room. At that moment, she did not see David.

He tried to remember how Steven had held his pencil, but to no avail. He did, however, recall that Kelly's nose had touched her paper so he decided to do the same. Unfortunately, when he mimicked his little friend's actions he couldn't see the lines on his own paper. He figured it would be best to give up that idea. As he sat immobile for the moment his earlier statement, "Me too" rang in his ears. He realized he had to do something. The problem was that he hadn't done this name-writing-stuff too much. He had colored a lot. Drawn circles and squares and pictures of King Kong. But name writing was something different. He knew his name, of course. He knew his parents knew his name. But knowing something and writing something were not one and the same. While at home, there had been a couple of attempts at writing his name but no big deal was made out of it. His parents had provided proud acclamations for his attempts but the exercise wasn't pondered over nor was any great attempt made for him to continue. It was like a lot of other things he did at home. At his parents' request, he would try things. Take a good shot at whatever it was. Enjoy it for whatever it was. Then try something else. There was no pressure and no requirement of excessive practice. He remembered that someone in his house had said that it was fun to be four-and-a-half. As far as David was concerned, it was.

But for some reason, he sensed the squeeze of pressure now. He knew he was to do something. He knew he was to do it right. He knew that Steven and Kelly had already done it. He was sure they had done it right.

Now . . . his turn. Without further delay he picked up his pencil. He held it in the palm of his hand as one might hold a lollipop. As he pointed the lead tip of the pencil toward the paper his right elbow moved toward the ceiling of the classroom. His fingers and wrist tensed. Had the pencil been made of clay it would have been squashed. He lowered the lead point to the paper. He remembered the straight line that had to come first. The initial movement was jerky, due in part to the tight muscles, the heavy pressure of lead on paper, and the slight movement of the paper. But the line was there and it was a good start. Next came the half-circle that turned out to be a full circle that surrounded the straight line. In rapid succession came several more lines, several more circles, various jabs and marks and finally the last straight line that was supposed to be vertical but turned out to be something less than that. He backed away from the paper and observed his effort. Suddenly something came to him. He had forgotten the dot. He knew that there was the letter "i" in his name and he knew that the "i" required a dot. But with all the lines and circles and jabs, he couldn't locate the little line of the "i." He knew there was supposed to be a dot, so . . . he made one. He made it, however, with such force that the pencil point broke. The slight curling of his lower lip was his way of saying "whoops!" The three children quietly laughed as they looked at David's name.

It was fun being four-and-a-half.

The events that were to follow went unknown to David. Just as well, for had he been aware of them he wouldn't have understood. Professional talk is usually understood by only other professionals. David was certainly not a professional. Nor was his mother who was to enter the preschool classroom shortly to pick up her son.

About ten minutes before the class was to be dismissed for the day, the teacher walked over to Steven, Kelly, and David to see how well they had done. It was a small thing, perhaps. Maybe just a capricious event that ordinarily would have little or no effect on the turning of an individual's own unique world. Whatever, the teacher did pick up Steven's paper first. Whether it set her into a particular direction probably wasn't even known to herself. She liked what she saw. The symmetry was perfect. It was clear, distinguishable, without error. "You are a very bright boy," the teacher said to Steven. Kelly and David joined their small friend in the quiet celebration. Kelly's was next. Not as good as Steven's, the teacher's expression suggested, but acceptable. "That was a good effort," the teacher commented. "A little more work and I think you'll have it." Kelly nodded. So did Steven and David. The three of them had done a nice job, David thought to himself. As he did, he caught a glimpse of his mother as she quietly entered the room. At that moment, the teacher moved over to David's paper. The child did not see the teacher's eyes as she looked at the name. All David saw was his mother's face. For him, that was enough. He quickly turned toward the teacher and was about to ask if he could go. It was then that he saw the face without the usual smile. The two other children noticed it also. There were no words either. No "bright boy," no "good effort." No "a little more work and you'll have it." The teacher looked up from David's paper and saw his mother. Reflexively, as if to hide something, a smile came to her lips. David's mother acknowledged the greeting but waited by the door. The teacher took the paper, rolled it up, and walked to the front of the class to say goodbye to the children. David was going to ask her for the paper to show his mom but the teacher was now too far away. "Walk out quietly," the teacher said, "and don't forget your jackets. I will see you all tomorrow." The children left their seats and were gone from the room almost immediately. David had walked over to his mother and they were about to leave when the teacher asked, "May I see you for a moment?" Mother nodded and she and David walked toward the teacher. "Why don't you ask David to remain out in the hallway while we talk for a moment," she suggested. "It will just take a few seconds."

Both Mother and David reacted to the teacher's suggestion. This was new. The expression, the tone of voice, the suggestion itself elicited a sense of uneasiness. Mother ushered her son out of the room and walked over to the teacher who was now sitting at her desk. "Please sit down," the teacher asked. As Mother did, the teacher unrolled the paper and presented it to her. Mother smiled as she recognized David's name and, more specifically, his style. The uneasiness left as quickly as it came. It was, however, to return again.

"David indicated that he was going to Washington School in the Fall," the teacher began.

"Yes," Mother replied.

"Well . . . I believe we need to talk about something," the teacher said as she looked at David's paper.

"Is there something wrong?" Mother asked. It was the only thing she could think of asking.

"David is almost five and quite honestly, he should be doing better than this," the teacher answered, pointing toward the name. "The other children, who are the *same age* as David, are doing much better."

"I wasn't aware that you were having problems with him," Mother said, grasping for something.

"Oh, I'm not," the teacher quickly responded. "No, I'm not having any problems with him. He is a most delightful child. A beautiful child. My concern is that *he* might have some problems."

"What kind of problems," Mother asked hesitantly. She looked to see if David could hear the conversation. Satisfied that he couldn't, she looked back at the teacher. Something in her said that she should run to her son's side, protectively. The word "problem" was clearly visible in her mind.

"Look at his writing," the teacher answered. "It is much below where it should be. Let me show you another child's work. I believe you can easily see the *difference*," she added, handing Mother Steven's work. The difference was clear. There was no denying it. For both Mother and the teacher, the concept "different" had a special meaning. A frightening meaning. "Do you see what I mean?"

"I do," Mother answered. "But I don't understand it." She silently groped for an appeasing explanation. None came. She felt an emptiness deep inside. "Can you tell me why his writing is so different?" she asked quietly.

The teacher's reply was not immediate. She already knew what she was going to say, but she wanted to wait for the right moment. As it was, no moment would have been any more right than another. When you are about to tell a parent that there is something wrong with her child, now or later becomes irrelevant. The effect will be the same. Hurt, despair, fear. "Many children today would like to do better in school," the teacher began, "but something prevents them from doing so. They have the desire, on the surface, even the ability. But *something* blocks them. Something gets in the way. Something interferes with the natural learning. David may be one of those children. I firmly believe that he has a visual-motor-integration problem. A processing problem . . . perhaps a perceptual problem. I know how to recognize the problem," the teacher admitted, "but I'm not sure of the appropriate treatment. I like your son David very much, but I would strongly urge that before you consider Kindergarten, you take him to see someone who can provide professional treatment. If you don't, he will probably have very serious learning problems when he gets older."

"Hi Mom," David said, as his mother returned to the hallway.

"Hi dear."

"Hey Mom, did you see my writing? I did it in class today. Not too bad, right Mom?"

"No Davey, not too bad," she answered, confused, sad, hurt.

The Acceptance of Differences and the Question of Expectations

Whether David's story had some significance for you will depend on where you find yourself in today's world. As a parent of a school age child, you might have experienced some empathy for David and his mother. You might have also experienced a sudden need to sit down with your child and help him learn how to write his name. As a teacher, with a classroom full of children, who are all performing at different levels, you might have agreed with David's teacher's evaluations and suggestions. On the other hand, you might have screamed, having recognized the circularity, the disease orientation, and the shirking of one's responsibility that was so evident. As a psychologist or physician, or someone just interested in children, you might have experienced considerable anger once having noticed the absence of alternative explanations for David's behavior, the assumption that age, in and of itself, somehow guaranteed some experience, and noticed the conclusion that differences amongst children somehow implied that one of the children had a problem.

The fact is, there was nothing wrong with David. Today, at the end of second grade, his writing is adequate — although still not on a par with Steven's. (There is no rule that ever stated that it had to be!) My purpose for writing this book is to show you the circumstances that led the teacher to incorrectly believe that David was the one with the problem. I am also going to share with you some ideas that would have enabled his teacher to avoid that conclusion entirely. Frankly, I am going to try to influence your thinking regarding the problems school children are said to have. With the exception of a few short sections that are a little "dry," the book should be easy to read, and enjoyable. At least, I hope so.

The matter before us is quite simple. Can we find alternative, healthy explanations for many of our school children's behaviors that seem to cause both parents and professionals great concern? If we can, we will make the lives of all the "David's" and their parents happier and more successful. If we can't, then know now that we will be stuck with the damn dragons that have been with us for thousands and thousands of years.

In a moment, we are going to meet a little girl named Molly. She, like David, was a little different. Nothing extreme, mind you, but sufficiently different to elicit a raised eyebrow from someone who should have been a little more tolerant. But the eyebrow was there, the difference was there, and the failure to meet an "authority's" expectation was also there.

Molly gives us the opportunity to briefly look at two very important concepts that govern our thoughts about the problems that school children are said to have. The concepts are "differences" and "expectations."

The two concepts are interrelated. To be different means that an individual's behavior deviates to a degree from a comparative group's behavior. David's handwriting, for example, was seen as being different only *after* it was compared with Steven's efforts. If Steven's handwriting had been similar to David's, and those were the only two examples of name writing the teacher had ever seen, the concept of "differences" regarding name writing, at least, would never have been considered. As is apparent, the concept of differences requires some form of comparison before it is invoked.

Comparisons, and the resulting evaluations, are a fact of life. For the most part they do not create much concern. We watch two tennis players, compare them, and with little difficulty, we can select which one we think is better. The same with the amateur and professional ballerina, as well as the seasoned and novice actor.

With school children, differences abound. While that should not be surprising to anyone, it often times is. The differences are observed, again, as a result of careful, and sometimes not-so-careful, comparisons. Teachers generally have no difficulty telling which students come to class better prepared, which students are most cooperative, and which ones make the working day seem short. They assuredly know which students cause them more problems, which ones occupy most of their time, and which ones create the need for thoughts of early retirement. Again, comparisons and evaluations are a fact of professional life. So is the determination that some children are acceptably different, while others are just a little "too" different.

The Meaning of Difference

Up to this point, I doubt that I have said anything to you that is unusually new about the concept of differences. Perhaps you have viewed differences as being just that. Perhaps you've never felt it necessary to add any special meaning to the concept of differences — special meanings such as one person being better, brighter, or more "normal" than another. Perhaps you have always been able to view a child as being uniquely himself; a product of unique endowments and events that no other youngster has ever been given or experienced. Perhaps you have been wary of comparisons amongst children, comparisons that lend themselves to conclusions such as one child being better, brighter.

I do not wish to totally dislodge your welcomed idealism, but understand that if you do believe as I have just suggested, then *you* are different . . . very different. One of the realities of today's educational and psychological world is that differences are more than just differences. Observed differences that have come about as a result of comparisons are used to determine —

1. Which children have educational and psychological problems and which ones do not.
2. Which children are to be labeled special and which ones are to be viewed like "everyone else."
3. Which children are to receive treatment A, B, or C, and which ones are to receive little or no special treatment.

And in selected cases —

4. Which children are likely to "make it," and which ones stand little chance to achieve the elusive and ill-defined "it."

The concept of differences has placed us in a very perplexing situation. On any given day, in any given classroom, one child's handwriting is seen as a sign of an organic problem — an organic problem that cannot be verified. A second child's handwriting is seen as being a sign of giftedness — a qualitative characteristic that at present is very difficult to measure or determine. A third child's handwriting is seen as being like most everyone else's and thus is not really even seen. One child is seen as a problem. One child is seen as an impending enigma. One child is seen as just fine.

Historical Precedent

Making comparisons, observing differences, and drawing conclusions that something might be wrong with the one who is different is not unique to the 20th Century. The practice had its inception from the moment that someone decided to behave in a way dissimilar to the majority of people who were *expected* to behave in a certain way. As you might predict, the first time that occurred was a long time ago. From that time to the present, one common thread has been readily apparent. The concept of differences, and the possibility that the differences mean something very special, have occurred as a result of our *expectations* that most members of a comparison group are supposed to behave in a very similar fashion. In the past, a small child was expected to behave in a particular way. If, however, he did what some said he was not supposed to do he was seen as being different *and* possessed by evil spirits. His "affliction" was treated! The purpose of the treatment was to remove the spirit and increase the chances that the child would behave as everyone else behaved. The child's differences were seen as being indicative of the presence of a serious problem.

Such a thing did happen some 7000 years ago. It happened because, at that time, no one could come up with an alternative explanation for the child being different than someone suggested he should be. As a result, the spirits were accepted as a responsible force in the child's life. Ironically, today, 20th Century A.D., parents and teachers, while not having to deal with evil spirits, still find themselves face to face with the relatives of the spirits.

The Blue Flag

The phone call came one early morning as I was readying myself for one of my graduate classes. The caller was a psychologist from one of the local hospitals. She was the director of the behavioral science clinic at the hospital and we had worked together on several occasions. "I've got a little problem," she said. "Do you have some free time?"

"Sure," I answered. "What's going on?"

"Have a six-year-old that's heading for trouble!"

"Serious?" I asked.

"Serious enough for the school where she attends to consider throwing her out," the psychologist replied.

"Throwing out a six-year-old!" I was only partially amazed. I had been involved with two other similar situations where the same consideration was proposed. "What seems to be the pressing problem?" I asked.

"I'm not sure," she answered.

"One of those, eh?"

"Yes . . . I think it is one of those. She tests out fine. I've observed her on three different occasions and I have seen nothing that would warrant raised eyebrows. I've talked with her. She's friendly, cute, vivacious, inquisitive, and six-years-old," she stated in a frustrated way.

"*Too* vivacious, *too* inquisitive?" I asked.

"Could be, I'm afraid," she said. "Would you take a look? I don't think we have much time."

"Sure. Let the principal and teacher know I'm coming. Tomorrow around ten o'clock would be good for me."

I arrived at the school a little before ten the following morning. As I worked my way toward the principal's office I noticed the empty, quiet hallways. The doors to most of the classrooms were closed but as I peered through some of the windows, I could see the familiar sight of young children with waving hands, smiling eyes, and busy pencils. I couldn't help feeling that the future was in good shape.

I found the office and after introducing myself I was ushered in to see the principal. An elderly lady, who wore the wrinkles of her difficult profession, greeted me. We sat for a few moments and talked.

"She's a lovely child," the principal began, "*but* if she doesn't change, I'm going to ask her mother to place her in a different school next year."

Somehow I knew the word "but" was inevitable. "Can you tell me what she is doing that's creating the difficulty?" Without hesitation, the principal explained that Molly had been sent to the office for discipline purposes three times this week alone. The major complaints from the teacher centered around the child's refusal to follow directions. This was very disconcerting to the teacher. She couldn't understand why the child behaved so differently from the other children. Apparently, the other children did exactly as the teacher requested. Molly, however, didn't. As a result, the teacher found herself spending too much time with the child — time that was supposed to be spent with the other children. The teacher expected Molly both to follow the clearly presented directions and to work independently as the other children were doing. When she failed to do so, the teacher would send her to the office where she would be talked to and then confined to a chair for a short period of time. The principal believed that this was all the school could do to help the child. Since the child persisted in her disruptive behavior, the school had little option other than to consider her dismissal.

I said very little as the principal spoke. I had heard the words before. I had, on previous occasions, felt the dismay and frustration that was elicited by teachers' attitudes regarding differences amongst children and how the differences implied that the child was the one who was expected to change — to be the same as the others. I did not feel very good as I left the office and walked to Molly's classroom.

Once there, I was silently greeted by the teacher and her aide as they sat off in a corner of the room while visually monitoring the children's efforts. There were about 26 children sitting at various round tables. Each child appeared to be doing some task. A quick glance suggested that the task was the same for all the children. For that brief moment, I could not see Molly. No child was particularly different from the next. All seemed intently involved in their activity. An additional minute passed. I walked quietly toward the teacher and aide. We smiled at each other. It was difficult to tell whether I was viewed as an ally or adversary. I turned toward the class. For the most part, my presence went unnoticed. However, as soon as I faced the class, two large brown eyes from the very back of the room caught my gaze. The two eyes looked at me for several seconds. When I took a few steps to the left, they followed. I smiled at the beautiful small face, but my action was not reciprocated. I was being inspected in a manner that suggested that the two eyes had seen someone, or several someones, like myself before. I looked at the other children almost in self-defense. The two eyes, seemingly satisfied, changed their focus back to the paper on the table top. The teacher had been watching the nonverbal interchange. When I glanced back toward the lady she nodded her head, confirming that the two brown eyes, set in the round, inquisitive face, were Molly's. Five more minutes passed. Again all the children appeared the same. Suddenly a buzzer went off signaling the end of the work period. As if cued, each child put down the various crayons that had been shared, each child raised his head, each child looked toward the teacher, who was now standing. It was then that she spoke to her students for the first time since I had entered the room. Her words were to the effect that she liked their hard work. Her tone, however, was quite flat and it matched the expression she carried on her face. I wondered for a moment how many times she had her previous students do the same task. The word "thousands" flashed through my head. Without saying much else, she visited each table and retrieved the assignment.

Most of the youngsters turned to a neighbor and quietly

talked about something that I could not interpret. I watched as the teacher walked to the very back table. Molly, like the others, handed the teacher the paper. Nothing special happened. It wasn't as if I was disappointed, but I did expect something. After all, I was there, was asked to be there, to watch this little girl who had previously been described as "hell-on-wheels." For this moment, at least, the wheels weren't even turning.

Then something happened. It wasn't anything overly alarming, but it was something. The teacher had begun to return to the front of the room. She had gotten fairly close to her desk, which was next to me. Her back was to the class. Out of the corner of my eye I noticed that one child left her seat. One child quietly, gingerly, began to walk to the front of the class. As she did, her two large brown eyes focused on me. I smiled at her. This time she smiled back. The only thing that came into my head was — "beautiful child." Her small hand touched the teacher's back that was now hunched over her book cluttered desk. It was almost as if the teacher not only expected it to happen, but knew who would be doing the touching. Before the teacher had completely turned around, Molly asked, "What are we going to do next?" It was a simple question that could have been answered in a simple way. However, the answer was not simple. As the teacher looked first at me, then at Molly, she retorted, "You know you are not to ask questions now! You also know that if you will wait for a few moments I will tell you what we will be doing. Now, take your seat!"

I reacted to the tone of voice. I felt myself step back. On the other hand, Molly didn't react at all. In fact, she asked a second question. I wanted to intercede; to ask the child to sit before the "axe" had a chance to make its mark. Had I interceded, I doubt I would have been in time. The teacher grabbed the child's right arm, turned her around to where she was facing the now frozen class, and led her back to the table. It was then I realized that her's was the only empty table. Molly had been sitting by herself throughout the entire exercise. Although I could not hear, the teacher "whispered" something into the child's ear. The child nodded. Then she became quiet and sat very still. Almost running, the teacher returned to the front of the room. "Did you see that?" she said to me as she whisked by. She did not wait for an answer. Had she, I'm not sure what I would have said. She lifted a stack of brand new papers from her desk and asked the aide to distribute them and give the instructions. Then she took the just handed-in papers and, while holding them, she ushered me outside. Before we had stopped walking she said to me, "She's always doing that. She's the only one I have that continually asks questions. She refuses to wait as the other children do." It was evident the teacher was quite upset. At the same time, she seemed pleased that Molly had "acted out." She obviously saw me as being a witness to the disruptiveness. Before I had a chance to say anything, she added, "I want you to see these papers!" I tried to clear my head, but there was little chance of that. The "axe," indeed, had fallen. I knew there was little I could do to forestall its downward motion. With a deep breath I began to thumb through the papers. After looking at the second one, I realized what the previous assignment had been. Both papers were very good reproductions of the American flag. The next one looked like the others. The next ten were almost identical to the ones I had looked at. Before too many more, I found Molly's. I tried not to look at the teacher, but her stare made it impossible to ignore either her presence or the "incriminating" evidence. Molly's flag was about the same size and shape as all of the other children's. Unfortunately, however, hers had a pole and, although I didn't ask, I was sure that was not part of the instructions. There was one other characteristic that also separated her work from that of her classmates. For some teachers the *different* characteristic might not have even been noticed. For some teachers, it might have been noticed, but not viewed as anything important. For some, it might have been viewed positively. For Molly's teacher, however, it appeared to be the proverbial straw.

"Do you see what I mean," the teacher said as she held the *blue flag* with no stars, no stripes, no reds, no whites. "I don't think the child is capable of following directions! I'm convinced the child is disturbed — emotionally disturbed. The disturbance prevents her from behaving as the others behave. I think the child belongs in a special school. I think the child needs special treatment. I don't think I can handle her," she added.

Unhesitatingly, I turned to her and said, "You're right. You can't handle the child!"

* * * * *

The saddest part of the above scenario is that it is completely true. Despite several conversations with both the principal and teacher, neither my psychologist friend nor myself were able to convince those in charge that the youngster was neither ill nor required special treatment — other than a change in the teacher's attitude, expectations, and approach she used in her classroom.

Because the school was a private institution, the child was dismissed. The youngster's parents had little recourse other than to find a school that would be more willing to accept Molly's individual differences, work with her own strengths and weaknesses, and not be so concerned with the fact that she didn't do everything "everyone" else did. With luck, she was too young to fully understand her teacher's assertion that she was sufficiently different and performing sufficiently below expectations, to prevent her from staying with her classmates.

Without being aware of it, Molly's teacher used the same logic of many early witch doctors who lived 7000 years ago to conclude that something was wrong with the child. Although that might not be apparent to you now, it will be before you finish this book. What differences exist between "evil spirits" and "emotional disturbance" as *explanations* for observed differences in children's behavior is something you will have to decide upon. In my judgment there is no difference. In fact, they have a great deal in common. Both are —

A. Safe
B. Irrefutable
C. Circular
D. Sick
E. and "Artifactual" Rather than Factual.

Both are offered as explanations only after differences have been observed and expectations have not been met. Both are accepted as accurate explanations because authorities are unwilling to look at other alternative explanations — alternatives that are neither safe, irrefutable, circular, nor suggestive of something being wrong with the child.

We will look at the meaning of the above five characteristics in awhile. For now, I would like you to consider what it means to be *different*, what it means to be compared with others, and what it means to have to perform to someone else's *expectations* that may or may not be realistic.

In the two previous stories, it was evident that both Molly and David were different than their comparative groups. What you must ask yourself is whether being *different* is sufficient to warrant the conclusion that something was *wrong* with either child.

It was also evident that both Molly and David were compared with their classmates. That would seem to be the logical thing to have done. However, while the two children were compared with their classmates, they *were not*, with any guarantee at all, compared with their peers! Peers are not necessarily children of the same age, who happen to be sitting in the same classroom and who are being taught by the same teacher. A peer is. . . "a person who is equal to another in abilities . . . "[1]* in interests, experience and endowments. Since the children were compared with other children who were not like themselves, you must ask yourself a second question. What could be gained by comparing one child with a group of different children? The determination that one child was better, brighter, more "normal," or simply different?

In the stories, it was further suggested that neither Molly nor David were able to meet their teacher's expectations. That could be extremely important. But another question from you is called for. What was the basis for the teachers' expectations? They used what might appear to be a logical way of establishing acceptable performance limits. They assumed that since all children in the respective two classes were very close in age, the children should be expected to behave and perform in a highly similar way. That logic might also lead one to believe that if a child isn't quite like the others in terms of behavior and performance, something must be *wrong* with the one different child. That conclusion is something you might like to question!

Perspective

Professional people greatly influence the lives of countless children and their parents. By their actions, they set the stage for feelings of optimism or despair. They can take a child and make him believe that he is worthy and important — regardless of where he might find himself in relation to others of similar age. But with a word, or a catchy professional phrase, they can accomplish the opposite. The professional can have the same effect on the parent of the child. They can inspire the parent, pointing out what can be done. Or they can drain the parents' enthusiasm, pointing out how different the child is and what he will never be able to do.

I'm sure that a professional rarely sets about to intentionally make matters worse for a child. Such a person's career would be very short lived. But intentions aside, such a thing does happen. It happens when we become regurgitators of the orthodoxy of the past without bothering

---

* For readability, I have numbered the various sources in this book, rather than including the author's name and publication date within the body of the manuscript. The listed numbers and complete citings are found under the bibliography section located in the back of the book. As you will see, number 1, the first listing, refers to the Random House Dictionary.

to determine if the past warrants our support. It happens when expediency takes the place of efficiency. It happens when we fail to monitor our belief systems regarding the meaning of *differences*, the purpose of *comparisons*, and the danger of unchecked *expectations*. It happens when we apply undue pressure in order to meet some artificially imposed time line. It happens when we assume that difference is synonymous with sickness. It happens, finally, when we fail to accept differences as real, as welcomed divergence, as something to be worked with. As we will now see, a lot of children, children who are different, have been told that they have a problem. Some of these children do have legitimate difficulties. Most, however, do not. The latter group have become victims of expediency. Their educational/psychological diseases have come from the logic of the past rather than the knowledge of the present.

Educational and Psychological Diseases: Their Prevalence

David and his "processing problem" and Molly and her "emotional disturbance" are not alone. It is not much comfort for them, or for their parents, but it is a fact. Lest you think I am the only one who feels that way, allow me to offer the following segment of a short, but meaningful poem. One wonders how many parents have felt the weight of its theme.

"D" Days

A child lives today
In dread of the "D's."
"He has," some will say,
"Disabilities."
"Dyslexic," they state,
"Disturbed," or just "dumb."
"Developing late,"
"Disordered," say some.

The verbiage is strong,
The labels profuse,
The check list grows long
With prescriptions to use.

At worst it's implied
He has a disease.
At best, it's denied
He's able to please . . .

–Irene Masinter, September, 1972

Facts

FACT: The prevalence of educational and psychological sickness in our country is higher now than it has ever been before. It seems to be increasing at a much faster rate than can be justified given the population growth.

FACT: Based on some rather frightening numbers that are available to all of us, there appears to be an inordinate number of youngsters who are presently experiencing some sort of serious difficulty with school activities.

FACT: We are presently in the midst of an epidemic. Each year more and more children discover — or more accurately *are told* by professional people — that they are sick.

FACT: A large percentage of these "sick" children are absolutely fine! Something else, however, isn't.

Let me show you some of the numbers I am referring to. Understand that the labels used to describe the "problems" can mean a multitude of various things. I would suggest that you not be overly concerned at this time with their ambiguity and just accept them for what you think they represent. We will look at them more closely later.

In 1971 there were approximately 5,914,121 preschool and school age youngsters who were diagnosed as having some sort of cognitive, behavioral, or physical problem.[2] A partial breakdown of these six million children were as follows —

Problem	**Numbers**
Retarded	1,338,866
Speech Impaired	2,145,647
Emotionally Disturbed	749,441
Other Health Impairments	1,089,147

The above figures do not include hard of hearing, deaf, or visually impaired. Of particular importance is the category of "Other Health Impairments." This group includes youngsters with Asthma, Cardiac Problems, Brittle Bone Syndrome, Epilepsy, similar difficulties, and "Learning Disabilities." It is difficult to say precisely how many of the "OHI" youngsters suffered from "learning disabilities" for the source did not divide the category into specific groupings. Without purposely meaning to overestimate or underestimate the actual numbers, I would cautiously guess that somewhere between 700,000 and 900,000 children were diagnosed as being learning disabled (LD). Perhaps the numbers were considered small and thus not of overwhelming significance — hence the reason for the absence of a separate LD classification. That is just conjecture on my part.

Some four to five years later, a relatively short period of time, new data appeared. Now we were told that the overall number of youngsters who were diagnosed as having problems increased to 7,887,000 — an increase of almost two million youngsters.[3] Again, a partial breakdown —

Problem	Numbers
Retarded	1,507,000
Speech Impaired	2,293,000
Emotionally Disturbed	1,310,000
Other Health Impairments	328,000
Learning Disabilities	1,966,000

Notice that learning disabilities had now attained its own classification and its own numbers. That probably accounts for the reduction in the "OHI" youngsters. Quickly, let's compare the two sets of numbers.

Problem	1971 Data	1975-6 Data	Increased Numbers
Retarded	1,338,866	1,507,000	168,000
Speech Impaired	2,145,647	2,293,000	147,000
Emotionally Disturbed	749,441	1,310,000	*560,000*
Learning Disabilities	800,000*	1,966,000	*1,166,000*

If charts and numbers turn you off, just look briefly at the "Increased Numbers" column and notice the problem referred to. Again, without intentionally attempting to make more out of the numbers than actually exists, it is evident that the "Retarded" and "Speech Impaired" groups increased only slightly. On the other hand, notice what happened to the "Emotionally Disturbed" and "Learning Disabled" groups. Their numbers jumped rather dramatically. One can't help but wonder why there was such a disproportionate increase. Why didn't all the groups increase at about the same rate? Is there something unique about "emotional disturbance" and "learning disabilities" that may account for their increase? Are there really that many kids that are sufficiently involved, sufficiently different, to warrant those diseased labels? Or is it possible that by sheer accident, or faulty logic, there were some misdiagnoses; that perhaps some of the children who were labeled disturbed and disabled were really okay?

"Emotional disturbance" and "learning disabilities" are not the only problems said to influence young school children. A "condition" known as "dyslexia" is another. This ominously sounding "thing" sometimes finds its way under the heading of learning disabilities. Other times, it is given its own wings. Either way, we are told that it, too, is very prevalent.

---

* approximate numbers

> Whether you call it specific language disability or by its more technical name, developmental dyslexia is a problem that affects between ten and twenty percent of all children born today. Two thirds of these children, about three million by a conservative estimate, are considered afflicted to an incapacitating degree.[4]

Technical words aside, three million kids are a lot of kids who are said to be suffering from this difficulty. The orthodoxy of the past tells us that the problem emanates from some physical deficiency that exists within the child — specifically the brain of the child. It tells us that dyslexia ("impairment of the ability to read, or to understand what one reads silently or aloud . . ."[5]) is a "thing" that can be treated with medication — specifically, antihistamines.[6] But the orthodoxy of the past has been questioned, as well it should be.

> . . . There is another, very different view of dyslexia. This more recently derived position does not make any presumptions regarding the presence of neurological dysfunction as the cause of the reading disorder . . . The cause of the reading disorder can be varied, including such factors as low intelligence, cultural disadvantage, lack of motivation, lack of stimulating home environment, emotional problems, and dislike for schooling, as well as presumed neurological dysfunction.
>
> The difference in conceptualizing the nature of dyslexia can cause confusion in the field and, at times, unnecessary concern to parents. When parents are informed that their child is dyslexic, they may well presume that he/she has some form of disease or 'thing' that causes the reading deficit when, in fact, the child may simply dislike school and refuse to work. . . .[7]

The conceptual differences represent two entirely different views regarding responsibility for academic deficiencies. I assure you the differences are much more than semantic. One view sees behavioral difficulties as resulting from some dysfunctional variable that exists *within* the child. The other recognizes that the exact same behavioral difficulties might be related to factors that exist from *without* the child. In the instance of "dyslexia," one view often proposes the use of medication as a method of treatment. The other view has a different idea.

Problems From Within, Problems From Without: A First Look

It is difficult not to reach the conclusion that the numbers of children who have been informed that something is wrong with them, and who are being treated by non-teacher oriented methodologies for that something, are growing at a rate that simply has to raise some suspicion. Some questions have to be raised. Are there really so many kids that have something wrong with them?

> In less than a decade, the ailment spread from virtual obscurity to something well beyond epidemic proportions. It has no single name, no universally accepted symptoms, and no discernible anatomical or biochemical characteristics which can be diagnosed in a clinic or laboratory. Yet it is said to afflict as many as 40 percent of all American children, to reflect an organic or chemical dysfunction of the brain or nervous system and to be the cause of most, if not all, pediatric problems in learning and behavior. Its most common name . . . is 'learning disabilities' (LD) but it is also associated, sometimes synonymously, with 'minimal brain dysfunction' (MBD), 'hyperkinesis,' 'impulse disorder' and a substantial number of other conditions and 'syndromes.' Before 1965 almost no one had heard of it, but by the beginning of the seventies it was commanding the attention of an armada of pediatricians, neurologists and educational psychologists, and by mid-decade, pedagogical theory, medical speculation, psychological need, drug company promotion and political expediency had been fused with an evangelical fervor to produce what is undoubtedly the most powerful movement in — and beyond — contemporary education. Learning disabilities, according to some 'authorities' in the field, account for nearly all school failure, most juvenile delinquency, a large proportion of broken marriages, and some part of virtually every other social affliction in modern life.[8]

And to treat that which seems to have *no* observable physical parameters that are readily diagnosable or testable —

> By early 1975 between 500,000 and 1,000,000 American children and adolescents were taking amphetamine-type drugs and other psychostimulants by prescription, but since their numbers have been *doubling** every two or three years, the total may well exceed 1,000,000 *before** the end of 1975. A small

percentage of those children suffer from some diagnosable *medical** ailment sufficiently serious to warrant chemotherapy. Most do not . . . .[8]

There are two important points made in the above quote that need to be remembered. First, the authors suggested the overall numbers of medicated youngsters could exceed one million by the end of 1975. Since the date of this present manuscript is some five years later, one can only imagine what total number of medically treated children are enrolled in our school systems. Without question, the numbers are large. Second, it must be apparent to you that sincere, concerned professional people do not medicate children on a whim. It is not something that is done haphazardly. Rather, such a decision is made on the basis of one's philosophy of causation or assertion of the primary, underlying problem. For the medicated children, the assumption has been made that the problem — the cause — rests *within* them, specifically within their physiological or psychological systems —

> . . . If the child does not learn academic skills at the rate or level expected, or if he does not behave emotionally or socially as expected, too frequently it is assumed categorically that the fault lies within the child.[9]

Further —

> . . . An attempt is made during the [educational and psychological] process to identify the presumed internal, underlying, 'within-the-child' variables that interfere with, disrupt, or block the acquisition of the teachings of the school program.[9]

Logically, if one is predisposed to believe that a child's failure to meet the expectations of a teacher is due to some problem that rests within the youngster, then it would follow, again logically, that treatment should deal with that which is perceived as being within. Today, many professionals in both education and psychology believe that differences among children often come about as a result of various physiological and psychological problems that are said to be *inside* the child. However, other professionals believe that there is often a viable alternative to the educational/psychological "within" view of causation that attempts to account for differences and failures to meet educational expectations. They see that several of the problems children — and teachers — encounter are related to factors that do not suggest that something internally is wrong with the child —

---

* Emphasis mine

> All teachers, whether they teach regular or exceptional children, frequently encounter youngsters at the preschool or elementary levels who are not responsive to instruction or who are disruptive in class. These children may evidence problems in reading, arithmetic, or other school subjects, in social adjustment or motivation, or in basic readiness skills such as language and perception. Most of these pupils are probably victims of *poor teaching,** *insufficient readiness experiences,** and/or *inadequate motivation.** No children are immune to the debilitating effects of these three factors; bright or retarded, sound or crippled, stable or difficult children can be affected at one time or another.[10]

The above authors have suggested probable outside sources that can be responsible for some of the problems our school youngsters experience. Their opinion is an alternative explanation to the "within-the-child" view of etiological responsibility. Their view does not categorically suggest that David's difficulty with handwriting was a result of an *inside*, organic processing problem. Nor does it suggest that Molly's difficulties were due to some psychological emotional disturbance that resides within her mind. It suggested that somehow teachers' methodologies and the educational system may have had a part to play in their manifested behaviors and their apparent differences.

If there is the slightest chance that a child's manifested difficulties are due to something, or several things, other than a problem that resides within him or her, we must know it. Otherwise, we may end up treating an *invented* condition instead of dealing with the major difficulties. We may, quite unintentionally, suggest to a child that something is wrong with him, when in fact he is fine. We may provide a willing teacher with an excuse not to teach by removing that responsibility from the teacher and conveniently placing it safely within the child. We may make it anything but fun to be either four-and-a-half or fourteen.

* Emphasis mine

The Suspicious Signal: Behavior The Critical Question: Why?

We have only a few more important items to cover before confronting the dragons. The information in this chapter is critical for it will give us a glimpse at the logic and foundation upon which the authorities of the past and the present have determined that one individual was disturbed and disabled, while another was free from such a burden.

Behavior: The Signal

If you are one step ahead of me, then you know that the major barometer used by authorities to suggest the presence of a problem is the behavior of the individual being looked at. The behavior becomes the sign or signal that alerts the professional that some dragon may be present. In the case of David, the signal was his name writing.

The Signal: **Behavior**

1. Name Writing

For Molly, it was several things she did that someone suggested were unacceptable.

The Signal: **Behavior**

1. Failed to Follow Requests
2. Did Not Do Assignments
3. Asked Too Many Questions
4. Out of Seat Too Often

Had the behaviors *not* been present, no signs of potential difficulty would have been observed. Nothing suspicious would have been evident and the suggestion would *not* have been made that either child was having a problem.

From the beginning of time, the behavior of an individual, be the behavior social, academic, or physiological in nature, has been the only indication used by competent professionals to formulate an idea that something might be wrong with the individual. With few exceptions, none of which I am personally aware of, people, in the past as well as the present, have been expected to behave in particular ways. Society, for the most part, determined what those acceptable ways were to be, and the acceptable was often very limited. The culture of Uwanga in 5000 B.C., for example, decided that children should not have tantrums. If a child was observed to have a tantrum, a spirit was said to have invaded the child's body. Why the tantrum was perceived as being so terribly serious, and thus indicative of a serious problem, is anybody's guess. But that's the way it was.

Today, the same situation exists. Professionals, operating within their *own cultures*, have determined that certain activities are not acceptable and thus certain activities are signs of problems —

> **Between-Meal Nibbling.** A commonly observed symptom of tension in many young children is between-meal . . . nibbling. This . . . child usually demands sweets . . . cookies, candy, cake, ice cream, and desserts of various kinds. He is ordinarily not hungry at mealtime and nibbles and picks at his food . . . . Such eating habits usually indicate an emotionally disturbed state.[11]

Behavior
1. Between-Meal Nibbling
2. Demands Cookies, Candy, Ice Cream, etc.
3. Not Hungry at Mealtime, Picks at Food

Why did the authorities, who suggested the above, perceive that between-meal-nibbling was a sign of a serious problem within the child? Frankly, I don't know. I would imagine that some youngsters might find ice cream more palatable than asparagus. But, the authorities made their decision and, no doubt, some parents were influenced by it.

In schools, the same circumstances are apparent. Signs are looked for and judgments regarding the seriousness of the signs are made —

> You will become increasingly aware that the behavior which angers you is a signal of illness, just as red spots are a signal of measles . . . .[12]

In the above case, it appears that the authority is suggesting that a behavior which angers a teacher is sufficient to warrant the conclusion of the presence of a disease. If that is the case, there are, indeed, an awful lot of kids who are diseased for I have met an equal number of teachers who are angered.

Why?: The Critical Question

Once a "significant" sign is observed, an important step follows. The question "Why?" is guaranteed. The two go hand in hand for the appearance of a suspicious behavior necessitates some explanation for its presence.

The question "Why?" is critical for it provides the professional with some direction regarding what needs to be treated. For the appropriate treatment to occur, however, the *answer* to the question "Why?" must have certain characteristics. The answer must be clear, precise. If it is, at least we will know what the authority is talking about. It must be capable of being verified — capable of being shown that it is true. If it doesn't have that characteristic, we won't know whether the authority is right or wrong. If the answer does not have those characteristics, the authority may be wrong! If such is the case, we may overlook some variable that is potentially critical. We may think we have found a very "significant" sign and received a very significant answer when, in fact, we haven't found or received anything helpful at all. Let me give you a quick example of how serious these characteristics are. Watch what can happen when the characteristics are not present.

The Adjective Versus The Noun

Recently, I received a call requesting some help with a seven-year-old who was still sucking her thumb prior to going to bed. The call suggested that the child had a problem. (In actuality, it was the child's parents who were having the problem — or were told by some authority that a problem existed. I found out that the child was not the least bit upset about the comfort of her thumb.) Prior to my learning of the thumb, the caller indicated that the child was an "insecure" child. The term "insecure," in that usage, was an adjective, describing the child. Note that the term told me *nothing* about the child. I had to assume what the child was doing to warrant the label of "insecure." For me, seven-year-olds who eat mashed potatoes with a straw are "insecure," so, I just assumed that the child ate mashed potatoes that way. My assumption was corrected once having been told of the thumb. (Note also, someone decided that seven-year-old girls should not suck their thumb prior to bedtime. Why? Well, with the possible exception of extensive dental bills, I can't imagine why someone would go bananas over that behavior. Some of us, considerably older than seven, put things in our mouth that are more "significant" than thumbs. We do it, no doubt, because it is enjoyable. Perhaps seeking enjoyment is also a sign of "insecurity." You will have to check with your own authority about that.)

As an adjective, the term "insecure" is purely descriptive. While it doesn't really describe anything particular, it's intent is to do so. It is like the term "good." A "good" child, for example, is doing something that someone believes is good. The word "good," however, doesn't tell us the substance of the child's actions. No one directly observes the act of being "good." In the same way, no one directly observes the acts of "insecurity" or "hyperactivity." Instead, we observe specific behaviors, such as helping a Mom or Dad with the dinner dishes, or thumb sucking, or a child who runs and jumps down a school hallway. After observing the behaviors, we attach whatever label we believe to be appropriate to the behaviors. Some adjectives are "pleasant." They cause no difficulties. Other adjectives, such as "insecure" carry a negative connotation. They scare people. In the case of the caller, she was definitely upset. Had the professional, who introduced the term to Mother, used the term "serene" to describe the appearance of the child, thumb in mouth, while she readied herself for sleep, I doubt I would have received the phone call. But "serene" was not chosen.

As our conversation continued, the mother of the seven-year-old nonchalantly pulled on a grammatical string and innocently suggested, "My daughter is sucking her thumb *because* of her 'insecurity.' "

Behavior	**Why?**
1. Thumb Sucking	"Insecurity"

Without realizing it, she had offered an etiological hypothesis. She had changed the adjective to a noun. Now, rather than *describing* something, she was *explaining* something. She had *answered* the question "Why?"

While I didn't tell Mother what she had done (she probably would have hung up the phone), I will explain what had transpired as a result of the grammatical switch.

1. She initiated circular logic that leads nowhere, and
2. Suggested an untestable idea to account for the observed behavior.

And, as a result of the above two outcomes, the following would likely occur:

1. Since the offered hypothesis is untestable, it can't be *disproven.*
2. Since it can't be disproven, it is likely to be accepted as true.
3. If it is accepted, alternative explanations for the same behavior won't be questioned.
4. The message within Mother's idea is that the child is perceived as having a problem. The problem is perceived as being *within* the child.

That's a lot to happen just because an adjective was accidentally used as a noun. But that's what could happen.

Now comes the important question. Could Mother's idea be correct? Could the concept of "insecurity" be the *cause* of a child's thumb sucking? That will depend upon whether the concept has the characteristics of being "circular," "safe," and "irrefutable." If it has those characteristics, it is not likely to be the cause of anything.

Circular. Mother's hypothesis was totally circular. It can best be described in the following manner. A child is observed to suck her thumb. Someone asks "Why?" The answer is offered that the child sucks her thumb *because* of "insecurity." Someone asks, "How do you know the child suffers from 'insecurity'?" The answer — "Because she is sucking her thumb." That's a circle.

Another child fails to follow a teacher's requests. She asks too many questions. "Why?" *Because* she suffers from "emotional disturbance." "How do you know the child is 'emotionally disturbed'?" The answer — "Because she fails to follow the requests and asks too many questions."

Circularity provides us with no usable information. The reason for this is that the offered answers to the question "Why?" are simply restatements of what was initially observed. The answers have no directly observable parameters. There is nothing directly to measure.

A child is observed to be delayed in academics and speech. Someone asks "Why?" An authority states, "Because the child is retarded." Can you see the circularity? Retardation, like so many other terms, is not a directly quantifiable entity. The term is supposed to be an adjective, meant to describe. Never to explain! (Even as an adjective, it doesn't tell us anything about what the child does or doesn't do. All it does is offer some negative characterization of the child. That doesn't help anyone!)

Because of their circularity, adjectives are not acceptable etiological terms. While they are frequently used in that manner, their usage is simply incorrect.

Safe and Irrefutable. The hypothesis that the child's thumb sucking is a result of "insecurity" is both a safe (untestable) and irrefutable (incapable of being disproven) explanation. Since "insecurity" is not an entity, with identifiable parameters, there is nothing to test or refute. All one can do is disagree.

Such answers are easy to offer but they are not scientifically acceptable. Again, an adjective-label is not a viable *explanation for anything.*

Sick. Once we attribute a behavior to "insecurity," the implication is clear and undeniable. We are saying that something is wrong with the child. The same is true when we suggest that a child *is* "emotionally disturbed," "retarded," "dyslexic," "immature," or "learning disabled." As adjectives, without a very specific definition, they tell us nothing. As nouns, as explanations, the outcome can be disastrous. Each of these safe, circular, irrefutable hypotheses tells someone that the child is sick. They tell us that a problem exists *within* a child. Unintentionally, they close alternative doors.

As is apparent, the mother's idea that her child's thumb sucking was *caused* by "insecurity" was incorrect. Her offered answer was neither clear, precise, nor capable of being verified. Thus it was not an acceptable answer to the question "Why?"

* * * * *

The Accountable "Why?"

It seems that consumer advocacy is higher today than ever before. Tires, and the machines they support, are being recalled when defects are noticed. No longer can television ads make claims that are unsubstantiated after being exposed to scientific rigor. Products that are eaten or drunk must list ingredients, both natural and artificial. School systems have been sued by parents for failure to provide acceptable educational services to all children. Presidents have been forced to leave their office when their behavior has been viewed as unacceptable.

The public is demanding accountability. The professions that provide physical relief, social aid, and psychological support are being watched with equal scrutiny. That, of course, is how it should be. The general public, however, is in a better position to question the credibility of tire claims, surgical outcomes, and promises of magical elixirs than the authenticity of educational/psychological assertions and explanations. Our professions are private and that which appears mysterious to the public is often equally mysterious to ourselves. New authorities enter stage-center almost daily. New answers are provided for the most complex manifestations of human behavior. Because of the "nature" of human behavior, professional accountability is often assumed, rather than challenged. Answers to the question "Why?" are often *accepted,* rarely *doubted.* That is not as it should be.

We are ready now to go back to the past. We are ready to see what the early-day authorities provided for us. We will see the foundation that was laid. As we proceed on our journey, remember the importance of the question "Why?" Remember, it is asked after differences in behavior have been observed, and the differences have been judged to be unacceptable. Remember also that the answer to the question "Why?" sets the stage for treatment. Remember further:

> If the answer is incorrect, the treatment might be incorrect;
> If the answer is circular, the question will not have been answered;
> If the answer is safe, no one will know if the answer has value;
> If the answer is irrefutable, it is likely to be accepted as true and an alternative explanation might be overlooked.
> If the answer is one that suggests the child suffers from an educational or psychological disease, it will take the child back into the land of the dragons, back into the darkness of the unknown, back to a time when accountability meant little more than inventing an easy answer that explained away one's responsibilities.

THE DRAGONS

Out From the Darkness

It was inevitable. It had to happen. The shroud of darkness had prevailed long enough. Thousands upon thousands of years of not seeing, not knowing, was more than sufficient to relegate even the hardiest into a state of utter, overwhelming fear. The small sphere that hung tenaciously in the heavens turned its predictable revolutions, but even during the brief moments of sunlight the darkness persisted. The new creature, the one with the two legs and the upright posture, was the most frightened of all. His cohabitants seemed unaffected. They were satisfied with just eating, sleeping, defecating, and procreating, although not necessarily in that order. They asked no questions, sought no answers. While the sudden clap of thunder and illuminating bolt of lightning sent the two-legged, upright one scurrying for both shelter and explanations, the others maintained their positions and activities, not caring much for a detailed account of what had happened. Indeed, they had neither the interest nor the equipment to ask the question "Why?"

But the two-legged one was different. He found himself with a large cranium, stuffed with a substance that would later be called gray matter. At present, however, he didn't care much about the substance's name. All he knew was that the stuff put pictures and thoughts into his consciousness, pictures and thoughts that for the most part gave him headaches and diarrhea. As far as he was concerned, the gray matter was a nuisance. Before he found himself with it, life was much simpler. If a falling rock came close to him, he simply moved out of its way. Now, however, he found his gray matter asking, "Where did that come from?" or "Why me?" Before, if he had been hit on the head by an icy hailstone, he just picked it up and ate it. Now he wanted to know what he had done to deserve such treatment. In earlier days, if one of his territorial-sharing neighbors was mistakenly perceived as being a banana and was accidentally devoured by a mammoth three-eyed gorilla, the incident went almost totally unnoticed. Not now, however. Now, the same event would produce the dreaded diarrhea for he could picture himself as being the chosen yellow, elongated fruit. He could think the thoughts of "Me next?" He, of course, only contemplated those thoughts after assuming a fetal position behind a huge tree. When the coast was clear, he would run. As he did, he would look toward the heavens and scream, "Someone help me with my thoughts and pictures. Someone, anyone, tell me why! I must know." When he realized that there was no one who was going to provide him with the needed answers, he would return, as he had done so many times to his cave, shivering, cowering, defecating. On one particularly frightening day he found a small, pointed rock and just prior to expiring he scribbled, "Ignorance is *not* bliss!" Unfortunately, he forgot to write his name or the date so we can only guess who he was and when the event actually happened.

Circa: 102,000 B.C., in a hilly, wooded area located in Northern Crameria

No longer concerned about falling hail, rolling rocks, and three-eyed gorillas, the two-legged creature flourished — perhaps continued to survive would be a more accurate description. He stayed close to home, venturing into the unknown only when the supply of toads needed replenishing. When that happened, the one who drew the short straw was appointed the chosen hunter. When the hunter made it back, if he made it back, he was able to choose which toad would be his. Most of the two-legged ones could have cared less. They were thrilled to have the last toad. Anything was better than going out into the unknown.

Because they rarely ventured out, they experienced a taste of comfort their earlier brothers and sisters had never known. Their gray matter had become more useful, and they had learned a few important lessons. They learned not to eat dirt. That was a big help for that lesson kept many of them alive for longer periods of time. They also learned to go into the nearby woods when they felt the urge to eliminate. That lesson helped them keep friends for longer periods of time.

All in all, they were fine so long as they had plenty of toads and so long as nothing new happened. If some never experienced event did present itself, they immediately stopped what they were doing and, while huddled together, held a life-saving prayer meeting. After each one of them had thrown a rock into the prayer hole, they rushed around the prayer fire while the tallest of them held the "Y" stick high into the air. The stick was actually a branch from a fallen tree that had the shape of what would much later be called a capital "Y." When the stick was steadied all of the two-legged ones would, in unison, chant, "Why did that happen?" "Why did that happen?" They would then wait for an answer. One rarely came. On one occasion, however, at the precise moment they had concluded their chanting, a giant pigeon, who had the misfortune of being in the wrong place at the wrong time, relieved himself. His droppings abruptly put out the prayer fire. The decision was made to cancel the "Why?" meetings for three weeks.

The history making event that was to occur this morning initially went unnoticed. It started with a high pitched scream that came from one of the bachelor caves. Everyone was used to screams, although admittedly those who were no longer sleeping were somewhat surprised that the scream hadn't come from the married caves, which was quite usual. No one was particularly alarmed, however, until the screamer ran from his cave and helplessly plopped himself next to the barely lit prayer fire. The commotion woke the remainder of the two-legged ones and everyone came out into the open to see what was happening. What had happened was that this particular two-legged one had awakened to discover a slight cracking of the skin between two of his toes. It was an exceptionally frightening observation. It was new. It was unknown. It was the worst.

"What is it?" the plopped one screamed toward the heavens. Terrified, he shrieked, "Why me?" To make matters worse, the inflicted one noticed that the crack was itchy! Despite his attempts at satisfaction, the itch continued. "Someone help me," he pleaded.

Mesmerized by what they were seeing, his neighbors forgot for the moment the "Y" stick. They cautiously joined him, watching wide-eyed his feeble scratching. They looked helplessly at each other, waiting for someone to do something, say something. They came close enough to the afflicted one to see the amazing crack. They somehow knew to contain their curiosity; they looked but did not touch. After several minutes of looking, they inspected their own toes. To their unquestionable delight, they observed no cracking, felt no itching. One of the observers, the most frightened, screamed, "He must have angered the gods. Stay away from him. Don't touch him. Leave him be." They all did. They left their former friend, sitting by the fire, scratching.

"Somebody get the 'Y' stick," one of them urged. They all turned and ran to the rock that housed the sacred branch. To their dismay, it was gone. Frantic, they dashed to and fro, searching. Unknown to them at that moment, one of the two-legged ones, the oldest one, had been watching the carryings-on. He was too tired to run, too tired to scream. He was even too tired to walk to the prayer fire. More so, he was tired of the prayer fire. Ever since the big pigeon, he had decided that the whole ritual was a big bust. Now, he sat on a large boulder. Behind his arthritic back, he held the "Y" stick. As he watched what was happening, he allowed his gray matter to do his thinking. "I can't believe this is the way it is supposed to be. Grown two-legged ones, running around, panicked, afraid of their own shadow. Unable to do a good days work without experiencing the fear of the unknown. Somebody must do something. But what?" he asked. "What could be the *answer*?"

He thought for a few more minutes while he watched his friends assume the fetal position behind whatever shelter they could find. Then he suddenly stopped thinking. He knew. "The *answer*! That's it! Give them an answer! Put an end to the ignorance. Tell them why! If they know the answer there will be no ignorance. Without ignorance, there will be no fear. Without fear, there will be no more diarrhea! It's worth a try," he thought.

He took a deep breath. He straightened his arched back and stood on the towering boulder. He held the "Y" stick in front of him. He calmed himself as best he could. "Hey guys," he yelled. The fetal bodies turned toward him. One by one they saw the "Y" stick. One by one they felt a little better. The old one, who had suddenly grown a long white beard, raised the stick high into the air. When he was sure everyone was watching, he methodically broke the stick in two. The onlookers moaned. They were sure life was about to end. "We don't need this anymore," the old one said, dropping the pieces to the ground. "Do you hear me? We don't need it!"

"But that was our 'Y' stick," one cried.

"Wait crying one," the old one urged. He took one more breath. "Do you want to know the *why* of the itch, the *why* of the crack?"

"For sure, for sure," the neighbors answered. "Please tell us why. We don't like the dark," they added as they looked hopefully at the old two-legged one.

He paused for a moment before answering. "That was the easy part," he said to himself. "Anyone can say that they know why; that's a piece of cake. Now the tough part," he thought. "I've got to come up with a good explanation. One, at least, that's believable. One that's believable and . . . one, maybe, that can't be argued with. That would be good. The answer might not be right . . . but . . . who will know." He stroked his beard and looked directly into the eyes of the waiting faces. A sudden sense of omnipotence filled his body. His face generated a warm, knowing glow. "Here goes," he said, his tongue a little heavy in his mouth.

"The gods are not angered," he spoke loudly, clearly. The eyes watched, listened. That was a good start. "They could care less about itchy feet. They have other things to worry about," he continued. He could feel his neighbors' relief. The afflicted one still scratched while he listened. He, too, felt better. "It is the diabolical demon from Northern

Crameria that has seen fit to play tricks on our friend." This was the moment of truth. "Would they buy it?" he thought. "If not, everything's down the tubes." He waited. Silence. Finally, someone spoke.

"Is that right?" There was belief in the tone.

"You betcha," the old one quickly answered. "The demon has punished our friend because he has been spending too much time in the forest. That is the *dragon*. That is the *why* of the itch, the *why* of the crack!" Again silence, but this time only for a brief second. As if a tremendous load had been removed, they all stood, even the afflicted one, and roared their approval. There was an explosion of applause and celebration.

"We all know why!" they sang. "We know why!"

The old one was shocked. "Damn, that was easy," he thought. He jumped off his rock and joined the merriment. He was hoisted on the shoulders of the strongest ones, carried, praised, adored. Suddenly, the darkness was gone, gone, that is, until the afflicted one hobbled over to him and asked, "But what am I supposed to do about it?"

The old one was dropped as quickly as he had been hoisted. A fickle group. A new problem had surfaced. "What good's an answer without a solution?" the neighbors said.

"Tough business, this giving of answers," the old one said to himself as he wiped the dirt from his long beard. "Fear no longer," he retorted. "We can handle the dragon." Without another word, and with renewed strength, he ran to the back of a prehistoric barn, grabbed a handful of moose dung, mixed it thoroughly with dead grass, formed it into a quarter-of-a-pound patty, and ran back to the afflicted one. "Stick your foot in this stuff," he commanded. "Keep it there for a fortnight plus three. When the itching stops, you'll know that the dragon has been slain."

"Thank you, thank you, thank you," the afflicted one said.

Behavior	Why?	Treatment	Outcome	Conclusion
1. Itchy, Cracking Toes	Demon From Northern Crameria	Moose Dung and Grass	Itching Stops	Demon Has Gone, The Dragon Has Been Slain

The laughter and celebration returned. Even the afflicted one smiled despite what he had his foot in.

Epilogue

After the seventeen days and nights, the itching stopped and the all-knowing one was adulated. He was catapulted into a position of supreme omniscience. From that point on, whenever a problem presented itself, the chosen one was sought out for the solution. Whenever the darkness of the unknown showed its ugly face, the giver provided the light. "Not a bad deal," the old one thought to himself. (By the way, four days after the itching stopped, the afflicted one's foot fell off. That was viewed as an unfortunate side-effect of the old one's wisdom. "No big deal," the afflicted one pointed out. "I don't feel the itch anymore.")

Circa: 5000 B.C., in a suburban village known as Uwanga

With the passage of time, things had changed. The numbers of people who inhabited the earth had grown significantly. Modern times existed and problems of the past were rarely discussed. Small communities began popping up all over the vast territories, and the people who lived in these communities were energetic, confident, and intelligent.

Uwanga was one of the first bedroom communities. Its major industry, the making of attaché cases out of banana peels, had been located far from the residential section of the town. Its chamber of commerce was rightfully proud of its clear, clean skies, its abundant lakes replete with fish and fowl, and its lush forests that provided all the comforts — shade, shelter, and tranquility. It was, by design, a quiet town with little in the way of unacceptable, exciting entertainment. Its population numbered approximately 300, but it was growing rapidly, due in part to the absence of exciting entertainment.

The children of Uwanga were very special. They were also very good. They were responsible, mature citizens almost from the moment they entered the world. By the age of three, they were already participating in family chores, already making important decisions regarding their own lives, and already helping their family survive and progress.

There were two major reasons for the children's advanced development. First, the unacceptable part of the modern world, with all its ills and distractions, existed on the other side of the largest lake and thus was unable to contaminate and influence. Second, and more important, the children appeared to have a built in immunity to both physical and mental disease. Their minds and bodies grew rapidly and their intellectual and emotional development increased geometrically with each passing moon. Nothing stood in their way. Nothing, that is, except the dreaded evil spirits and damn *dragons.*

One of the children living happily in Uwanga was Yjerkie Yjerk. (The "j" is silent.) As expected, Yjerkie was a good boy. He had always been a good boy. There was never any reason to assume that he would be anything but good for the rest of his life. His parents, quite naturally, had a great deal to do with his goodness. They dutifully said the special evening prayer and liberally spread the special green dust, purchased from the town's spirit and dragon watcher, over the sacred fire. The prayer, dust, and the fire were the most effective methods, according to the watcher who had cornered the market, for keeping the spirits and dragons a safe distance from the Yjerk's children. The parents' efforts had been very successful — at least up to this day, Yjerkie's fourth birthday. Beautiful Yjerkie. Four-years-old. My, how time flies.

The sun rose brightly over the eastern hills. The chirping birds and croaking frogs signaled another cherished day in the lives of the Yjerks. Although Mother had to work at the attaché factory (Father did the housekeeping), Yjerkie, and the rest of his family played together as all anticipated the joyous party that would occur when Yjerkie's mom returned from the office. There was great excitement as everyone guessed what special present Mom would bring home. Toward the afternoon, Father left his children and busied himself with straightening the residence and smoothing out the dirt that made up the kitchen floor.

Everyone watched the sun gradually move across the deep blue sky. When it rested for a second or two at 45 degrees above the western hills, the family knew Mother would soon be home. Quickly, Father ushered Yjerkie into the birthday chair, located in one of the darker areas of the home. Custom had it that the birthday child was not allowed to watch Mother as she entered the house. Nor was the child allowed to inquire about the special gift that would be his after dinner was finished. In Uwanga, no good, healthy child ever asked the question, "What did you bring me?" In Uwanga, no healthy child ever would.

Mother walked into the house when the sun reached 42 degrees above the hills. She was a degree late, but business was brisk this time of the year. Just in case Yjerkie was peeking, she hid the present she had purchased. She was, however, having a problem. It was difficult to hide the six foot Uwanga spear behind her four foot Uwanga frame. She was warmly greeted. Quiet exclamations filled the house as everyone, minus Yjerkie, saw the present. Mother shushed her family as she hid the spear behind the family's Uwanga log.

All this time, Yjerkie fidgeted in his chair, isolated from the happenings in the other room. He had heard the greetings and the shushing. His curiosity had reached uncontrollable proportions. He strained his neck hoping to catch a glimpse of the present. As he did, his active brain reminded him of the custom, of the danger in breaking the custom, of the spirits and dragons that would certainly be angered if the custom was even slightly vilified. He silently cursed the custom, the dragons and spirits, as he had done on two of his previous birthdays. (When he was a year old, he accepted everything.) He had tried to understand his parents' explanation for the custom, but their answers never made much sense to him. He had been applauded for his inquisitiveness, but severely punished when he questioned the purpose of the custom, and more seriously, the very *existence* of the dragons.

"I've never seen them," he had said once to his mother, who had turned as white as a snowflake.

"Yjerkie, don't ever say that again!" Mother admonished, as she firmly placed her hand over his still moving mouth. "You are never to question the existence of the dragons! No one has ever questioned them, no one ever will!"

"But Mom, I've never seen them. No one has ever seen them. If no one has ever seen them, how do we know they are real?" It was then that he had been severely punished.

Despite his remembering of the incident, he continued to stretch his neck. "Damn dragons, wherever you are!" he whispered, while looking toward the ceiling. "I don't think you are real, do you hear me?" he added, now standing bravely, proudly. He was about to point his middle finger of his right hand toward the invisible sky when his father came running into the room.

"We're ready," Father happily proclaimed, unaware of his son's blasphemy. Yjerkie was too upset to be happy. His grumbling and mastications went unnoticed. He was fuming as he walked with his father. "Dumb dragons," he thought to himself as he sat down at the Uwanga table.

While Father served the rabbit soup, Yjerkie let his eyes dart to each of the four corners of the room. Nothing. He looked behind the chairs, the benches, the tables, the shovels, but again, nothing. His teeth, still grinding, mutilated one of the flat, green leaves that had previously been floating on top of the rabbit broth. His family's excitement went unperceived as his disappointment, his anger increased. The wooden spoon held tightly in his hand began to shake as his small fist trembled. Unable to contain himself, and unwilling to accept the need for the custom and the dragons, he uncharacteristically slammed his fist to the table. Before the sound of small muscle and bone hitting the wooden table top had been fully processed by his family, he rose from his chair and in total defiance of tradition, he iconoclastically challenged the very fiber of the accepted. He tilted his head toward the flat beamed ceiling and yelled with all his strength, "I WANT MY PRESENT!!"

His brothers and sisters were startled by the sound rather than the content. His mother and father were startled by the content rather than the sound. Before anything could be said, Yjerkie again voiced his demand. Everyone was startled. Mother and Father stared at each other, knowing the seriousness of the situation. They quickly ran to him, hoping to protect him from the inevitable onslaught. Before they could reach him, however, he was down on his knees pelting the kitchen floor with his fists. He was screaming at the top of his lungs. His face had reddened, almost purpled. Without further hesitation, Mother ran to the Uwanga log and fetched the Uwanga spear. She almost impaled her husband, who was standing, mouth open in disbelief, as he watched his young son rearrange the house's foundation.

"Here, Yjerkie," Mother said. "Here is your present. Please quiet down. Please stop screaming." Yjerkie did not hear. He was too caught up in his own activity.

"Son," Father spoke, "please."

His father's voice, soothing, comforting, caught his attention. He looked up from the floor. He saw his mother and father, standing, quietly pleading. He saw his brothers and sisters, their startled gaze still frozen on their faces. He saw the spear, but it was too late. Too much had happened. He stood, body still trembling, and grabbed the spear. He raised it, pointing its tip toward the kitchen window. He let his mouth silently utter several brand new "four-letter" words. Then he rather calmly said, "Hey dragon, up your Uwanga!"

He let the spear fly. He missed the window by just a hair. It smashed, instead, into the kitchen wall. Now it was two spears, neither of which was particularly useful nor attractive. He saw what he had done. He saw it from its beginning to its untimely end. He saw it, and what he saw angered him more. Back to the floor he went, pelting, screaming, purpling.

Mother and Father were shocked. They were scared and confused. This was new, different, unknown. "Something must be wrong," Father said. "Do you think it could be . . .?"

"Don't say it," Mother begged.

"But . . . ."

"No, it can't be."

"Then maybe it was the soup,"Father offered, groping for an answer.

"Can't be the soup, dumbo," Mother reacted angrily. "We ate the same stuff and we're not on the floor going bananas."

"Well, I'm worried," Father admitted, feeling the darkness, the fear. "I think we should . . . should . . . call the mind doctor immediately. Maybe he can tell us what is wrong with our Yjerk. Something must be wrong. Look what he is *doing.*" What Yjerkie was doing was digging a twelve inch depression in the kitchen floor.

The mind doctor arrived almost the moment after he was summoned. Everyone in Uwanga was so good; there was so little darkness, that he rarely had an opportunity to practice the trade he had studied so diligently. After courteous introductions, Mother, Father, brothers, sisters, and mind doctor stood watching Yjerkie as he continued to dig, pelt, and scream.

Several minutes passed, then the mind doctor spoke. "Ah yes, I see," he said. "Yes," he added in a highly professional tone. Mother and Father were impressed by the depth of the doctor's voice. The children weren't; they were too young to be impressed by such things. "I have seen all I need," he stated. "Why don't we go outside and talk."

The mind doctor sat on a large rock just outside the Yjerk's house. He pulled an untattered scroll from his small black bag. While the parents and siblings watched, he carefully unrolled the parchment and read intently the material before him. "As I suspected," he murmured. He placed the parchment back into his bag, closed it, and placed it next to him. He closed his eyes and allowed his arms to hang limply by his sides. Cavernous wrinkles appeared on his aging forehead, that was bounded by a shock of thick white hair. His narrow body remained motionless. It was obvious he was deep in thought.

"Tell us, please, what is happening," Father said, breaking the silence. "We must know."

The mind doctor's eyes abruptly opened. A vibrantly reddish color filled his worried face. "As I suspected," he repeated, as his head jerked toward the early evening sky. "Your son is having a tantrum!" It was simply said, factual, without undue emotion.

"A what?" gasped Mother.

"A tantrum."

Behavior

1. Tantrum

"Holy bananas," Father whimpered.

"Can you tell us *why*?" Mother pleaded, grabbing her husband's clammy hand.

"Yes, dear parents, I can," the mind doctor said authoritatively. Then he paused and returned his gaze toward the sky. The moon was well off in the distance; a full moon that had the potential of providing wanted light. Overhead, however, it was dark, very dark. As the doctor stared at the darkness, familiar thoughts began to run through his mind. Rather than holding them back, he allowed them to flow . . . .

> "I know I am supposed to say that I can tell them why," his thoughts reminded him. "My teachers have always assured me

that we authorities know the answers; that we can always come up with satisfactory explanations for behavior, but . . . ."

His lips continued to move as silent concerns pulsed through his brain. Their movement, however, was difficult for the dryness that had taken over his mouth prevented his tongue from flickering in any direction. He had fought this battle with himself before — and had always lost. He was, to be sure, a professionally sound individual. He prided himself on his self-imposed credibility. He despised dishonesty of any kind, but particularly professional dishonesty. He hated being put in the position of coming up with an answer to a question that almost defied answering. But there he was again.

". . . I wonder if satisfactory and correct are necessarily one and the same. Maybe it's *not* too important to be correct. Maybe the only thing that really counts is to have something to say. I *can't* admit that I don't know why. I don't have that option. I can't just admit my ignorance. I must say something. Imagine how these nice parents would feel if I had nothing to say. The darkness would return all over again. Something else, too. I'd be out of business in a second if I admitted my ignorance. The parents would simply go to someone else. Those other guys always have answers. I'd better come up with something. Who knows, maybe they will believe me. Maybe they will feel better. Heaven knows I won't. What a drag . . . ."

He looked toward the parents and offered them a feigned smile. He had used it before and it had always been effective. He took a deep breath and readied himself for his explanation. As his words passed his chapped lips, he winced reflexively. His eyes were tightly closed, protectively closed, as if he expected to be smacked by a dried cow chip that had been shredded by a moving fan. Prepared for their challenge, for their denial of his authoritative assertion, he opened his eyes and said, "Your son has been taken over by an evil spirit." Then he quickly shut his eyes and cowered.

To his surprise and relief there was no challenge. Nobody asked, "How do you know?" "What kind of evidence do you have?" Nothing. Instead, the parents just stared at him as if they were asking for more. The brothers and sisters sat, totally confused. But in Uwanga, children were expected to be seen and not heard, so they said nothing. Feeling a drop of confidence, the mind doctor added, "Yes, good parents, your son has been taken over by a devilish spirit. His goodness has been replaced by a force that has the ability to alter. In a nut shell, the reason *why* your son is behaving as he is, is because of this evil, defiling spirit." Suddenly the moon, the light, was directly overhead.

Behavior	Why?
1. Tantrum	Evil Spirits

"Thank goodness for that," Father said, relieved. "At least now we know. You just don't know how difficult it is not to know," he added, satisfied. He turned and hugged his wife who immediately reciprocated. For a brief moment there was joy.

"But what can we do about it?" Mother asked, after letting go of her husband.

"I was afraid someone would ask me that," the mind doctor said to himself. Then out loud he indicated, "To cure the malady, we must drive the spirit from its newly acquired home. Once done, your son will no longer be diseased." The parents nodded. There was nothing else they could do. He appreciated their nods — nothing more disconcerting than parents who do not nod at the right time. Unnoticed, one of Yjerkie's brothers moved closer to his parents. It was as if he wanted to say something.

"We have several treatments for this disease," the mind doctor explained. "The first is known as trephining."[1] Immediately, the doctor pulled a small "saw" from his black bag. He showed it to the parents, then to the brothers and sisters. The youngsters seemed to sense that whatever this thing was, they didn't like it. "This is called a trephine."[1]

Behavior	Why?	Treatment
1. Tantrum	Evil Spirits	Trephining

TREPHINING: Trephining, often considered the first known surgical procedure, involved a process by which a small crown saw, a trephine, was used to remove circular discs of bone from the skull. This surgery was performed to provide escape routes for evil spirits. Evidence strongly suggests that this procedure was used up through 19th Century A.D.

Rationale: The assumption was that the evil spirit had settled inside the body. "Windows" were therefore provided to facilitate the spirit's escape.

"What we do," the mind doctor continued, "is drill perhaps three holes in your child's head. Then, we watch his *behavior* very carefully."

"What do you watch for?" Mother asked.

"We watch to see if the tantrum stops."

"And if it doesn't?" Father said.

"You can be reasonably assured that the tantrum will stop after three holes are drilled into his head," the doctor stated confidently.

"But if it doesn't stop?" Father persisted.

"Then, we'll drill three more holes."

"If it then stops?"

"When it stops, we know the evil spirit has gone," the mind doctor answered.

Behavior	Why?	Treatment	Outcome	Conclusion
1. Tantrum	Evil Spirits	Trephining	Tantrum Stops	Evil Spirit Gone

As soon as the doctor had finished his explanation, Yjerkie's older brother raised his hand as if to ask a question. Mother, however, quickly grabbed the hand and sat on it. "The second procedure is known as BDOK," the doctor pointed out.

Behavior	Why?	Treatment
1. Tantrum	Evil Spirits	BDOK

BDOK: BDOK, pronounced "beedock" was a procedure used with young children who had been taken over by evil spirits and were observed to do any of the following: having tantrums, thumb sucking, showing disrespect, not doing chores, not going to bed on time, fondling genitals — theirs or someone else's. The procedure involved placing the child on a hard surface, usually a table. Hard ground was acceptable. Volunteers were called to assist in the procedure. Once the youngster was sufficiently restrained, everyone gathered around the child and proceeded to **B**eat the **D**evil **O**ut of the **K**id.

Rationale: The evil spirit had obviously settled inside the child's body. The key to successful treatment was to make the "home" an unpleasant place to be. This was accomplished through repeated pummeling of the young child's body.

"Usually, the beating lasts about seven to nine minutes, depending upon the determination of the spirit," the doctor stated. "After the beating, the tantrum usually stops. We then conclude that the evil spirit has decided to go elsewhere."

Behavior	Why?	Treatment	Outcome	Conclusion
1. Tantrum	Evil Spirits	BDOK	Tantrum Stops	Evil Spirit Gone

Again the older brother made an attempt to be recognized. He raised his free hand, but his father grabbed it and sat on it.

"Finally," the mind doctor said, unaware of the older child's attempts, "we have a brand new technique. This treatment involves the use of a very powerful medicine that can be used to help rid Yjerkie of his problem. It has been used with other diseases, but until very recently, never with evil spirits. It is called a prune.

PRUNE: Prune, a variety of plum that dries without spoiling. To be ingested in large quantities. Research has proven that prunes facilitate the moving of evil spirits out from the body.

"Our experience indicates that after approximately 63 prunes have been consumed, and after 22 trips to the Uwanga forest, the affliction will terminate." ("Either that, or the child is simply too tired to have any tantrums," the good doctor thought to himself.)

"And do you then conclude that the evil spirit has gone?" Mother asked.

Behavior	Why?	Treatment	Outcome	Conclusion
1. Tantrum	Evil Spirits	Prunes	Tantrum Stops	You Guessed It, Mom!

With great effort, the older brother pulled himself free from his protecting parents. He stood as tall as he could and said quite clearly, "WAIT A SECOND!!"

The mind doctor almost fell over backwards. The relied upon silence and acceptance had ended. Uwanga's mind doctor knew that the chip was about to hit the fan!

"That's my brother you're playing with!" the youngster exclaimed. "I'm not going to let you drill holes in his head, beat him, or make him eat prunes!" Father fainted. Mother was on the verge. "Your logic is for the bananas!" The mind doctor had grabbed his lower lip. He was pulling on it furiously. He suddenly needed to eliminate.

"First you tell us that Yjerkie is having a tantrum," the brother said. "Big deal," he added, silently.

Behavior
1. Tantrum

"Then you tell us that the reason he is having a tantrum is because of an evil spirit that has taken over his body."

Behavior	Why?
1. Tantrum	Evil Spirits

"If I may be so bold to ask," the brother said, "did you see the evil spirit go into his body?" He pointed his finger at the doctor. The authority immediately shook his head "no." "Did any of us see the evil spirit go in?" the brother asked his family. His mother, revived father, and brothers and sisters also shook their heads "no." "Then how do we know that it is in there? How do we know that it is real? You don't, do you?" he asked the mind doctor. "Of course not," the brother said, answering his own question. "You just guessed that the spirit was there, was real. Next, you tell us you're going to treat this thing that may not even exist. Are you kidding?"

Behavior	**Why?**	**Treatment**
1. Tantrum	Evil Spirits	Trephining BDOK Prunes

"Then you have the nerve to tell us that you will conclude that the evil spirit has gone as soon as you see the tantrum stop. Don't you see how meaningless that conclusion is? You are just talking in circles!"

Behavior	**Why?**	**Treatment**	**Outcome**	**Conclusion**
1. Tantrum	Evil Spirits	Trephining BDOK Prunes	Tantrum Stops	Evil Spirit Gone

"You don't see the spirit go in. You don't see it come out. All you are doing is guessing that it is there. And the basis for your guesses? Yjerkie's behavior. You are using my brother's behavior as a sign that the spirit exists. But, point in fact, all you are doing is inferring the presence and absence of the cause. Since you are not willing to honestly say that you don't know why he's going bananas, or you are not willing to look at other alternative explanations, you decide to drill holes. That's the way you are going to slay your invented dragon? Well, not with my brother, you won't! I don't have to believe your explanation. I am not enamored by your authority. Unless you can come up with some good evidence to back what you are saying, I won't believe you. My parents can. That's their choice. Not mine!"

"I'll tell you something that's really scary," the brother continued. "I'll bet that someday in the not too distant future, some mind doctor will use the same logic you have used to reach your same conclusion. The only thing that's going to be different will be the terms. They'll be longer, more impressive, more difficult to understand. Maybe the new doctors won't drill holes anymore, but they will invent something. Something! You watch," the brother said, angrily. "It's going to happen."

The brother went over to a now sleeping Yjerkie. He picked up his little brother, held him tightly for a moment, then placed him gently into his warm bed. "It's okay, sweet brown eyes," the brother said softly. "I won't let them hurt you."

The mind doctor, knowing the youngster's prediction would come true, quietly placed his "saw" and prunes back into his bag. His white robe clung tightly to his wilted, wet body as he walked alone into the darkness of the Uwanga forest.

Circa: 20th Century A.D., in the beautiful city of Cucamonga, California

Twentieth century A.D. was truly an amazing time to be alive. The wonders of technological and scientific growth were everywhere. Only the most hard core skeptic still believed that the earth was flat. People were now very willing to take long ocean cruises without fear of falling into oblivion once past the horizon. The moon had been visited. Scientists and space explorers, breathing oxygen from tanks and eating food from plastic containers, provided seemingly undeniable proof that there was no man on the moon. They also proved that the sphere was not made of green cheese. They further reported that while they explored the surface of the moon, they never once saw a cow jumping anywhere.

Shiny metal birds, called airplanes, could take travelers places in hours where previously it would have taken months, even years. For those people who preferred not to fly in the skies, there were automobiles and trains. The former, according to many, caused more problems than they were worth, while the latter suffered from the disease of never arriving on time.

The most noticeable of all changes that came to man along with the 20th century was the way he thought of himself and the influential forces that touched his daily living. New technology had helped him to better understand why he behaved as he did. Although he still experienced problems with the unknown, the new technology provided him with a multitude of answers that seemed to satisfy his need to know. For awhile, it appeared that the darkness that came with ignorance would never again be a problem.

So pervasive was the new technology that every citizen in every city and town of America was exposed to it. One could randomly select any community within the confines of the two great oceans and see the new technology and the new thought. Cucamonga was no exception.

A sleepy, historic town located in one of the numerous lush canyons found in the great state of California, Cucamonga was fast becoming a mecca of industry and tourism. This beautiful town was once named "Our Lady of the Basin of a Fountain of Cucamonga" (rough translation!). Sadly, the romantic name had to be shortened because the post office, which was to come around in 1867, couldn't fit all those letters on the cancellation stamp.

The people of Cucamonga were, in the true sense, pioneers. They were best characterized as ruddy, strong-willed, proud Americans who built their town with their bare hands and strong backs. During the blizzard of '23, with shovels only, they fought the elements and cleared a path through the main street so business could go on as usual — a proud heritage that was passed on to every son and daughter. To many, the town symbol was a shovel.

The Whipples were a typical Cucamongan family — a hard working husband and wife and two bright, lovely children. Kerkie Whipple, who had recently turned five, and his older sister Sara, were considerate children, fun to be with. With few exceptions, they were easily manageable children and the result was that the entire family participated in many activities together. One of these activities was roller skating. Every Friday night, the entire family would pile into the family car and spend several glorious hours at the rink. Kerkie truly loved skating. Not only did it give him the chance of feeling the air conditioned wind as it raced by his young face, but it gave him the opportunity to collide into his somewhat inept father who was just learning how to stand on the skates. According to Kerkie, the collisions were accidental. Perhaps, but they were occurring rather frequently.

Kerkie was a joy to his mother. He helped her clean up his room. He went to bed on time. His little underpants were always as "clean as a whistle." He liked to describe them that way. His school work, what there was of it, was good. After dinner, he would help clean the table and, when Mom would allow, he would even help with the dishes. If Mom asked him to do something, more times than not, he would follow her request. They had a warm, trusting relationship.

As of late, Kerkie was not quite as cooperative for his dad. It wasn't as though he didn't like his dad, because he did. He just seemed to like his mother more. Whether Father wanted to admit it or not, Mom was more fun to be with, so Kerkie stayed closer to her. In the evening, after everything was cleaned up, Kerkie would wrap himself around his mother and rest his head on her full breasts while she read to him. This was disturbing to Father. "Can't he put his head someplace else?" Father often asked. Mother would respond, "Don't be so silly. Besides, *I* like it." Father would become angry and often scold little Kerkie for not showing him equal affection. Mother would always intervene and point out, "You are not built like I am." It was a fact Father could not deny.

Father was certain that Kerkie realized he was jealous. He even felt that Kerkie enjoyed making him feel left out. At times, Dad believed that Kerkie would be very happy if he were not around. On one very significant occasion, Kerkie asked his father if he could have his long raincoat when he decided to die. Father said that was proof positive that Kerkie wanted him gone. Mom tried to convince her husband that Kerkie was just a little boy and really didn't understand what he was saying. Mother's statement did little to appease Father. He was openly upset about the incident for several days.

Weeks had passed since the episode with the raincoat and Father had finally forgotten about it. For some reason, things had been going pretty smoothly between Kerkie and his dad. They played together, talked together, and took long walks into the hills. They really enjoyed being with one another. But . . . today was Friday. Something was about to happen.

It was about 5:30 p.m. and Mom was busy making dinner. Kerkie and Sara had washed their hands and were sitting at the table when Dad came home. He gave a quick hello to his kids, a peck on the cheek to his wife, then he ran upstairs to put his metal lunch box by his bed.

"What's for dinner?" he asked while walking down the stairs. He had his brand new white tennis shoes on that he had purchased specifically for wearing to the rink.

"Pancakes," Mother answered.

"You know I don't like pancakes," Father responded in a grumpy tone.

"Mom made them because she knows I like them," Kerkie quickly said. It was not the best thing to say at that particular time. Hearing his son's comment, Father said something under his breath that went unnoticed.

"Yes, Kerkie," Father said out loud. "Now eat your pancakes so we can go. I don't want to miss the opening music. One more thing, don't play with your milk! If you spill it like you did last night, you won't go skating with us. That's a promise." Once again under his breath — "Why am I taking him anyway? He's always knocking me over. I'll just bet he's doing it on purpose. It's his mother's fault. She lets him get away with everything."

"Did you say something dear?" Mother asked pleasantly.

"No dear! I just asked Kerkie not to spill his milk."

"We aren't going to spill our milk, are we Kerkie?" Kerkie and Sara both shook their heads "no."

"Fine," Father answered, satisfied. "But let's hurry."

"I will Dad," Kerkie answered.

Sometimes little events that ordinarily would go unnoticed become catalytic triggers for major explosions. Such was the case with the glass of milk — eight ounces, colored unfortunately with deep chocolate syrup, that happened to spill, then roll off the table and end up permanently staining a brand new pair of initially white tennis shoes. On another day, no critical situation. But today, Friday, it precipitated a scene that can best be described by the following dialogue that took place between several members of a very happy family. The conversation had something to do with whose fault it was for the spilt milk.

"It was his fault!" Father yelled after looking down at his now brown, wet sneakers.

"No!" Mother screamed, "it was your fault for asking him to hurry. He was just doing what you asked!"

"No! If we hadn't had pancakes tonight, this would never have happened. It was your fault!" Father retorted intelligently.

"No! If you hadn't come home tonight, Kerkie wouldn't have had to hurry, so it was your fault," Mother offered as she joined her husband on a trip down the phylogenetic scale.

"No! If we'd never gotten married in the first place . . . !"

"No! If you'd never been born . . . !"

"Excuse me," Kerkie broke in before his parents killed one another. He was holding Sara's hand. "You know, if today was Thursday instead of Friday . . . ."

So much for family conversations.

The next few words were a simple, plain dictum. It was spoken by Father. Like other things, it was inevitable. "You are not going skating! You will stay home! You will never go skating! You will always stay home!"

Kerkie could not remain silent. Something had to be said. "It was an accident, Dad," he whispered.

"Accident my foot!" Father remarked, looking down at his feet. "Never . . . never going," he mumbled.

"But I want to go skating."

"Never!"

"Mom, I want to go skating." Mom said nothing. In fact, for the next several moments the dining room was silent. Somehow Kerkie surmised that silence meant the question had been resolved. He further determined that the resolution was not in his favor.

"But I want to go skating." It was said softly. No reaction.

"I want to go skating." A little louder, staccato-like. No reaction.

"Hey . . . I want to go skating!" Louder with waving arms. Mother looked up at him. It was a good sign.

"Will someone listen to me . . . I want to go!" There was a cry to the voice. It was loud enough to elicit an eyeblink from Sara. Father looked up. A better sign.

"Go! Go!" He screamed, waved, cried. It had worked.

"Kerkie," Mother said comfortingly. "It's okay. Relax. I'm sure your father will let you go."

"Go! Go!"

"Son, I've changed my mind. It's all right. We will all go. Just quiet down a little," Father said. Kerkie's screaming was so loud that he didn't hear what his father had said. The crying continued, accompanied by wildly thrashing, waving arms.

"What's happening?" Mother asked her husband.

"I don't know. I've never seen him this upset before. Have you?"

"No, I haven't." She, too, had become concerned. "Kerkie, honey, it's Mommy. Everything is all right." She put her arms around him, but to no avail. He did not calm down. "Something must be wrong." Sara nodded her head in agreement.

"Why don't you hold him. I'll call Dr. Clarity. He'll tell us what to do," Father said, running to the phone.

Father already felt more at ease having talked with his psychiatrist friend. Clarity had that ability. His voice and manner were soothing. Father knew everything would be fine once Clarity had a chance to find out what had happened. Kerkie was nestled up against his mother as Father walked from the phone. The youngster's arms hung limply. His cries were softer, weaker. Mother continued to gently rock her son until little Kerkie was fast asleep. The roller skating rink was suddenly thousands of miles away. Something else was much closer. It pervaded the house. The darkness, the fear of the unknown, had entered the Whipple's abode. Somebody was needed. Somebody who could provide light.

The following morning Clarity sat patiently as he listened attentively to the parents' report of the previous evening's events. He rocked back and forth in his leather swivel chair, sometimes looking directly at the parents, sometimes looking toward the ceiling of his dark wood-paneled office. The large caduceus at the end of a bronze letter opener that he held in his hand was easily visible to the parents. During the minutes the parents spent describing what had happened, Clarity said very little other than an occasional "yes" or "uhmmm." There was, however, a definite soothing quality to his seldom used voice that compensated for his bespeckled, ectomorphic, balding appearance. He looked as if he knew what he was doing. According to the new technology, the "look" was fifty percent of the curative process. As the parents talked, Clarity was busy listening, hunting, Un-Raveling, and Un-Tangling the hidden meanings behind the obvious. Finally, satisfied with their descriptions of Kerkie's actions, Mother and Father asked, "Why . . . why did it happen?"

"The question is not an easy one to answer," Clarity began, adjusting his silver rimmed glasses. "No question asked of a psychiatrist is easy," he added, touching his rounded nose. "But the information you have shared with me has enabled my mind to formulate a hypothesis as to what *caused* your son to behave as he did. I will share my ideas with you. Together, we will find the light." Clarity then paused for a moment. He liked to pause for it gave him the opportunity to review the subtle phrases the new technology had provided him. It gave him the time to consider the new answers that explained the complex "Whys" of human behavior . . . the new answers that a boy, living 7000 years earlier in a little town called Uwanga, had prophesized.

"First, I think it very critical to tell you," Clarity began, "that Kerkie's behavior, his tantrum, is really not too important . . . ."

Behavior

1. Tantrum

". . . You see, it was merely a symptom of other events that are much more critical."

"I'm not sure I am following you," Father said tentatively. "Last evening, in the midst of the chaos, we thought it was important."

"Yes, of course," Clarity answered. "To you the surface behavior is of primary concern. To us, it is very Un-Important. We recognize the surface behavior for what it really is. Namely, surface behavior." The parents looked at each other quizzically, but said nothing. "We also recognize that of greater import is what the surface behavior symbolizes. That's the nuts and bolts," Clarity continued, pleased with his expression. "That is why you are here. Without realizing it, you are Un-Consciously concerned about the symbolism. You might think you are here because of your son's behavior last evening. Sorry, such is not the case."

"Isn't that amazing," Mother thought out loud. "All this time, I thought we were seeing you because of what Kerkie did. But you are saying what he did really doesn't matter; what matters is not what he did."

"That's exactly correct," Clarity said, praising Mother for her astuteness.

"Then we should forget what he did and think about what he didn't do?" Father asked, hoping to find something to hold onto.

"That would be wise," Clarity said, this time with no praise.

"Wasn't the tantrum important in the beginning? Didn't it tell you that something was wrong?" Father said.

"In the beginning, maybe. Now, it's Un-Important. It was a sign, a clue. But now that the sign has been given, the clue seen, now . . . it's Un-Important."

"Oh."

"What's important now is 'why'," Clarity explained.

Behavior	**Why?**
1. Tantrum	???

Father interrupted Dr. Clarity before he could continue. "My wife and I thought about that on the way over this morning. We have decided that the 'why' is obvious . . . ."

As quick as Father had interrupted, Clarity was twice as quick. "Nothing is OBVIOUS!!" Clarity exclaimed. He abruptly stood from his chair and looked at the parents. "Remember the rule: What appears obvious is always the most Un-Obvious!!"

"Oh."

"Now that we have settled that, let's get down to the answer." Clarity returned to his chair and composed himself. After a short pause, he began. "Your son is going through something that all boys go through. I will explain it to you in a moment. First, understand that Kerkie is in conflict."

"No!"

"Yes."

"But we've never seen him behave as he did last evening. He's always been such a good boy. We've never seen him in this conflict until yesterday," Mother explained.

"No, my dear," Clarity said softly, affectionately. There was something about this woman that made Clarity feel pleasantly funny. "The conflict that your son is experiencing has nothing directly to do with what happened last night. The conflict to which I am referring is not something that you can actually see happening. The conflict is one that is occurring *within* your son. It is a conflict that is occurring Un-Consciously, inside young Kerkie."

"No!" Mother gasped, suddenly frightened by the term "Un-Conscious."

"What you saw last evening was a symptom, surface behavior. It tells us that the conflict is taking place. Your son is experiencing an Un-Conscious conflict. It's that simple," he said, sympathetically. "His personality has been taken over by forces that are battling within him.

These forces are now in control. What he did last evening was caused by these forces. These are the youngster's enemies that will have to be reckoned with."

Behavior	**Why?**
1. Tantrum	Un-Conscious Conflict, Forces, Enemies

"How do we reckon with them?" Father spoke.

"Treatment. Psycho. . .psycho. . .therapy." Clarity always had trouble with that word. "We will treat your son until his conflict has been resolved."

"How will you know that the conflict has been resolved?" Father inquired. It was a fair question.

"When your son doesn't do anything he isn't supposed to do, then we will know that there is no longer a conflict."

Behavior	**Why?**	**Treatment**	**Outcome**	**Conclusion**
1. Tantrum	Un-Conscious Conflicts, Forces, Enemies	Psycho. . . Psycho. . . Therapy	Doesn't Do Anything He Isn't Supposed to Do	Conflict Resolved

After thinking of all the things that Kerkie had done that Father thought he shouldn't have done, he stated, "It sounds hopeless."

"Not hopeless," Clarity said. "We have had plenty of practice practicing with these problems. You see, all boys go through the same conflict. They have been ever since the conflict was discovered."

Looking directly at Father, Clarity continued. "I want you to trust me. The facts I am about to relate will not be pleasant. But we must be strong. We must be willing to accept the authority's answers even when the answers cause deep pain. As it turns out," Clarity said, "*all [little] boys want to murder their fathers. This . . . is usually unconscious. They wish to murder the father and to have. . . .*" Clarity quickly changed his focus to Mother. He reached out with his hand to touch and comfort her trembling fingers that were now jumping nervously on her legs. He felt that pleasant, funny feeling again. "*. . .and to have sexual intercourse with the mother . . . .*"[13]

"My God!" Mother sputtered. "My little boy wants to do that?" she asked, not wanting an answer.

"I knew it! I knew it!!" Father screamed. "That little kid — your little kid," he said, pointing his finger toward his wife. "That's *why* he tries to run over me when we go skating. That little kid! He's trying to murder me. Did you hear that Ethel? Remember the raincoat? Huh? Huh? You said it was nothing. Nothing!! Murder me!!" Sara, who was quietly sitting with her brother in the reception room, heard the screaming. Fearing something was wrong she silently walked into the office and took a seat off in one of the corners. Because of her diminutive size, she went unnoticed.

"Yes," Clarity agreed. "There is an excellent chance that the accidents you spoke of earlier, and the incident with the raincoat, are additional signs of your son's conflict. . . ."

Behavior	**Why?**	**Treatment**	**Outcome**	**Conclusion**
1. Tantrum 2. Skating Accidents 3. Request for Raincoat	Un-Conscious Conflicts, Forces, Enemies	Psycho. . . Psycho. . . Therapy	Doesn't Do Anything He Isn't Supposed To Do, e.g., Tantrum, Skating Accidents, Request for Raincoat	Conflict Resolved

". . . The accidents are indicative of Un-Conscious attempts to get you out of the picture so your son can have his mother all to himself . . . intimately."

"My God!" Mother mumbled.

"You see," Clarity added, "we have learned a great deal about the relationships of sons and mothers, and daughters and fathers."

"Are you saying," Father interrupted sharply, "that our daughter also wants to kill me so she can have . . . have her mother too?" Sara's eyes popped open. She rapidly shook her head "no!"

"No, that would not happen," Clarity answered. "It is a little different for girls. Whether you wish to admit it or not," he said as he glanced toward Mother, " '*all women feel that they have been injured in their infancy and that through no fault of their own they have been slighted and robbed of part of their body.*' "[13]

"I don't want to hear anymore," Mother pleaded as her hands fell protectively over her pubes.

Not listening to Mother, Clarity said, " '. . .*that the girl recognizes the fact she lacks a. . . .*' " He loosened his tie. It was becoming very tight due to the pool of perspiration that had formed around his neck. " '. . .*lacks a penis, does not mean that she accepts its absence lightly. On the contrary, she clings for a long time to the desire to get something like it, and believes that possibility for an extraordinary number of years; and even at a time when her knowledge has long since led her to abandon the fulfillment of this desire as being quite unattainable,* [the new technology] *proves that it still persists in the unconscious . . . . The wish with which the girl turns to her father is, no doubt, ultimately the wish for the penis, which her mother has refused her and which she now expects from her father.'* "[13] Sara wanted to ask what a penis was but decided not to. She figured it couldn't be that big of a thing anyway.

"Ethel! Ethel!" Father shouted, "Get rid of Sara. I don't want her in my house. I don't want a daughter who wants my . . . my . . . Ethel!!"

Sara whispered, "I don't want it . . . whatever it is."

Impervious to Father's ranting Clarity continued. *"Girls and boys, therefore, are different. Little girls suffer from penis envy . . . ."*

"Stop. You must stop. I don't want to hear anymore."

". . . While little boys – since they already have one – suffer from something else." Clarity was "on." No amount of protesting would stop him. He loved his funny little words. He was at home with them. He used to repeat them while taking a shower and listen joyfully as they echoed off the sweating tiles. They gave him more of an intense orgasmic sensation than anything else he had ever discovered or experienced. His knuckles were white as the grip around his bronze letter opener tightened. " '*When a boy, from about the age of two or three . . . feels pleasurable sensations in his sexual organ and learns to procure these at will by manual stimulation . . . .*' "

"Please, no more."

" '*. . . He becomes his mother's lover. He desires to possess her physically in the ways which he has divined from his observations and intuitive surmises of sexual life and tries to seduce her by showing her the male organ . . .of which he is the proud owner . . .*' " he continued, raising the letter opener above his head. " '*. . . His father now becomes a rival who stands in his way and who he would like to push aside.*' "[13] Clarity stood up. He raised his arms toward the ceiling. His left hand was in a tight fist. His right hand was welded to his metal phallus. He took a deep breath. He proclaimed the new technology "AND. . .WE. . .CALL . . .THIS. . .CONFLICT. . .THE. . .OEDIPAL. . .COMPLEX!"

Behavior	**Why?**	**Treatment**	**Outcome**	**Conclusion**
1. Tantrum 2. Skating Accidents 3. Request for Raincoat 4. Showing Mother His Organ 5. Wanting to Murder Father 6. Wanting to Have Sex With Mother	Oedipal Complex	Psycho. . . Psycho. . . Therapy	Doesn't Do Anything He Isn't Supposed to Do, e.g., Tantrum, Skating Accidents, Request for Raincoat, Keeping His Organ to Himself, Not Wanting to Kill Father, Choosing Manual Stimulation in Place of Mother	Oedipal Complex Resolved

There was silence as the words reverberated off the office walls. Nobody moved. Nobody spoke. It was difficult to tell who was in the greatest state of shock. Then . . . .

"For what it's worth, I don't buy it!" It was as unexpected as a clap of thunder from a clear blue sky. The little voice from the corner. It caught Clarity totally by surprise. He almost stabbed himself with the letter opener. Mother and Father turned abruptly. Diminutive Sara, not noted for her public speaking: "I don't buy it. Period. I'm sure my little brother wants to kill his father and have sex with his mother. I'm sure." Her voice was innocent, naive, yet very clear. Clarity stared immobilized. No blinking. His breathing almost stopped. "You're saying that this Edible Compost Conflict is inside my brother? Inside? You don't know it's there. You can't see it. You can only guess it's there. What do you use to make your guess? What Kerkie did! I hate to be the one who has to break the news to you, but he could have done those things for hundreds of reasons." Clarity slumped in his chair. Still no blinking. His breathing began to vacillate. There was a chance he wasn't going to pull through. "Why would you tell my parents that there is something wrong *inside* my brother when you don't have the slightest idea if you are right? Did you want to scare them? An inside dragon — one that nobody can see? Why didn't you just admit that you had no idea why he had his tantrum? Wouldn't that have been more honest? Why drum up that sex and death stuff? There's no way you can prove anything you said. Or . . . is it not too important to be able to prove it?"

Young Sara stood up. She walked over to her parents and lead them from the office. Before she closed the door behind her, she looked at Dr. Clarity. "It would have been okay if you had just said that you didn't know. We could have handled that," she remarked. "Honest ignorance is better than erroneous, irrefutable, dragons." Then she closed the door and took her brother's hand. When they were away from the office, she whispered into Kerkie's ear, "That guy's a flake."

"Yeah, I heard," Kerkie answered as he held his sister's hand very tightly.

"Hey, by the way," Sara whispered again to Kerkie, "do you know what a penis is?"

"Sure. Those are the things you buy at the circus. You know . . . in the shells, with salt on them."

"Oh."

Dragons — The Metaphor

As you may have gathered, dragons are answers. They are the explanations the authorities have given us when we have asked the question "Why?" They are the causes, the reasons for our behavior. They are the demons that made our feet itch, the evil spirits that caused our tantrums, the Oedipal complexes that made us run over our fathers and run after our mothers. They are the perceptual-processing problems that made name writing difficult. They are the emotional disturbance that somehow accounted for our refusal to follow directions, refusal to stay in our seat, refusal to be like someone said we were supposed to be. And, with very exacting, very specific characteristics, they can be the legitimate answers to legitimate problems that seriously affect children, their parents, and their teachers.

Birth of the Dragons

Dragons were born the moment man was forced to face his own ignorance. In this usage, "ignorance" should *not* be interpreted to have negative connotations. It should be interpreted to represent the fact that at certain points in history, various occurrences and experiences were inexplicable, given the knowledge we had during those points in time. Things happened and the reasons for the events were simply unknown.

Although that fact should have been understood, it wasn't. Ignorance, rather than being something that needed to be worked with, was very frightening. Thus, man sought out answers to his questions; questions that in his view were germane to his very survival. Questions that when left unanswered, often rendered him confused, and unable to function. He sought out people who had the answers and, because of his fear, it is probable that it made little difference whether the answers were correct or incorrect. The answer itself eased his state of fear. It momentarily resolved his state of not knowing. There simply was no way man would allow himself to admit his ignorance and go from there. He had to know "Why?" And he had to know immediately. Dragons, therefore, served their purpose.

With the birth of the dragons came another need. Someone had to be found who could provide the answers. An authority was needed. Somehow, either by choice, chance, heritage, or education, certain individuals, often whether they liked it or not, accepted the responsibility for providing answers. If they did a good job, which meant they had something half-way believable to say, they were honored, adulated.

It was not an easy job, however. By definition, the authority had to constantly keep talking. There was no way an authority would ever be allowed to admit his own ignorance. If he did, he would have faced either a ventilated skull or numerous trips to the Uwanga forest. Along with the rewards for his wisdom, the authority was under constant pressure to disseminate. When a question was asked, the authority would answer it. This is not to say that he would answer it correctly, but he would answer it. When he was presented with an unusual occurrence, he would explain it. This, again, is not to say that his explanation would be accurate, but at least one would be offered. When the authority was informed that a problem existed, he would be quick to tell why it existed — regardless of whether he had the necessary information to support his assertion.

In the beginning, few two-legged ones questioned what the authority said. There were few, if any, alternative explanations available. The authority had control of the market. Thus the "Neanderthal" man with the itchy, cracky feet had little option other than to accept the idea of the demon. Since the knowledge of fungus was not around yet, he plopped his foot in the poop rather than considering athlete's foot ointment.

The Irrefutable Dragon — The Suspicious One

As suggested, answers did serve a purpose. They calmed and comforted. At the same time, they had the ability to cause great pain, unnecessarily. In many cases, it was anybody's guess as to what effect they would have. Borrowing the overused simile, there were "white-hat-dragons," and "black-hat-dragons." The sinister ones were the latter that were potentially injurious because of one major characteristic.

Quite simply, a good dragon is one that is a correct, valid answer. It is one that has been researched carefully; one that has withstood the rigors of the scientific method, and one that has maintained its explanatory properties despite many attempts to prove it false. The "black-hat-dragon," on the other hand, has either of two characteristics. First, it is one that is *wrong*, yet still used to answer the question "Why?" Second, it is one that could be either *right or wrong*, but there is simply no way to know whether it is right or wrong. An example should help clarify the distinction I am making.

Suppose one of our youngsters awakens with the following signs. He has a fever, a headache, and is experiencing stiffness of the back and neck. He is also unable to hold down his breakfast. The child is taken to a physician and it is discovered that there is an increase of lymphocytes in the youngster's cerebrospinal fluid. Little question that the child's parents will want to know what is responsible for the child's illness.

Suppose further that a well-meaning individual tells Mother or Father that the reason for the child's symptoms are a result of the child consuming too much sugar in his diet. That would be an answer — a dragon. In this instance, it would be a *bad* dragon for the answer is *wrong*. A physician would be able to refute it with little difficulty. The physician would be able to demonstrate that the offered dragon, "excessive sugar," did not have the power to serve as a causatory variable for the observed signs or signals.

Another individual comes along and offers his idea. He indicates to the parent that the child's ailment is due to evil spirits that have moved into the child's body. That would be an answer — a dragon. It would also be a *bad* dragon. It is bad, however, for a different reason than the one given for the sugar dragon. If you will allow me to stretch my point to its limit, the evil-spirit-dragon *might be a correct one*! Although presently no one can prove the existence of evil spirits, no one can *disprove* their existence either. Since we can't scientifically disprove their existence, their existence is possible. The dragon could be used to explain the occurrences of the child's signs and signals. Someone could disagree with the answer, even deny it, but that someone would have an impossible time arguing the question of the dragon's validity from a scientific standpoint. That's the problem with those types of dragons.

Finally, the physician informs the parents that before offering an answer that might explain the child's problems, more tests are necessary. These tests verify that a virus is present. According to the laws of good scientific methodology, the virus is identified. It is called "poliovirus" and it is the etiology or cause of poliomyelitis. Now when the parent asks "Why?", the physician does provide an answer — a dragon. The dragon is a valid, correct one. It has the ability to explain. It can be tested.

In order for dragons to be of the good kind, the "white-hats," they must be correct. They must be testable. They must be capable of being substantiated and capable of being refuted. The polio virus dragon had those characteristics. The evil-spirit-dragon did not have those characteristics. It was neither capable of being substantiated or refuted. It represents the most dangerous of all "black-hat" dragons, for *irrefutable* dragons are easily accepted as being correct even in the face of absolutely no evidence.

Let me quickly present the three dragons that were described in the earlier fables and the ones that were offered to explain Molly's and David's behaviors. Consider them in light of the distinction of "white-hats" and "black-hats." If they are "white-hats," no arguments. If they are "black-hats," some questions have to be raised.

	Behavior	**Dragons Why?**	**Treatment**	**Outcome**	**Conclusion**
102,000 B.C.	Itchy Toes	Demon	Moose Dung	Itching Stopped	Demon Gone
5,000 B.C.	Tantrum	Evil Spirit	Trephining, BDOK, Prunes	Tantrum Stopped	Evil Spirit Gone
Twentieth Century A.D.	Tantrum, etc.	Oedipal Complex	Psycho-Therapy	Tantrum, etc., Stopped	Oedipal Complex Resolved
David	Poor Hand-Writing	Processing, Perceptual Problem	— — —	— — —	— — —
Molly	Too Many Questions, Not Following Requests, etc.	Emotional Disturbance	— — —	— — —	— — —

First: The Behavior Column

As can be seen, all five "cases" started from the same point — the child's (and caveman's) behavior. The behavior was observed and seen as a sign of some problem. Had the behavior not presented itself, there would have been no indication that something was wrong. Without the indication, the question "Why?" would not have been asked and no treatment would have been undertaken.

Second: The "Why?" Column

Since the behaviors were observed, the question, as to what was responsible for them, was asked. The "Why?" column provides us with the answers that were offered. In the fables, the personally involved parties were unable to answer the question to their satisfaction. They sought out an authority who told them why the behaviors occurred.

Look carefully at the answers that were provided. Do you have a feeling that something is unusual about them? Although you might initially disagree, the truth is that *none of them were directly observed.* They were not actually seen by any of the authorities who suggested they were responsible for the behaviors that were viewed as signs of pathology. I'm sure you have no problem with that assertion when thinking in terms of the demon and evil spirit. Obviously, no one saw them. But what of the Oedipal complex? The processing problem? The emotional disturbance? Were they observed? The answer is no!

Since they were not directly observed, what did the authorities use to determine their presence? The answer is both confusing and ironic. The authorities used the *presence* of the puzzling behavior to infer the *presence* of the dragon which, in turn, was used to explain the *presence* of the puzzling behavior. As you now know, that's a circle — and circularity doesn't tell us much.

Evil spirits, Oedipal complexes, processing problems, and emotional disturbances, are not entities that lend themselves to direct observation. To the best of our ability to know, they are not things that have measurable physical parameters. They aren't like chromosomes, or fractured bones, or tomatoes, or lightning bolts. You can't take pictures of them, or measure them, or bring them into a laboratory and expose them to scientific exploration. Until the day comes when they can undergo such scrutiny, their existence is based purely on inference. Until that day comes, their existence must be questioned.

Third: The Treatment Column

Logically, if one believes that the answer to the question "Why?" has been determined, the next step would be to develop a treatment approach to remediate that which purportedly has been found. If a physician discovered the presence of a virus, the physician would treat the virus. If a speech pathologist discovered that a child was having problems coordinating tongue and lip movements, thus influencing the child's articulation, the authority would develop a program to help the child's coordination.

In our five cases, a special problem regarding appropriate treatment presented itself. No one was really certain what it was that warranted treatment. All that was known was that the behaviors of the individuals were different and, according to someone's standards, unacceptable. Despite that, the hypothesized underlying causes were treated (or almost treated) even though no one was sure that the causes existed, or that a serious problem existed.

It was suggested that David receive some treatment for his supposed processing problem. His parents, however, questioned the existence of the organic difficulty. Instead, they helped the child learn how to hold a pencil, learn how to keep a piece of paper from slipping off a desk, and learn how to write. That was the parents' choice. Another parent, however, whose child was also having difficulty producing his name to the satisfaction of an authority, might have believed the assertion of a processing problem and might have accepted the suggestion that special help was needed — not to solve the handwriting difficulty, but to resolve the organic dysfunction. The parents might have accepted the assertion that if something wasn't done immediately, the child would suffer further serious learning problems.

Under that pressure the parents might start searching out other *differences* manifested by the child. The parent might change the way he or she normally responds to the child for fear of doing more harm. Sensing the change, the child might begin to pick up on his apparent differences as well as the differences now being manifested by his parent. Fairly soon, both parent and child might begin to believe that something, indeed, is wrong.

Iatrogenic Disorders. Unrealistic concern for a child's happiness can lead to iatrogenic disorders. Literally, an *iatrogenic disorder* is a problem that is produced by efforts to prevent or treat a presumed or actual disorder or disease. Specifically in relation to special children, iatrogenic disorders may arise from premature diagnostic labeling or attempts at treatment. . . .[14] The outcome of such efforts may be anything but desirable if adults then begin to view the child as 'disturbed' and in need of 'treatment.' Parental anxiety is then created or intensified, and normal parental reactions may become stilted and artificial as parents fear doing or saying the wrong thing. Classroom teachers and other adults may become sensitized to any unusual behaviors. Eventually the child may begin to develop some awareness that things are amiss, and adult anxieties may become the spur for the child to develop a concept of self as different or inadequate.[7]

The question "Why?" leads to the decision regarding what treatment plan would be most judicious. That decision, however, requires an identifiable, observable, measurable underlying problem. *Irrefutable dragons do not* have those characteristics. When they are accepted, they do not allow room for alternative ideas as to what might be happening. They also rarely allow for the opportunity to conclude that the child is okay. Rather, they set the stage for the conclusion that the child has some inside problem. Ironically, the child may not have any problem, but our insistence that he does, might literally create one.

Fourth: The Outcome and Conclusion Columns

After treatment has been employed, it is helpful to determine what effect the treatment has had on the identified underlying problem. It is hoped that a surgeon's attempt at an appendectomy results in the successful removal of the appendix. If by accident, the surgeon removed the spleen, leaving the infected appendix securely fastened to the intestines, one might conclude that the treatment was a bust. An "outcome" study of the surgeon's efforts would strongly suggest that the authority should change professions.

In our cases, the **outcome** column represents what happened after the various treatments were actually, or hypothetically, completed. A quick look at our chart shows us that what happened was that the original behaviors that were seen as signs of difficulties stopped. One might have predicted that drilled holes and unappetizing dung would have accomplished that result! The outcome column, however, does *not* tell us what effect the treatment had on the hypothesized underlying problem. That should have also been predicted since the purported "causes" were never seen. Their presence was assumed, not known. Thus, it might appear impossible to determine if the treatment influenced the primary problem. Such is not the case, at least according to the authorities who suggested 1) that a problem actually existed, 2) that they knew why the problem existed, and 3) that they had a treatment plan for the dragon.

If you will look at the **conclusion** column, you will see that the authorities concluded that the underlying problem was resolved. What was the basis for that conclusion? No one saw the demon, spirit, or complex leave. No one saw them "come in," so there would be no reason to assume that the authorities would be any more likely to see them "go out." A look at the chart will tell us the basis for their conclusion. Since the behavior — the signal — was no longer occurring, the authorities simply inferred the absence of the problem. That was all they could do. Not very accountable, but certainly expedient.

As to the original question of the effectiveness of the treatment, who knows? Something happened, that's for sure. Whether that something was related to the hypothesized dragons is difficult, if not impossible, to figure out. A check on David's and Molly's progress will demonstrate the difficulty. After both children were informed that they were suffering from an educational/psychological disease, they encountered new teachers. Neither of the new teachers knew of the purported disease. Both, however, knew that the children were having some difficulty — one with writing, one with social classroom behavior. After a period of time, the name writing and classroom behavior improved. In other words, the *original signs* of the disease were no longer present to their initial degree. What conclusions could possibly be drawn? I'll list a few.

1. Molly was no longer suffering from emotional disturbance.
2. David no longer had his processing-perceptual problem.
3. Molly was still disturbed but she had learned how to handle it.
4. David still had a brain problem, but he had learned to compensate for it.
5. Molly wasn't disturbed in the first place.
6. David never really had a processing problem.
7. Molly's problem was being in a system that attempted to ignore her individuality.
8. David's problem was a lack of experience.

The entire business is confusing, to say the very least. That is the problem with *irrefutable* dragons. We don't know whether they are real or a product of some authority's imagination. Since that is not known, knowing what to treat, or knowing if treatment is necessary, is difficult to determine.

M.I.A.H.I. + A.A. = B.H.D.

The above formula depicts the conditions that have produced the confusion we have just discussed. Dr. Clarity and Harvey Layman will explain the component parts in just a moment. While we wait for them to get ready, a word about the pressure professionals and parents experience is in order.

All of us experience pressure when observing a youngster's behavior that deviates from what is either expected or desired. We face it when trying to explain why the deviation has shown itself. We face it when accepting the fact that the easiest answer is not always correct or helpful to anyone.

The pressure is not unique to us, today. It existed 7000 years ago in Uwanga, and 7000 years before then. It has been around ever since the question "Why?" was asked, and someone took the responsibility to answer it. Some of the answers that have been offered to man to help him better understand his ills and actions have been nothing short of humorous. Others have caused him both great pain and kept him in the darkness from which he has tried so hard to escape. It is important to be aware of the past's answers, for the knowledge of what has happened might prevent the same from happening again. E.T. Worthington, a noted medical historian, said it in the following way: Knowing something of our past will . . . "help preserve us from two opposite errors, excessive trust in authority, and overeagerness to adopt anything which seems to be new and original."[15]

The authority faced with the responsibility of having to explain why something has happened must constantly remember that people, who are asking for help, will be influenced by what is said. The Davids and their parents are susceptible to something called "authoritative validity." They will believe what the authority says because the authority has said it. It has been that way for years. The dependency is not likely to change, easily. All of us would be better off if we could learn to both admit our ignorance and accept the ignorance of the times. It is better to admit and accept ignorance than to offer or adopt an irrefutable answer that distracts us from the problem at hand.

The laypublic must be willing to accept the authority's absence of available knowledge. The authority must be equally willing to concede the absence of the information. If we fail to be honest with each other, we will ultimately have to face two people — the skeptic and ourselves. Both can be unruly and unrelenting critics . . .

It had not been a good day for Harv. His golf game had totally fallen apart despite the ten individual lessons, despite the countless hours of practicing, and despite the brand new dimpled, nippled golf balls that had promised a straight, high trajectory. He had tried to do everything his golf teacher had shown him, but it wasn't working. Although he rarely used the excuse, he was certain that part of his problem was the instructor's manner of teaching. When the guy was sober, which wasn't too often, he would intimidate Harv to a point where holding the golf club was a formidable task. Most of the time, the old geezer would pick up his own club, point to a tree some 200 yards down the practice range, and smack the ball to where it would rest within three feet of his target. Then he would turn to Harv, whose mouth was wide open, and say, "See if you can hit it like that, you turkey!" Something less than supportive, Harv had thought to himself as he tried to hit the little white ball that was becoming smaller each time he stood over it.

It had also been a bad day because of the conference that had taken place earlier in the morning. He and his wife had been called to school to discuss a problem regarding their son. It was the first Harv had been informed that a problem existed.

When they arrived at school, they were immediately ushered into a small room where they were greeted by their son's teacher, the vice-principal, and the school's psychologist. This was the first time he had met the authorities who were seated around the table.

The apparent difficulty centered around his son's seeming inability to do well on the tests the teacher gave him in class. The child's teacher indicated that she felt the boy was bright. That was pleasing to hear. However, she felt that he was not applying himself to the fullest. She believed he was preoccupied with something that was interfering with his work and preventing him from scoring the "A's" the teacher believed he was capable of. It was then that the school psychologist brought up the issue of "test anxiety." He asked if the parents were aware of any signs of severe anxiety prior to a test-day. Neither Harv nor his wife were able to offer any information. They did state that they would be on the lookout for signs if it would be helpful. Their offered help was appreciated.

As the conference continued, the conversation kept returning to the possibility of severe test anxiety. Feeling unsure of what was being said, Harv asked for an explanation of the term. The psychologist obliged, but his words and phrases were unfamiliar to both Harv and his wife. Rather than asking for an additional explanation, the matter of meaning was dropped. Harv remembered that he had experienced some degree of discomfort before taking tests while he was in college. He silently concluded that, despite the professional opinions, the problem wasn't all that severe. As the conference ended, the psychologist and the child's teacher assured the parents that they would keep a close watch for any further behaviors that were inappropriate or significantly different. The parents thanked the authorities, and left.

On the way home, Harv's wife was noticeably upset. He tried to assure her that getting a little nervous about a test was not a terribly serious situation. He promised her that he would talk to his son after the child returned home from school. That made her feel better.

If the school's conference and Harv's poor performance on the golf course wasn't enough, Clyde was. Harv had made the mistake of telling his friend about the morning's conference while walking down the first fairway. Although Clyde was a good friend, he had the annoying habit of knowing everything there was to know about everything. Ask a question, Clyde would have an answer. Have a problem, Clyde would have a solution. For the most part, Harv was able to handle Clyde's omniscience. Today, however, with all that had happened, he wished that Clyde would, for once, keep his mouth shut. For the first several holes, he was able to put up with the offered opinions by reminding himself that Clyde's habit wasn't all his responsibility. Most of the answers he disseminated were the echoed words of Harv's and Clyde's mutual acquaintance, J.F. Clarity, M.D. Clarity was one of the foremost psychiatrists in the city. He was constantly in the news, constantly in demand for answering questions, and constantly available for explanations and solutions. Fortunately, Clarity didn't play golf. That limited the meetings between himself and Harv. But anytime Harv would wonder out loud about something, Clyde would unhesitatingly point out what he was sure Clarity would say. This day was no different. By the fourth hole, Harv had heard every possible theory that could account for the phenomenon of test anxiety.

When Harv arrived home in the afternoon, he promised himself, as he had done no less than one hundred times before, to sell his golf clubs for fifty cents. He had an early dinner with his family. Afterwards, he and his young son went outside and sat under a tree. They had been sitting for only a few moments when the child began to cry. It was evident that he was aware that the conference had taken place. "I try Dad, really I do," the child said. "It's just that sometimes I don't understand the questions that she asks. She uses words that I've never heard before. But I do try . . . ." Harv took the little boy in his arms. He felt his own tears coming. He loved this little boy and was determined to do whatever was necessary to guarantee that the child would be happy and pleased with himself. He was determined to keep this testing business in its proper perspective. He was not going to act hastily nor would he be upset by what had happened at the conference. He certainly wasn't going to believe what Clyde had said to him. There was no way he was going to allow the pressure cooker of *time* and *illness* to get in the way of his son's happiness. No way!

He went to bed a little earlier than usual. He assured his wife and son that he was fine, just tired. In truth, he was tired. More than that, he was upset. He could not justify why his son had to experience the irrefutable dragons. He was never able to find any value in them. He promised himself that he would not accept them unless they were shown to be real. If necessary, he would challenge. He would not be intimidated, he said to himself, as he slowly approached his restless sleep . . . .

The room was large, larger than any he had ever seen before. Rows upon rows of dark blue velvet cushioned seats that gently rocked after being touched with the slightest pressure filled the room. The cathedral ceiling reached 70, perhaps 80 feet into the air. Its deeply dark-stained wooden beams complemented the yellows, reds, and blues of the stained glass windows that surrounded the huge hall. Mammoth chandeliers hung almost to the floor. Although they provided more than sufficient light, they used no light bulbs. Instead, white, squared, dimpled-nippled golf balls were attached to the many branched sockets. An elevated stage occupied the very front of the hall. In place of curtains, several large, fully-leafed trees appeared to be growing from within the stage floor itself. The trunks and arms of the trees were dotted with Latin crosses that designated the point of impact where brave golf balls had attempted to penetrate the fence-like barrier created by the dense foliage. Located on the stage were eighteen metal folding chairs that had seats covered with soft, green bent grass that had been freshly mowed.

Suddenly, a towering figure appeared from nowhere. He walked omnisciently toward the lectern located front-center stage. At that precise moment, Harv found himself standing in the middle of an exquisitely manicured putting green whose surface rolled and swayed unpredictably as if controlled by undersea currents and light atmospheric winds.

"Knock the ball into the hole," the old teacher on stage demanded.

"I can't" Harv answered after losing his balance and falling down.

" Pick yourself up, turkey, and knock the ball into the hole!"

"I'm trying, but I can't see where the ball is supposed to go," Harv cried.

"Is there something wrong with you?" the teacher said in a tone suggesting that he had already made up his mind.

"Really, I'm trying. I'm trying. I'll try again . . . and again," the small voice promised.

Just then a huge wave came tumbling over the bow of the stage, washing away everything in its way. Harv held tightly to the stainless steel arms of his velvet chair, checking quickly that his life preserver was securely fastened. He closed his eyes hoping to avoid the oncoming disaster. Nothing, however, happened. When his eyes opened, he saw Dr. Clarity standing behind the lectern. He was using a three-wood to point to something that was written on the blackboard. The letters of the words were too small for Harv to see, but he knew the message must have been important for all the other students, who were sitting around him, were busy taking notes. Harv strained his eyes but was still unable to see. Finally, he turned to the student sitting to his immediate right. It was Clyde. "Clyde, it's me, Harv." Clyde did not answer. "Clyde, I need some help!"

"Why? Is there something wrong with YOU?" Clyde finally said.

"I don't think so," Harv answered. "I just can't see the teacher's writing!"

"Then there must be something wrong with you because I can see it," Clyde answered.

"When you decide to be quiet," Clarity pointed out, "the lecture will begin." Quickly, Harv turned to face the front.

Behind Clarity sat eighteen very elderly teachers all dressed in long black gowns that left only their eyes and mouths uncovered. While their chalk-white faces were completely hidden, their glaring stares sent shivers up Harv's spine. He wanted to leave, but he was suddenly immobilized by a stack of text books that held his feet to the ground.

"Today, I am going to tell you why all pupils suffer from test or examination anxiety," Clarity began, after rapping the three-wood on the edge of the lectern. "You are to listen carefully for we will have a test after my lecture. Those of you who do not answer the questions to my satisfaction will have to go to a special class for handicapped learners."

Harv felt his own anxiety build. He was almost unable to hold his pencil, but he gripped it with both his hands and said, "I will try." One of the teachers got up from her chair and wrote his name on the blackboard. She placed a small slash mark after it and indicated that he would be punished for talking out of turn. "I'm sorry," Harv said, bringing a second slash mark.

"Now to the disease of test anxiety," Clarity said, smiling at the teacher as she took her seat. "We have proven beyond a shadow of a doubt that . . . '*all children have some degree of examination anxiety.*' "[16]

"All children?" Harv whispered. His voice carried further than he had intended — resulting in a third slash mark. The spotlight that had suddenly fallen directly on him returned to the front of the stage to Dr. Clarity's face that had ballooned to twice its original size.

" '. . . *One cause of examination anxiety is the fear of disgrace,*' " Clarity continued. " '. . . *The child dreads that his teachers and parents will find out that he has not applied himself diligently, will discover his shortcomings, and will humiliate him.*' "[16]

"Now wait a moment," Harv broke in. The eighteen teachers turned toward him. How dare he speak out in the middle of a lecture, their eyes said. Ignoring their stares, Harv said, "What parent in his right mind would ever humiliate his child simply because he didn't do well on a test? Tests are not that serious. Getting a little panicked before taking a test is even less serious."

"Wrong!" the teachers said. "Tests and test anxiety are very serious."

"How could that possibly be?" Harv asked, surprised that the teachers thought everything was so serious.

"Serious because of the *fear*!" Clarity answered. "And . . . '*if this fear is associatively connected in the unconscious with the memory of the humiliation the child suffered earlier when he discovered how much smaller his genitals were than those of his father the examination anxiety will be enormously increased, even though he has applied himself diligently to his pre-examination studies.'* "[16]

"You're kidding!" Harv exclaimed. "Humiliation because a child sees that he has smaller genitals than his father's?"

"Smaller genitals are no small thing," the teachers pointed out.

"You mean smaller genitals are no *big* things, don't you?" Harv stated.

"That was disgusting," the teachers remarked. Four slash marks were placed after Harv's name.

"Are you quite finished?" Clarity asked the unruly student.

"More important, are you finished?" Harv retorted.

"Not by a long shot," Clarity answered. Then he continued. "Further, '. . . *instead of the fear of disgrace, examination anxiety may be the fear of being found out and punished for lack of diligence. If the fear of punishment is associatively connected in the unconscious with strong fears of punishment by castration for masturbation, the examination anxiety will be increased because examinations are identified with proof of sexual capacity and failure is equated with impotence and castration.'* "[16]

"You're nuts, do you know that? You're a looney bird, a fuzzy-headed dingbat!" Harv screamed, pointing his fist at Clarity. The other students in the classroom disappeared. The spotlight shifted from center stage to the one blue velvet rocking chair that took up the entire floor of the hall.

"Identify yourself this minute," Clarity demanded. "Who are you and what gives you the right to call *me* a nut?"

"I am Harvey Layman. And you are a nut because you are!"

"The gentleman does have a good argument there, Dr. Clarity," the teachers pointed out.

"Screw the gentleman's argument," Clarity responded, losing himself for the moment. "You out there," Clarity screamed, "I'm not finished, so knock it off!"

"There's more?"

"There's more!" Clarity stated. " '*There is another cause for greatly increased examination anxiety. To be successful in the examination is to progress onward in ambition. If this idea is connected associatively in the unconscious with the oedipus fan-*

tasies of killing the father and taking his place, and if these fantasies are not yet resolved but still dreaded lest the father retaliate in like kind, then there will develop fear of succeeding and perhaps also a desire to fail . . . .' "[16]

Silence fell over the room. It was as if everyone was waiting to see if the intruder would react. Clarity, himself, was the most restrained. He had never been challenged by a layman before. His medical books never suggested that such an event would happen. For a moment, he felt fear. He knew he was being examined. His own anxiety streamed through his associative Un-Conscious. He wondered what the cause was for his discomfort. Could it have something to do with his father? With the size of his genitals? Or because he was once caught masturbating in the attic?

"You don't really believe what you have just said, do you?" Harv asked, ending the silence. There was strength in his voice.

His back was to the wall. "Of course I do," Clarity said authoritatively. "I have searched my storehouse of wisdom and those answers are the only ones I have for test anxiety." he added.

"Would you mention those explanations to a parent if the parent's child was having difficulty taking tests in school?"

"I can't see any reason why not," Clarity answered.

"How about the possibility that you might scare them half to death," Harv said.

"The truth is often frightening," Clarity said.

"What truth? You can't prove what you said. YOU CAN'T PROVE WHAT YOU SAID!" Harv bellowed, using his Orson Welles' voice. The powerfully eloquent tone was effective immediately causing Dr. Clarity to shake his head.

"No . . . I can't," Clarity stated feebly. The teachers became incontinent.

"He can't prove it!" they exclaimed, as they went to change their clothes.

"But . . ." Clarity said, holding the teachers in their place, "but . . . *can you disprove it*?"

"Of course not," Harv reluctantly admitted.

"He can't disprove it!" the teachers said.

"No, he can't disprove it," Clarity echoed. "The answers are still *safe*!"

"Safe," Harv whispered. "You know and I know that there is no way to disprove what you have said," he continued. "Your causes and explanations are totally irrefutable. You have successfully placed most parents at the mercy of your authoritative irrefutability. Not only does that take us back into the darkest of darkest times, it is totally misleading, and not helpful to anyone."

"You have forgotten one word," Clarity pointed out. "It is *easy* . . . and smart to use safe, irrefutable explanations. Why say something that can be proven false?"

"Because then we could hold you accountable for what you say, that's why. As it stands now, we have no way to know whether you are right or wrong."

"So what's the hassle?" Clarity said, confidently.

"I'm going to be the hassle! I'm going to be your nemesis. Do you hear me? Your funny authoritatively spoken words aren't going to count anymore. You're going to have to back them up with evidence that everyone understands. No more mysteries. No more double talk. From now on, straight, honest, testable answers. We will accept nothing less!" When he had finished, he ran to the front of the stage. Clarity saw him coming. He ducked behind the lectern. Harv approached Clarity and grabbed the three-wood from his hands. With all the delight in the world, he broke the wood over his knee. Then he ran to the blackboard and took a piece of chalk. He pushed Clarity to the side and turned to the teachers, asking them politely to take their seats. After they had done so, he thanked them for sitting so nicely. With his thanks, came a change in their appearance. No longer were they cold and uncaring. No longer were they bound by the tradition of the past.Symbolically, they removed the chains that had prevented them from doing what they loved the most — teaching. Their warm smiles gave Harv the courage to proceed. He knew his son would now be fine. He took one long, satisfying sigh, returned to the blackboard and wrote:

M.I.A.H.I. + A.A. = B.H. DRAGONS

Then he took a seat by the teachers. While looking at them he said, "**M**an's **I**nability to **A**dmit **H**is **I**gnorance, plus the **A**bsence of **A**lternatives, equals **B**lack **H**at **D**ragons.

"It seems," he continued, "that man has an inherent inability to admit his ignorance. He is afraid to say that he doesn't know the answer to a question. Thus, when a question presents itself, man answers it despite the fact that he may not know what he is talking about. If there are no suitable alternatives to his contrived answer, the answer becomes accepted. Man has been doing this since the beginning of time. In the beginning, it was probably justified for he knew no better. But not today. Yet today, he continues to offer his unsupported answers and the public relies almost exclusively on the authority to tell him what is wrong. The public often accepts the authority's disseminations unquestioningly. Man has bought the dragons of the authority either because alternative explanations have not been available or because man simply will not bring himself to admit that something might not be explainable given the technology of the moment. This has resulted in an unbelievable number of safe, circular, sick dragons that have done little more than impede the needed growth of knowledge. It has resulted in the perpetuation of darkness. Unless we are willing to challenge, to demand professional credibility, the darkness will remain."

Clarity heard what the layman had said. He noticed that the teachers were affected by his words. He felt his omnipotence waning. He knew he had to do something . . . something *intelligent.* Without Harv noticing, Clarity dashed from the stage and ran to one of the large chandeliers. He grabbed a square golf ball and threw it toward the stage. One of the teachers yelled for Harv to duck. A second ball came, creasing Harv's cheek. A teacher ran to get a bandage. A third came flying. Harv saw it. He saw the dimple. He saw the dimple's dimple. He saw the dimple's dimple's nipple. It was coming right at him. He tried to move, but he couldn't. Someone was holding his arms. Someone was preventing him from dodging the oncoming projectile. Just as it appeared right before his eyes, he woke up.

His wife was shaking him, screaming at him. He was soaking wet from perspiration. His arms were trembling. He reflexively looked around the bedroom for the teachers, for Clarity. He shook his head, blinked his tearing eyes, and brought himself back to reality. Then he remembered. He remembered Clyde telling him about Clarity's theories. He remembered throwing Clyde into the lake that bordered the fifth hole. He remembered how good he felt after seeing his friend immersed in the green, murky water. Now that he remembered everything, all he had to do was to handle his wife who was demanding to know whose dimples and nipples he was playing with while on the golf course.

Medicine's "Germs": The Precursors to the Irrrefutable Dragons of Psychology and Education

The authorities of the past started with what you might expect: a strong drive to help, hope and faith that they were doing the right thing, but not a ton of wisdom. This statement is in no way meant to fault their efforts. They tried, and in many instances, they succeeded in helping those who suffered. As it turned out, their early efforts established what would be a logical framework for future exploration and experimentation in the field of physical medicine. These roots would enable medicine to advance significantly. But the roots would also do something else. They would suggest that the same logical framework that was so beneficial to medicine would be equally beneficial to the professions of psychology and education. Today, many educators and psychologists believe that supposition to be highly problematical.

Early Medicine's Demons, Devils, and Dung

Medicine probably had very little choice other than answering the early questions the lay-public asked about their problems with the concept of saints, demons, and a host of various gods. As late as the 4th century A.D., the physician held to the notion that . . . "Just as plagues and epidemics were universally ascribed to the wrath of God, so particular diseases came to be attributed to the anger of particular saints."[17] The reason for this view, in all likelihood, was that not many alternative explanations were available. Evil spirits and the like were in, and dislodging them from the times was not an easy task. Since they were assumed to be capable of causing all sorts of difficulties, they had to be treated. As has been pointed out, "the . . . medicine man, who treats his patient on the . . . principle of removing the cause of the disease . . .

discovered . . . different methods of getting rid of a demon. First, the body of the patient may be rendered an unpleasant abode for the intruding spirit . . . . The sufferer may be vigorously squeezed and pommelled, beaten, starved, fumigated by evil-smelling substances . . . ."[15] I think you will agree that none of the above "treatments" were particularly appealing. This may partially explain why relatively few people complained of the same ills, that resulted in the same treatment more than once.

Hippocrates (c460-360 B.C.), known to many as the father of medicine, tried to convince his colleagues of the futility of the spirits. His words were not always heeded and the thought continued to persist that early man ". . . was literally regarded as possessed, and his body as motivated by a spirit or demon which had driven out the habitual and natural resident."[15] Hippocrates, however, did not give up the fight.Since logic would not work, Hippocrates decided to propose an alternative to the spirits. On the surface, his dragon appeared more credible than the saints and the demons. "Black Bile" was his alternative. It was one of four elemental fluids of the body that purportedly helped to determine a person's physical and mental constitution. If someone wasn't feeling well, or if someone was doing something another someone said he shouldn't be doing, the difference and deviation were accounted for by a disproportionate amount of black bile.Sadly, despite the efforts of countless technicians and physicians — and who knows how many unwilling bodies — the mystical, mythical substance turned out to be both mystical and mythical.

In the early days, a variety of explanations and treatments for various problems were suggested by different authorities. I will list a few of them for you.

Problem	**Treatment**
1.Scratch orSlight Wound.	"Take the dung of a bull and apply thereto."[18]
2. Warts.	"Apply the urine of a dog or the blood of a mouse, and the warts will be infallibly cured."[19]
3. Child with Whooping-Cough	"Put one of the child's hairs between slices of bread and butter and give it to a dog to eat. If the dog then coughs, it is a sign that the ailment has been transferred to the animal."[18]
4. Deafness.	"Ram's urine, eel's bile and the juice of ash expressed and place in the ears."[18]

5. Baldness.	"Take an onion, cut it in half, and rub in well on the top of the head."[19]
	"Locate some fat from a bear and rub the fat into the head."[20]
6. Convulsions.	"Take cuttings of the sick person's nails, some hair from the eyebrows and a half-penny, wrap them altogether in a cloth which had been round the patient's head and place the package in a gateway, where four lanes meet. The first person who found and opened it would then take the disorder and relieve the afflicted one."[18]

Early "dentistry" wasn't in much better shape than early medicine. Some of the "cures" proposed for toothaches might make you feel pretty fortunate about today's treatment methods. For example, this first cure, although painless, apparently would only work under very specific conditions. Accordingly, if a toothache . . . "occurs on a Tuesday or Thursday, and if the moon is waning, [it] may be cured by repeating seven times c'argidum margidum stargidum."[19] Pretty, but of questionable effectiveness. The inventor of the above cure was a fellow named Marcellus. He lived sometime around 480 A.D. He undoubtedly was big on nonsense syllables for he advised, one time during his professional career, that . . . "if a man's nose bleeds, whisper in his ear on the same . . ." (side as the bleeding nostril, I guess) . . . "socsocam, sykyma; thrice nine times . . . ."[20]

A gentleman named Priscian also had some interesting ideas about toothaches and what to do about them. His treatment was much more advanced than Marcellus' for he used "medication" rather than songs. Of course, this advancement was to be expected since Priscian lived some three hundred years after Marcellus. Priscian suggested that ". . . asses' dung dried and used as a dentifrice will immediately cure a toothache."[20] Little question of that! He also added, ". . . and it is equally effective when mixed with vinegar and held for some time in the mouth." Unfortunately, Priscian failed to tell us how long one must hold the solution in the mouth. We can only hope, for the sake of the patient, that the time period was brief. On the other hand, the time period may not have been too important. It was likely that as soon as the patient gargled the solution of vinegar and asses' dung he went into a state of shock. At that point, the pain from his tooth wouldn't have mattered much.

Toothaches, coughs and warts were not the only things that occupied the authorities' minds. Some effort, albeit not a great deal, was spent on the development of birth control methods. The following is one such method. I do feel compelled to warn you that this approach, if you should try it, may be hazardous — not necessarily to your health, but most assuredly to the size of your family.

Direct from the "Code of Health of the School of Salernum," described as a practical medical guide written sometime around 1096 A.D. —

> ". . . to prevent a woman from conceiving, all that is necessary is to bind her head with a red ribbon during the sexual act."[21]

Whoever came up with that one gargled too long with Priscian's toothache formula. So taken by the above procedure, I tried to find additional information about it. I met with little success. I was unable to determine when the ribbon was to be removed. I was unable to determine how tightly the ribbon was to be tied. Frustrated, I talked with one of my colleagues about the technique. She pointed out . . . "If the ribbon was tied very tightly, the approach might work. After all," she continued, "what woman in her right mind would be at all interested if her head was experiencing considerable pain." There was, I believed, a good deal of logic in her view. I studied the matter for a few more days and concluded that this early birth control method may have accidentally set the stage for a truly historic event. Namely, the very first time that an important and highly useful phrase was ever uttered —

"Not tonight, dear, I have a headache."

* * * * *

Fortunately for all of us, medical science was not satisfied with its state of affairs. In time, many of its invented, safe, irrefutable dragons were beheaded by findings emanating from its research laboratories. The medical scales began to tip in favor of science and away from the "arts." The myths, the incantations, the sorcery, and the inventions of dragons born out of ignorance were slowly, ever-so-slowly, replaced by well-studied, well-researched explanations and descriptions which were based on experimentation rather than "hand-me-down" allegations. Assuredly, medical science experienced the two step forward, one step backward dance, but with the likes of Harvey, Pasteur, Koch, Lister, Curie, Salk, and many others, the frustrating terpsichorean efforts were destined to lead medicine out from the "dark ages."

The Microscope. I doubt it would be possible to pinpoint any one particular event or discovery that could be considered solely responsible for the type of medical treatment most of us experience today. Somewhere on top of the list, however, would be the names of Leeuwenhoek — who discovered bacteria, which helped lead medicine to the formulation of a germ theory of disease, and Pasteur and Koch — who proved that certain bacteria were responsible for certain diseases. The work of these scientists was aided to a significant degree by the work others, namely Spencer, who made the first American microscope; Janssen, who probably discovered the principle of the compound microscope some 250 years before Spencer's work; and by unknown engravers who used glass globes filled with water as magnifying glasses some 5000 years prior to Janssen's work.

The invention of the microscope was a tremendously important event. Without it, it is most unlikely that medicine would have ever discovered its "germs." Without that discovery, you and I would still be hearing "c'argidum margidum stargidum" when visiting our family physician. In addition to the incalculable humanitarian gains man received from the finding and understanding of "germs," he received a viable *alternative* to his invented demons, gods, saints, and dragons. He no longer had to believe that many of his ills were caused by supernatural beings. He learned that real, *observable*, living organisms were responsible for many of his physical troubles. He no longer had to invent explanations —invent safe dragons. He learned that these living organisms were subject to experimentation, verification *and refutation*. He also learned that these real, observable, living organisms could live *inside* of him.

The "Germ Theory" of Physical Disease. The first observation of bacteria (April 24, 1676, referred to as the birthday of Bacteriology[17]), or as Leeuwenhoek called them, "little animals," set the stage for still another monumental finding by two of our previously mentioned scientists. Some two hundred years later, Robert Koch and Louis Pasteur showed that certain germs were capable of producing certain diseases. Their work helped substantiate an idea known as the "Germ Theory of Physical Disease," which stated, among other things, that various diseases were caused by underlying factors known as "germs." Although this idea had been suggested some 400 years prior to their work, there was little hard evidence in favor of it. However, once Koch and Pasteur completed their work with anthrax (an infectious disease of man and animals), sufficient evidence was gathered to validate the theory. (Their findings, by the way, killed about 28,000 fallacious medical dragons.)

Physicians soon discovered that certain diseases and certain "germs" almost always accompanied one another. They discovered that if a large group of people contracted the same illness or disease, most, if not all, would be found "carrying" the same type of "germ." Equally important, physicians found that a particular type of "germ" (or physiological problem such as a genetic deficiency) produced very similar types of symptoms or complaints from those suffering from the illness. The finding that a lawful, reliable relationship existed among specific "germs," diseases, and symptoms was very beneficial to the practicing physician. It enabled him to begin to categorize types of "germs," names of diseases, and constellations of symptoms that seemed to go together, more times than not. Once these categories had been thoroughly researched and validated or refuted, the physician found himself in the highly favorable position of being able to *predict* the presence of a "germ" or symptom, even though he only had minimal information about the patient's difficulties.

Accurate Prediction of the Underlying "Germ." Accurate diagnosis of the "germ" or disease increased the chances that the physician would determine the correct treatment for his patient. The physician believed that he would first have to discover the *real cause* of the patient's difficulties before the difficulties could be effectively dealt with. The germ theory reminded him of an axiom: to cure the patient of his ills, the physician should determine the *underlying cause* of the problem and alleviate that which was determined. The physician might *not* be curing the patient by simply extricating his symptoms or complaints. The physician, of course, was well aware of this admonition long before the validation of the germ theory. Even the early medicine man had adopted the philosophy of first predicting or identifying the "cause" of his patient's difficulties before working on the problem. Remember the sequence that was previously discussed. In Yjerkie's case the sequence was as follows:

Step one: Observation of the tantrum.

Behavior
1. Tantrum

Step two: Determination of the underlying cause.

Behavior	Why?
1. Tantrum	Evil Spirit

Step three: Treatment, based on the determined cause.

Behavior	Why?	Treatment
1. Tantrum	Evil Spirit	Trephining, etc.

The mind doctor would not prescribe a treatment method until he was satisfied that he had discovered the "cause" of the problem.

The early physician's task of prediction and identification was relatively simple compared to his modern-day counterpart. Usually, if he made a mistake, no one would know about it. He was very good at pointing his finger at safe dragons, and relatively few people would ever disagree with him. Take the case of Pextus Antonious. He ran a small, fairly successful floral shop sometime around 327 A.D. On a very busy day in late December, he must have walked in and out of the shop's refrigerator cooler two dozen times. He hadn't slept well for several days because he had stayed up with his young son who had been coughing and sneezing for almost a week. When Pextus left his little shop that evening, he felt his neck stiffening. He noticed that his swallowing was becoming more difficult, actually painful. By the next morning, he felt worse and after much deliberation agreed to visit the neighborhood physician. He carefully described his complaints to the doctor. The physician checked his medical book and concluded that his patient's difficulties were due to his "diseased" blood. The doctor went to work to rid the patient of his "germ." He prescribed bleeding as the treatment. Logically, if the blood is bad, simply remove it. Makes sense. Despite Pextus' apprehension, he was bled four times that day, then sent home.

To the surprise of both Pextus and the physician, the treatment procedure was successful. According to the historical accounts of this case, Pextus was so weak after the day's treatment, that he did not have the strength to complain that he wasn't feeling well. He decided therefore, to skip the next day's appointment. That decision made him feel a lot better. Since he was feeling better, he concluded that the doctor knew what he was doing. Sitting back in his office, the doctor came to the same conclusion. He assumed that his procedure had been quite effective since Pextus did not visit him again. He did, however, bump into Pextus several weeks later. He noticed that the symptoms Pextus had complained about were no longer present. He concluded that the treatment had been successful, and also that his assertion as to the underlying cause had been correct.Since the patient was no longer complaining of his symptoms, the cause of the symptoms must have disappeared.

Pextus' fictitious medicine man couldn't lose. He was dealing with safe dragons (bad blood would be pretty difficult to argue with) and "logical" treatments to deal with the dragons. In his time, correct identification of the "real cause" was an exercise that probably made him feel potent, while doing little for most of his patients.

Soon, however, physicians would not have it so easy. They would begin to deal with problems and "causes" of problems that would not be so safe. These new problems and their solutions would be open to public *and* professional inspection. Both the public and the physician would know whether the patient was helped or maltreated. The physician's identifications and predictions would be subject to accountability. This would mean that he or she would have to be very careful about what was said and what was prescribed.

Circa 1550 B.C. (The following is an actual case found in the "Ebers Papyrus.")

> When thou findest a man with an obstruction — with pale face and beating heart — and findest on examination that his heart is hot and his belly swollen, that is an inflammation . . . that cometh from irritant food. Treat it with something that cools heat and opens bowels . . . .[15]

(Those good old prunes!)

Let's assume that the word "obstruction" refers to the condition of constipation. It appears that is what the physician was talking about —or based on his treatment, hoping for.

Step one: Symptoms, complaints, behaviors: Obstruction, pale face, beating heart, hot heart, belly swollen.

Behavior

1. Obstruction
2. Pale Face
3. Hot and Beating Heart
4. Belly Swollen

Step two: From his description, he attributed the cause of this condition to irritant food. That would be the proposed dragon or etiology. There might have been other "causes" for the obstruction, etc., but the physician may have been correct.

Behavior	Why?
1. Obstruction, etc.	Irritant Food

Step three: After diagnosing the cause, the physician prescribed treatment. On the advice of his doctor, the patient consumed several doses of the elixir.

Behavior	Why?	Treatment
1. Obstruction, etc.	Irritant Food	Prunes

Now to some important questions. What effect resulted from the physician's treatment? What was the *outcome* of his technique?

Behavior	Why?	Treatment	Outcome	Conclusion
1. Obstruction 2. Pale Face 3. Hot and Beating Heart 4. Belly Swollen	Irritant Food	Prunes	1. "Went to the Bathroom" Several Times 2. Color Returned to Patient's Face 3. Heart Cooled Off, While Continuing to Beat 4. Patient Reported He Was Feeling Better	?

Was the patient cured? Since the symptoms disappeared and the patient indicated that he was feeling better, we probably would say that he was cured, at least for the moment. Did the physician diagnose the correct dragon? That is a little more difficult to ascertain. All we can say is that the symptoms disappeared and the patient said he was all right. We might, therefore, cautiously conclude that the physician was correct. It is possible, that the symptoms might have disappeared even without the physician's help. Nevertheless, we would probably agree that the physician did a pretty good job. At least, no one got hurt.

To be sure, the physician was heavily rewarded for his astuteness. It is nice to know that you have helped someone. Rewards sometimes do that, but they also do something else. They suggest that the treatment method should be used again the next time another patient manifests the *same*, or very *similar*, symptoms. In the early days, "small," yet critical differences, often went unnoticed. Given the state of technology, that was to be expected.

Circa 1550 B.C. plus one day! (*Not* taken from the "Ebers Papyrus.")

"I vould like to schpeak to Dr. Clarityonious. This is Dr. Clydeonious schpeaking."

"I vill try to find him, doctor," the receptionist said. "I believe he is on roundings."

Several minutes later, "Clarityonious here. May I help you?" "Dis is Dr. Clydeonious, Dr. Clarityonious. I have here dis patient who is suffering gargantuously. I vould like your opinion."

"Fine mine young colleague. Relate to me de symptoms. Hokay?"

"Yes sir. I vill do dat."

Step one:

"De patient has, I believe, an obstruction. She has a pale face, a hot and beating heart, and a svollen belly."

"Anything else," Clarityonious asked.

"Nope. Dat's it."

Behavior

1. Obstruction
2. Pale Face
3. Hot and Beating Heart
4. Belly Swollen

Step two:

"Vell my colleague, no big deal. I had vone just like dat yesterday. Dose symptoms must be going around dese days. Probably the weather. De patient is obviously suffering from constipation due, no doubt, to irritant food."

"Dat's marvelous," Clydeonious marveled.

"Yes, dank you."

"Vat should I do?"

"You should help de patient, dumbo," Clarityonious answered, somewhat perturbed. His time was very valuable.

Behavior	Why?
1. Obstruction	Irritant Food
2. Pale Face	
3. Hot and Beating Heart	
4. Belly Swollen	

Step three:

"Give de patient an elixir dat cools heat and opens bowels."

"Prunes! Vhy didn't I dink of dat?"

"Because you are not Clarityonious, dat's vhy," the modest doctor replied.

Behavior	Why?	Treatment
1. Obstruction	Irritant Food	Prunes
2. Pale Face		
3. Hot and Beating Heart		
4. Belly Swollen		

Our lady patient was given several dosages of prunes as per the doctor's orders. As was evident, treatment was determined only after the underlying cause was determined, and that was determined only after the symptoms were determined. Unfortunately, one "small" item went undetermined.

The patient made several trips to the Uwanga forest. Despite that, the symptoms persisted. Clydeonious, not knowing what else to do, took it upon himself to prescribe more elixir. The result: several more trips to the forest. The patient complained of being tired. "Dats de vay it goes." Symptoms persisted. More prunes. More trips. Finally, completely out of breath, perspiring profusely, and complaining of sharp pains in the abdominal region, the patient plopped supinely on the floor and with no help from the confused Clydeonious, gave . . .

Behavior	Why?	Treatment	****Outcome****	Conclusion
1. Obstruction 2. Pale Face 3. Hot and Beating Heart 4. Belly Swollen	"Irritant Food"	Prunes	**. . .Birth to a Six Pound Baby Girl of Slightly Brown Color.**	??????

(As a result of their combined genius, Clarityonious and Clydeonious probably were forced to conclude that either prunes were not the panacea initially thought, or that they accidentally happened upon the first known fertility drug.)

* * * * *

These sometimes unexpected and unpredicted outcomes actually served a very useful purpose for both the public and the medical practitioner. If out of ignorance, a physician invented an explanation for the cause of a patient's difficulties, and if the prescribed treatment for that cause did not produce the desired outcome, people would find out about it. There would be public and professional scrutiny and, in many cases, the public would avoid him. The charlatan's professional existence would be short-lived.

No longer would he be in the comfortable position of attributing causes to *irrefutable* dragons. The public would demand credibility. They would find themselves in a position to be able to determine the authenticity of the physician. Authoritative validity would be less potent. The layman would be less dependent. The subject matter the physician dealt with would be more observable and much less mysterious. It would, therefore, be open to verification and refutation.

With verification and refutation would come the growth of knowledge, the death of ignorance, and the demise of erroneous dragons.

Psychology's "Germs":* The Case of the Wandering Uterus

> We may recall . . . that not so long ago it was devils and witches who were held responsible for man's problems in social living. The belief in mental illness, as something other than man's trouble in getting along with his fellowman, is the proper heir to the belief in demonology and witchcraft. Mental illness exists or is 'real' in exactly the same sense in which witches existed or were 'real."[22]
>
> —Thomas Szasz, M.D.
> Psychiatrist

The fact that medicine had begun to clean up its act and rid itself of its unwanted dragons, should not be interpreted to mean that psychology and psychiatry were ready to do the same. In fact, the opposite was to happen. With the discovery of the microscope, the discovery of bacteria, and the formulation and verification of the germ theory of physical disease, clinical psychology and ultimately education were about to "discover" an entirely new strain of dragons — a strain that would eventually infect millions of unknown children.

Some Early Dragons and Their Treatment

Early mental health workers used the same logical pattern of the early physicians to determine the presence or absence of a problem. They observed what people were doing, namely their behaviors. They decided whether the behaviors were sufficiently different to warrant concern. If the signals were viewed as being "too" different, the question

* The term "germs" in its present context represents whatever underlying problem is hypothesized to account for the presence of behaviors and actions that are deemed unacceptable, different, or pathological. As will be apparent, the term "germs" does not necessarily refer to any physiological entity such as bacteria or virus.

"Why?" was asked. Whatever means they had at their disposal were then employed to answer that question. Based on that answer, they guessed at what treatment method might change those behaviors and bring them in line with what most everyone else was doing. In the early days, alternatives to the proposed dragons were few. However, varying treatment methods were plentiful.

Continuing our journey, allow me to suggest that you were alive and almost well back around 100 A.D. Let me further suggest that you had the unfortunate habit of doing something like "talking with your hands," or "using foolish gestures,"[23] to convey some ideas that you thought were important *but* others thought were just a drop too different to be acceptable.

Behavior

1. Using Foolish Gestures
2. Conveying Ideas that Were Different

No big deal, right? Wrong. You would have had a disease. The name of the disease was "phrenitis."[23] Phrenitis was responsible for your "abnormal" behavior.

Behavior	**Why?**
1. Using Foolish Gestures	Phrenitis
2. Conveying Ideas that Were Different	

The treatment you would have received for this dreaded mental disease would have depended upon which therapist was living in your neighborhood. If the therapist happened to be a nice methodist fellow named Soranus of Ephesus, some of the following would have been recommended to stop your hands from waving and your mouth from moving in the wrong way. If you were lucky, your head would have been sensuously massaged with a cloth dipped in warm oil. You might have been gently rocked (presumably in a chair, although I was unable to determine precisely what Soranus had in mind) while being given a careful diet (of what I was also unable to ascertain.) Probably prunes.

If you weren't so lucky, you would have been subjected to "careful blood-letting." On the third or fourth day of treatment, your head would have been shaved and your now bald skull would have been treated with cupping[24] — a process of drawing blood to the surface by the application of a cupping glass; with leeches, and with scarification — your head would have been cut and scratched and the blood would have been cupped. During the procedure, you would have had to endure the pain solely on your own. Soranus made it known that he was totally against the consumption of wine during the treatment.

Behavior	Why?	Treatment
1. Using Foolish Gestures	Phrenitis	Warm oil
		Rocking
2. Conveying Ideas that Were Different		Diet
		Shaved head
		Leeches, Cupping, Scarification

New Differences But Same Logic

Besides shivering over the possibility of being shaved, cupped, and leeched, you should have twitched a drop over the logic that was used to suggest that such treatment would even be necessary. Obviously, Soranus had to account for the behaviors that someone suggested were indicative of "phrenitis." In 100 A.D., one couldn't allow a person to walk around waving his or her arms, uttering statements that were viewed as profane. Imagine the danger in allowing a housewife to approach her husband with a poised, closed fist while exclaiming, "I will not take out the garbage!" Obvious blasphemy! Soranus had been somehow trained to view those actions as "symptoms" of an underlying disease. Although he preceded in time the "germ theory of physical disease," he apparently knew it was coming. What he failed to recognize, however, was that these new "symptoms" were not quite like the ones the early physicians had talked about. There is a major difference between an overgrown wart and a behavior or two that is simply upsetting to whomever it is that is responsible for making the rules as to what actions are appropriate and which ones aren't. Soranus ignored the differences and concluded that the only possibility for the behaviors was the condition of "phrenitis." He, of course, never observed the disease. There was nothing to observe. All he observed were the actions of the individual. After observing the behaviors, he inferred the presence of the disease. After treatment, once the behaviors stopped (which they would have after several cuppings and leechings), he had little alternative but to conclude that the phrenitis had been cured.

Perhaps he had one other alternative. He might have concluded that there was nothing wrong with gestures and different ideas. Had he concluded that, the patient would have been able to avoid the loss of his or her blood. That would have been the humane, and correct, thing to do.

But the technology of the times would not allow that to happen. Everything was set to identify an enormous number of unacceptable behaviors. Everything was set to state that these behaviors were "symptoms" of a serious underlying problem. Everything was set to invent whatever dragon would be necessary to explain the presence of the behaviors. The acceptance of alternative explanations or the admittance of ignorance was not a possibility. The possibility that the symptoms were not symptomatic at all, but were expressions of different ways of life was also not a possibility. The authorities had total control. They dictated what was acceptable and what was pathological. Relatively few people asked them for the basis of their dictums. Had they asked, they would have discovered "Catch-22." Had they asked, the authority would have used their questions as evidence of "phrenitis." Challenging the authority was the same as suggesting that the authority might have been wrong. That idea would have been too different to tolerate. It was not tolerated, and "phrenitis" was only the beginning.

* * * * *

Suppose instead of phrenitis, you were told that you had a severe case of the "mania's." According to the best definition I could find, mania was manifesting "any sort of violent abnormal conduct or action."[5]

As to the treatment for this "mental disorder," our friend Soranus suggested that if you were unable to sleep during your attack of mania, listening to the sound of dripping water would somehow lull you into a state of sleep. During the day, you would have been cupped and leeched once again. Traveling and playing chess were also part of the treatment. Soranus, however, did reject a few treatment alternatives some of his colleagues had used. Under his care, you would not have been placed in a closet! He was opposed to darkness as a therapeutic approach. Neither would you have been deprived of food; he was against starvation as a means of teaching you to be like he thought you should be. However, under his care, you would not have been allowed to have an enema! You would not have been allowed to listen to music. And there would have been no love making until you shaped up.[23]

As to the dragon responsible for your abnormal conduct, unrestrained sexuality was one. Over-exertion was another. Alcohol was still another. And, believe it or not, "the absence of relief afforded by bleeding from haemorrhoids or menstruation" was an additional one.[23] This last dragon was "maintained in all seriousness until the nineteenth century."[24] That's nineteenth century A.D.

Moving right along, we come up against one of the most colorful of all the dragons the early mental health workers used to explain the unacceptable actions of certain people. This one is of particular interest for it could only affect women! The men were happy about that, I assure you. Come to think of it, it was the men who indicated that only women were susceptible to this horrible problem. Not very fair, but that is the way it was. The following story is an almost real account of what happened to a nice family that was caught up in the technology of the times. In order to protect the innocent, I have changed the names of the principal characters.

> Claudia Rectus and her family decided to go on their picnic despite the cold temperatures and falling snow. To do otherwise would have disappointed the children. Mr. Rectus fastened the team of horses to the family's chariot. After the horses were covered with warm blankets, the family proceeded on their way.
>
> Since it was cold as they drove toward the lake and the picnic grounds, the children huddled together in the back seat of the open chariot in hopes of keeping warm. Claudia and her husband weren't so fortunate. They had to stand and face the blustery north wind. If the children hadn't been along, they might have stopped at one of the local inns and spent the day producing another Rectus. But the kids were there and the picnic had been promised.
>
> After lunch, the four children danced and played in the snow. They didn't seem to mind the weather or realize that the temperature had dropped some twenty degrees since their arrival at the lake. Before it became too dark, the children were summoned, and the family set about to return home. The trip to their house was not as pleasant as the trip to the lake. The children were tired and very cranky. They were shivering and complaining of the cold. Each took their turn crying and expressing their discomfort. Most of this went unnoticed by Mr. Rectus, for his full concentration was on the horses who also were not thrilled with what was happening. Claudia did what she could to ease the children's discomfort, but it was beyond immediate repair. Twice the chariot had to be stopped so two of the little Rectuses could find a suitable tree. Claudia had to walk each one of them through three foot drifts, and as a result, her waterproof boots were now soaking wet. Before they were half way home, Claudia began to lose her temper. After asking the children to be quiet several times, she uncharacteristically warned them to be quiet. When this failed, she threatened to throw them out of the slow moving chariot if they didn't cool it. On one occasion, some five minutes before they arrived home,

Mr. Rectus had to drop the reins and grab his lovely wife who was screaming at the three-year-old while holding him up by his small ears. As he held his wife, Mr. Rectus noticed that Claudia's nose was running a bit; he saw that her eyes were tearing, and finally that she had a most unusual look on her face. It was almost as if she were about to leap from the chariot to find a quiet place to hide. All of this was most uncharacteristic.

By the time they arrived home, Claudia was ranting and raving. She was screaming at the top of her lungs. She was waving her hands all over the room. After the children were placed in their beds, she collapsed into one of the small chairs located next to the fireplace. She told her husband that she was too tired to eat and she spent the next hour blowing her nose and wiping her reddened eyes.

Mr. Rectus became very concerned over his wife's behaviors. Everything was so uncharacteristic. Sometime around nine o'clock, he slipped quietly into the bedroom and phoned The Mental Illness Clinic for Disturbed and Sick Behavior. The soothing voice on the other end of the line turned out to be a Dr. Claritus, a young physician who was on call. He suggested that Mr. Rectus bring his wife over to the clinic immediately. After a baby sitter was hired, Claudia and Mr. Rectus walked to the clinic. For some inexplicable reason, she refused to get into the chariot.

They were met at the clinic by the resident nurse who led them to a small room. Moments later, Dr. Claritus joined them. He was much younger than Mr. Rectus would have guessed, yet he looked exhausted. He had dark circles under his eyes and was unshaven. His clothes were a mess, almost as if he had slept in them, and he seemed to be having difficulty walking. After taking his seat, as far away from the nurse as possible, he quietly asked Mr. Rectus to review the symptoms his wife had manifested. After hearing of the ranting and raving, the physical assault on the three-year-old, the runny nose and teary eyes, the refusal to eat, and the general fatigue, Dr. Claritus nodded understandingly as he smiled in the direction of Claudia, who had fallen fast asleep.

Behavior

1. Ranting and Raving
2. Physical Assault On Child
3. Runny Nose, Teary Eyes

4. Refusal to Eat
5. General Fatigue

"It's a clear cut case of '*hysteria*' — '*emotional instability, weakness, with possible somatic symptoms,*' "[5] Dr. Claritus explained. "It is a disease we are not unfamiliar with," he added as he wiped his nose.

"It sounds dangerous," Mr. Rectus said after hearing the explanation. "What could cause such a thing to happen?"

Claritus paused for a moment. His hesitation was not due to his ignorance. He knew the answer. It was just that he would have liked to have been able to say something else. The thought crossed his mind to say, "I don't know," but his supervisor would have been very upset upon hearing of such a response. So, he looked at Mr. Rectus and let it fly. "It is caused by the . . . '*malposition of your* [wife's] *uterus,*' "[24] the good doctor said.

"You're joking, of course, aren't you?" Mr. Rectus asked.

"Kind of wish I was, but I'm not. My supervisor says that the disease of hysteria is a result of . . . '*a wandering uterus that has been loosened from its moorings in the pelvic cavity.*' "[24]

Behavior	**Why?**
1. Ranting and Raving	A Wandering Uterus!
2. Physical Assault on Child	
3. Runny Nose, Teary Eyes	
4. Refusal to Eat	
5. Fatigue	

"Don't you think there could be another explanation for her actions," Mr. Rectus asked. "Something a little less serious? After all, it was cold out there and the kids were a pain. I was a little tired myself," he added as he wondered if he had a uterus.

"It's the only explanation I've ever been taught," the doctor admitted.

"Well, what do we do about it?" There was a plea to the husband's voice.

"We have to treat it."

"Why?"

"So the thing will come back."

"Come back from where?"

"From wherever it wandered to."

"How will we know when it has come back?"

"When your wife doesn't do what she's not supposed to do," was the doctor's answer.

"Oh," was the husband's response.

"We have two treatments," the doctor pointed out.

"One of them I don't even want to think about," he added as he watched the nurse fumble with the buttons on her blouse.

"How about the other one?"

"It's called 'fumigation.'[24] We use it . . . *'hoping to lure the vagrant uterus back to its natural position.'* "[24]

Behavior	**Why?**	**Treatment**
1. Ranting and Raving	A Wandering Uterus!	Fumigation
2. Physical Assault on Child		
3. Runny Nose, Teary Eyes		
4. Refusal to Eat		
5. Fatigue		

"I'm almost afraid to ask what it is."

"If I were you, I'd be afraid myself," the doctor stated. Then he whispered to himself, "If I was your wife, I'd get the hell out of here quick."

"What is it?"

"Fumigation involves inserting a hose into your wife's vagina. Once accomplished, we force hot, acrid smoke into her."

"Does it work?"

"Well, let me put it to you this way. After being fumigated *once*, the patient never does whatever she did that got her fumigated in the first place!"

"I'd like to hear of the second procedure, if you don't mind," Mr. Rectus requested. "The first one sounds pretty heavy." Claritus remained silent. "Dr. Claritus, please! My wife's uterus has gone. The second procedure, please!"

Reluctantly, Claritus sputtered, "The second procedure is to have frebglu semrxw intipiewquzn."

"I'm sorry, I didn't quite get that," Mr. Rectus said.

Dr. Claritus took a breath. It was a shallow breath, but it was all he could muster. "I said the second procedure is to have frequent sexual intercourse!"

"No!"

"Yes!"

"Does it work? Does it lure the vagrant uterus back into

place?"

"Does it work? Is that what you want to know? Let me tell you," the doctor said in short, choppy sentences. "It may do wonders for you and your wife. It may cure all your ills. For me, it's killing me. Do you hear me? It is killing me. I can't handle anymore," he added, his voice trailing off into the quiet night. With that, Dr. Claritus, the young physician, whose clinic specialized in one of the two treatments designed to cure "hysteria," keeled over and passed on to a less demanding land.

* * * * *

As time passed, some of the invented dragons disseminated by the authorities became more sophisticated. That was to be expected. The life span of "wandering uteri" as an acceptable explanation for anything couldn't have been too long, regardless of the need to reduce ignorance. For a while, decaying matter in the nervous system was suggested as a possible cause for various types of "neuroses," but that ultimately gave way to the proposal that scars in the brain were causes of all kinds of "mental derangements." Interestingly, "scars" was a pretty good guess. Further, some very good minds suggested that "mental illness" was a result of "animal spirits," of "body humidity" — whether your insides were wet or dry, and of "magnetic forces emanating from the planets."

Ideas were plentiful, but rarely were the ideas satisfactory. They were neither verifiable nor refutable. This unfortunate state of ignorance placed the well-meaning practitioner in a most uncomfortable position. As Alexander and Selesnick (1966) pointed out, when King George III, in 1788, suffered from the frighteningly named disease of "depressive psychosis," the layman and physician alike didn't know whether to treat the King's problem by having his head blistered, his intestines purged, whether to bleed him, make him vomit, or simply have him walk around the royal gardens while listening to soothing music.[24] One can only hope that for the sake of the King, and for those who finally decided what to do, the King was asked which procedure he preferred.

As with early man and early medicine, ignorance was not a state of bliss. Because of ignorance, the "insane" were chained, beaten and burned. They were seen as witches and carriers of evil spirits. They were either avoided or viewed as one views animals at a zoo on a pleasant Sunday outing. Because of these attitudes and means of treatment, the thinking physician and psychologist continued to pursue better answers and more humane treatments to deal with the "Whys?" Sadly, they made little progress.

> The position of the psychiatrist around 1900 [A.D.] was not a particularly happy one. Although he was better able to classify . . . and predict . . . than his predecessors a century before, he still suffered the same ignorance of the causes of mental illness and he still had to be content with the same miserable methods of treatment.[23]

The ignorance and miserable methods could be found almost everywhere. Psychotherapy, as viewed by Boerhaave (1668-1738), consisted of blood letting, consumption of substances that would cause bowels to move, dunking in ice cold water, and other procedures that were designed to induce a state of shock. One of these other methods was an invention by Boerhaave. It was called a spinning or gyrating chair. It was used to induce shock and render a patient unconscious. A patient, who was seen as someone who was doing something Boerhaave said he shouldn't be doing, would be placed in the chair and spun around at great speeds until he became unconscious.

One of the next authorities to come along had the name Darwin. Not Charles, however. This Darwin was Erasmus Darwin, Charles' grandfather. Erasmus thought the chair was a good idea. He also thought that one of the most viable dragons had been overlooked by his colleagues. Darwin believed that all diseases arose out of something he called "disordered motions of the nervous tissue."[24] To many of the unsuspecting laypeople of the time, the dragon sounded good. The fact that no one had ever seen nervous tissue in "disorder" made little difference. If Darwin said it, it must be true. Thus if someone would do something that Darwin believed to be unnecessary, different, or strange, the unfortunate someone would be placed in the chair and spun around. Darwin believed that, as a result of the spinning, the disorder and the disease would somehow become ordered. Verification of the success of the treatment was based on whether the patient complained of the same problems that got him placed in the chair. Since that didn't happen too frequently, Darwin concluded that the procedure was successful.

Benjamin Rush, "the founder of American Psychiatry" also liked Boerhaave's chair, but he wasn't fond of Darwin's logic or rationale for its use. Ben had invented his own dragon, and it wasn't disordered tissue. He believed that congested blood in the brain produced mental illness. (Everyone was entitled to his own dragon.) Ben's treatment of choice? Decongest the congestion. He would violently spin the patient around by means of the chair. If the patient stopped doing whatever Ben thought were the signs of the "mental illness," he concluded that the blood of the patient was no longer congested. If Ben had not been satisfied with the effects of the chair, he would have taken a shot at blood letting in order to relieve the brain of its vascular clog. If that didn't work — and the patient was still alive! — Benjamin probably would have concluded that he had postulated the wrong dragon. He would thus find a new one. Masturbation was a likely choice. He believed that masturbation was a major dragon for disturbed psyches. I was unable to find out what Dr. Rush did to prevent masturbation, but I didn't look too hard. Ben also believed that too much sex was bad. He wasn't much in favor of pregnancy, either. All in all, Ben must have been a real thrill to live with.

From an over-stimulated sex life, we move to an under-stimulated body. That was Dr. John Brown's dragon. He believed that nervous weakness and nervous illness was somehow caused by a lack of stimulation. To take care of that dragon, John believed that huge doses of stimulating drugs would be in order. "As the medical historian Guthrie report[ed] Brown's system killed more persons than the French Revolution and the Napoleonic Wars taken together."[24]

Whereas one mind doctor would try one approach, another was bound to come along and try the opposite. Samuel Hahnemann, M.D. decided that instead of giving huge dosages of drugs that would stimulate the unstimulated, he would give very small dosages of drugs which caused reactions similar to the symptoms — giving stimulants to patients already stimulated. The best that was said about Sam's approach was that "if it did not cure, at least it did not kill."[24]

There were others. One psychiatrist, out of total frustration with his profession, simply concluded that sin was the ultimate cause of mental disturbances. Others stayed with the physiological approach, suggesting that too much blood in the brain was the dragon of depression, while not enough blood caused one to become extremely excited. Others stopped dreaming up new dragons and just began to rename the old ones. New terms were invented such as "mneme" and "glial proliferation" and "sthenic" and "allopathy" and "super-us."

Irrefutable dragons abounded. The pets were safe, for they were described and discussed in ways that kept them light years from scientific investigation. Ironically, some of them might have been extremely beneficial. But it was almost impossible to make that determination because of their irrefutable idiosyncrasies, and the idiosyncrasies of their inventors.

Each inventor waved his own flag and few of them would have anything to do with those who would disagree, or demand credibility. Whether it was Hippocrates' "humors," Gall's "lumps on the head," Mesmer's "animal magnetism," or Hartmann's "unconscious," the story remained the same. New dragons were born to take the place of those already discarded. Yet each new dragon did little more than maintain man's ignorance. Each stayed around until there were no more believers. Each would then die quietly, only to have another take its place.

The New Dragons — The Breed that Lives Within Us All

> Primitive man's explanation of abnormal behavior was that some outside power, an evil spirit, must have taken possession of the sufferer. In short, mental disease . . . was to him caused by evil spiritual forces. In principle, man was right when he associated mental disease with psychological forces; what he did not recognize until recently was that these forces *were not outside** him, were not caused by magic, but were *his own* unacceptable desires, fears, and impulses.[24]

Enter psychology's INSIDE dragons.

From the beginning when physicians and psychologists talked about evil spirits, demons, diseased blood, too much blood, they were attempting, as best they could, to help free man from his suffering. Rather than being content with locking "mental" patients in dark closets, hoping everyone would soon forget them, they experimented. Despite their noble efforts, few helped. Some did more harm than good. Fortunately, for the patients, those scientists who were committed to finding answers, were not satisfied with what was available. They realized that most of the previously disseminated answers and speculations did not ameliorate the suffering. They realized that most of the speculations were not testable. They realized that to help man, a method would be needed to scrutinize new hypotheses to see if they had any value. The cry for professional credibility ran high. But the scientists also realized that before they would be able to scrutinize new ideas, they would have to find some *new* ones to consider.

Where would they go to find other explanations? Where would the new speculations and new answers come from? Where?

They needed to find a new frontier to explore. The old territories had failed to yield the fruit they so desperately desired. The magnetic influences of the planets had, for the most part, been discounted. The secret influential fluids that supposedly ran throughout the body remained

---

* Added emphasis mine

elusive. The demons and spirits, said to infiltrate the body and soul, had never been seen so their existence was strongly doubted. In truth, the number of possible alternatives to these "dead and discarded" dragons was limited. By discounting the heavens, by negating the fluids, by belittling the magnetic charges, man had literally limited the possible alternatives to be investigated. The pressure from this limitation was too great for man to remember that in the absence of suitable alternatives .... Too great for him to remember his "inherent" inability to admit his ignorance.

To save man from his ignorance a new dragon needed to be discovered. Or if necessary, invented. And . . . one was.

"Germs! Why not germs?" Dr. Claritimen stated as he removed his glasses and cleaned them with a tissue. The other members of the group were quite surprised at his suggestion.

"What do you mean, germs, Dr. Claritimen?" Dr. Clydimen asked, "We are talking about psychological problems, *not* physiological diseases."

"I am aware of that, Dr. Clydimen" Claritimen said curtly. "I, too, am a physician. I do know the difference between physical and psychological difficulties." That was only half true. Claritimen was a very competent physician. His specialty was internal medicine; he was known throughout the world for his expertise in that area. Psychological problems, however, were as mysterious to him as they were to the rest of his colleagues. "I am speaking of *psychological* germs. Real germs that somehow work themselves into the insides of people and cause grevious psychological abnormalities. We have a precedent for such an idea and I believe we would be foolish not to consider it. I am referring to Pasteur's and Koch's work with anthrax. Remember, their work helped confirm the idea of the germ theory of physical disease. With a little adjustment, we could develop a germ theory of mental disease."

"Granted it's an intriguing idea, but are we talking about bacteria?"

"No, silly. Not bacteria. But we could talk about traumatic past experiences, about inadequate psychosexual development, about serious internal psychological conflicts," Claritimen suggested. "We could talk about divorce as a germ for all sorts of things. Being the first born child could be a biggy. Being the middle child could even be bigger. And think of the possibilities for being the last child — the one that came late, unexpected."

"And the symptoms of these germs?" Dr. Clydimen inquired.

"Well my friend, let me ask you a question. Do you have patients who talk funny and do funny, strange things?"

"For sure."

"Do you have patients who continue to wet their bed long after we believe they should?"

"For sure."

"Do you have a few patients who are not thrilled with their sex lives?"

"For sure, for sure."

"Have you been able to *explain why* these people are so strange?"

"I have not," Dr. Clydimen unhappily admitted.

"Then why not germs? Psychological germs responsible for psychological symptoms?"

"Sounds exciting," the other members of the group commented.

"But we don't know that there are such things as psychological germs," Dr. Clydimen stated.

"True. But that's not overly important."

"Well, I do like the idea of inside germs. Never cared much for outside explanations. Things like present day problems in social living are too clear, too simple. Things like habits and ways of adapting to what the environment requires are too logical. Things that have real physiological underpinnings are too tight. Not enough pizazzz," Dr. Clydimen added phonetically. "But psychological germs? I just don't know. Maybe too much pizazzz. Personally, I think we should concentrate more on the brain. Something like too much brain, or congested brain, or a wandering brain, or a wet or dry brain. The brain is inside. That would certainly satisfy me."

"No way, Charlie," Claritimen retorted. "We've played around with that thing long enough. Besides, it might be nice of us to leave that for *someone else*."

"Who?"

"I don't know for sure," Claritmen said. "Some group, in the near future, might be able to use it. Maybe our colleagues in education might find some value in it. I can imagine that educators one day might be able to explain all of the academic imperfections of their pupils with the idea of a disordered brain or a hyper-brain or even a no-brain. They might like that a lot.

"And further, Dr. Clydimen, I remind you that time is moving quickly. We can't afford the luxury of debate any longer. If we don't come up with something soon, someone will beat us to it. In my judgment, inside, nonphysical, psychological germs are the ticket. I suggest we stop our bickering and take a vote."

"Can you vote on something like this?" the other members of the group asked.

"Sure. Professionals do it all the time. You sit around a table, you make your best case, and you vote. If you don't have a clear cut answer, you have to get everyone to agree on something. Hippocrates' group voted in favor of black bile and that did all right for awhile. Soranus' group had some good times with phrenitis. It was obvious they didn't know what they were talking about. I needn't tell you how popular the wandering uterus was. Lots of people got a bang out of that one!"

* * * * *

The logical place to look for new dragons had to be *inside* man himself. Most of the supernatural outside sources had been discounted. The small number of other possible locations for the dragons just about guaranteed that man's own inner make-up would be the next target. But part of his inner make-up had already been considered. The bile, blood, humidity, and brain had already had their shot and none had provided a permanent, suitable answer. The scientists faced a perplexing problem.

Then it happened. Sometime during the 19th and 20th centuries some of the more prominent mental health workers began to propose that the dragon they had been looking for had been discovered. The vote was taken and counted. Once the results were in, the scientists issued a proclamation that the dragon did live inside man. Their proclamation clearly stated, however, that the dragon was not part of man's physical insides, rather his mental insides. With effort, they found a way to incorporate their findings into the trusted and respected germ theory model. This appeased some of the skeptical physicians, for it offered them something they were familiar with. They liked the idea of "germs" and "diseases" and "symptoms," even if the germs weren't biological, even if the diseases were given new and confusing names, even if the symptoms seemed to be everyday behaviors that a lot of people manifested. They were comfortable with such terms as "diagnosis" and "prognosis" even though they knew that their tools for diagnosing were no better than feeling bumps on someone's head, and their guesses as to what would happen in the future of a patient's "mental" life were as accurate as their guess of whether a coin would turn up to be a head or tail. Nevertheless, psychology's inside dragons were born. They were hailed as one of the most important discoveries — or inventions — to have come along since clogged blood in the brain.

Before the passage of many moons, in place of the previously accepted physical and supernatural explanations for "insanity," phrases such as "unconscious conflicts," "unconscious hostility and anxiety" began cropping up. Strivings, passions, emotions were given high priority as being possible causes of mental illness. Thoughts of sex, of Mother, Father, Sister, Brother and Self were hoisted high on the list of likely "germs" that were responsible for a variety of "diseases," which showed themselves through an endless variety of "symptoms." The germ theory of mental illness was here!

Within no time at all, previously unknown explorers who had spent most of their waking day looking at nervous systems, blood systems, and breathing systems, discarded their valued armaments and began with great fervor to investigate the new frontier. Since the frontier was virgin, everyone had an equal shot at it. Each explorer was on his or her own. The entire affair could have been likened to a California gold rush. Each staked out his own mental territory. Each with pickax, textbook, and on occasion, stethoscope, went searching. With very little trouble they found! They discovered and Un-Covered. They Un-Earthed, Un-Raveled, Un-Riddled, and resolved. It was very exciting.

The Balloon

While the explorers went on their individual excursions, they were guided by several accepted principles. First, psychological "germs" were real and were capable of producing never ending difficulties. Second, although everyone was potentially susceptible to the "germs," not everyone would catch the "germs' " diseases. Somehow, certain people were able to handle the "germs" while others were not so fortunate. Third, the "germs" were inside man. They weren't directly observable, but they were there nevertheless. Fourth, the "germs" would have to be discovered and purged. If they were allowed to remain active, they would continue to cause serious everyday problems. Fifth, and perhaps most important, the explorers accepted the idea that man was more than just a man. Man, the two-legged upright one, was now viewed as being a balloon.

"Yes, my friends, man is a balloon," Dr. Jason Clarity said to the audience at the first annual conference on the "Germ Theory of Mental Illness." The professionals in attendance sat in the provided chairs, writing down everything the Keynote speaker was saying. Their eyes left their papers only to catch a glimpse of the most prestigious authority in the field of psychological diseases. "And like a balloon," Dr. Clarity continued, "man is full of hot air." The audience nodded in agreement. "Not your typical hot air, however," Clarity pointed out. "A very special type. We will call this hot air 'psychic energy.' This air has the properties that can cause man to do strange things. That's the bad news," he added. "The good news is that man has the ability to cork his hot air." The audience was relieved upon hearing that. "This corking device is something we will call a defense mechanism." Clarity paused for a moment, walked over to the chalkboard, and picked up a piece of chalk. As he drew a large circle on the board he said, "Picture the inside lining of the balloon as representing man's defenses. If this lining is strong, and the hot air or energy inside the balloon is stable, the balloon — or man — will appear to be intact, symmetrical, or in a state of satisfying equilibrium. Please notice," Clarity continued, "the picture I have drawn on the board represents an intact, symmetrical, satisfied balloon.

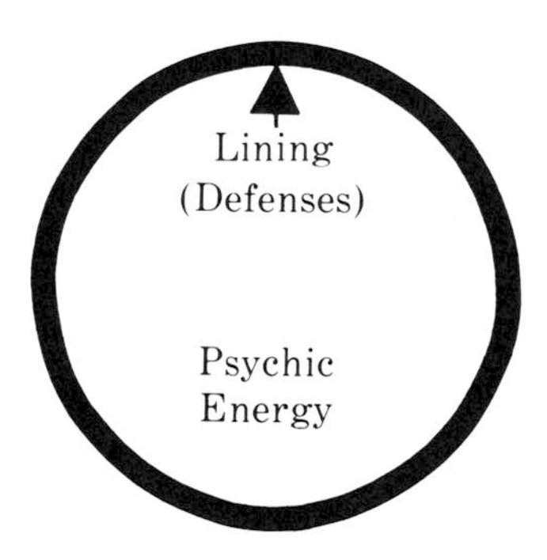

BALLOON #1

"However," he pointed out, "if the energy inside the balloon builds up to a sufficient degree, pressure or stress will be placed on the inside lining. What happens next depends on the strength of the lining, or the strength of man's defenses. If the lining is weak, and the pressured energy becomes too intense for the balloon's wall to handle, something has got to pop out. The following," he said as he drew a second balloon, "is a picture of a balloon whose psychic energy is too great for its wall to deal with.

BALLOON #2

"We want you to consider this pop-out as being a representation of an abnormal behavior. We have decided that an abnormal behavior is anything a person is doing that he or she is not supposed to be doing.

"Now, with a little imagination," Clarity said, "it should be very easy for you to make the transition from balloon to man. Let me draw you a picture of a man whose psychic energy is intense and whose defenses are weak. Notice the similarity between balloon and man.

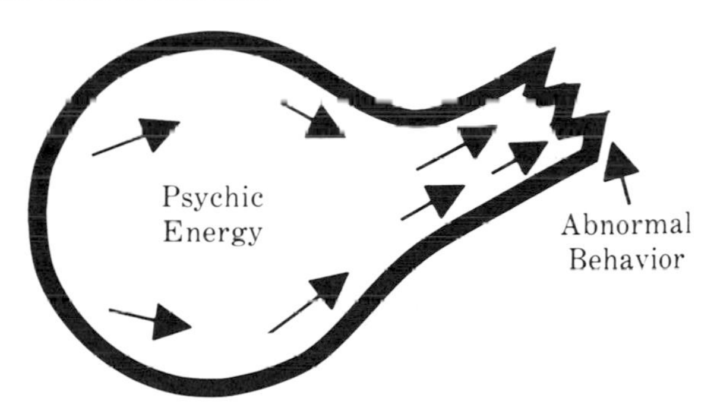

MAN

"To help you appreciate the importance of this model, allow me to draw a picture of a man who presently has just the right amount of psychic energy and whose defenses can handle the pressure from within.

AN O.K. MAN

"It is obvious from the drawing that this man is stable, intact, and symmetrical. His conflicts have been resolved and his traumas haven't been too traumatic. He's not doing anything he's not supposed to be doing. In fact, he is doing just what we think he should be doing. There are no signs. Everything is fine.

"This next picture is slightly different," Clarity explained as he drew. "We have a man who is still going to work, who is not saying anything particularly unusual, and who does not appear to be overly concerned with the size of his genitals.

NOT AN ALL-AROUND O.K. MAN

"If you will look carefully at this man, however, you will see that he's not quite as O.K. as the previous O.K. man. His psychic energy is beginning to boil a bit. Notice the small nodules at the surface of his wall. He is showing signs of stress. These nodules, according to our germ theory, are telltale signs that something is brewing. He is doing something, minor perhaps, that he shouldn't be doing. Probably something like not shaving for a couple of days and forgetting to tie his shoelaces.

"Finally, I will draw you a picture of a man who is falling

apart. It is apparent that he can no longer handle his psychic energy. He can no longer defend himself against his internal conflicts. His traumas have overtaken him. The pressurized energy, stemming from his Un-Conscious germs have caused a weak psychological area to give in. He has just manifested something that was totally uncalled for and cannot be explained by the average layman. Perhaps he just emerged nude from the lavatory of a crowded 747 while it was flying over Salt Lake City.

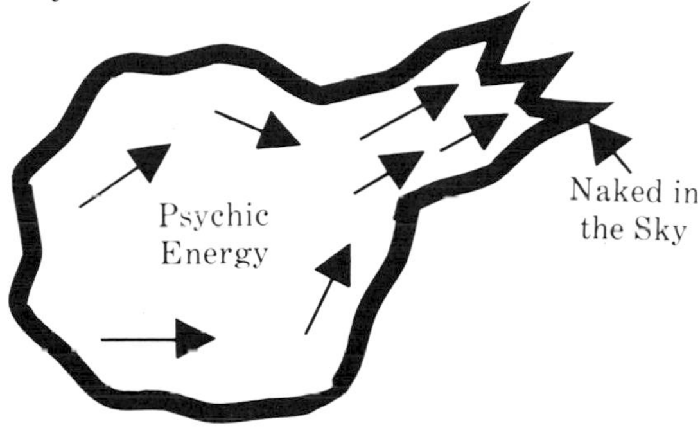

A SICK MAN

"The man is sick! We know he is sick because of his pop-out. We also know that his pop-out would not have popped out if a serious problem did not exist within his inside psychological system. It is apparent that to help him we will need to go inside of him and locate the nature of his germs."

Clarity replaced the chalk and walked back to the front of the stage. He looked around the room and smiled at those colleagues who had finished writing and were now paying homage to his expertise. "If you have any questions or comments, I will entertain them," he said.

"I would like to clear something up," a distinguished looking gentleman said as he stood.

"Anything," Clarity answered.

Before speaking, the gentleman straightened his black satin-like robe that draped his shoulders and flowed to the tips of his newly shined shoes. He cleared his throat, adjusted his Ben Franklin spectacles, and carefully moved his gold colored tassel that adorned his impressive mortarboard so its strands would not obstruct his vision. "I am a little ahead of my time," the quiet, soft spoken educator began, "but I believe the time is right to set the stage for the future." Clarity nodded.

"If I understand, you are suggesting that we should watch very carefully what a person is doing, specifically his or her behavior. We should then use that behavior as a means to determine whether that person is functioning as we believe he should. If we determine that his behavior is not acceptable, we should assume that there exists an inside psychological problem that is responsible for the observed, outside behaviors."

"That is correct," Clarity indicated.

"Would you agree that in the future we might wish to use the same logic to explain some of the problems school-aged children might have?"

"I see no reason why you wouldn't be able to," Clarity responded.

"That is very interesting," the educator said, more to himself than to Clarity and the audience. "If we were to observe a child whose handwriting was not as accurate as we believed it should be, we could then explain the differences by some inside problem — psychological or otherwise. We wouldn't have to consider any other type of alternative explanation. We could simply conclude that something was wrong with the *child*."

"If I were in your shoes, that's exactly what I would do," the authoritative expert stated.

"We could do the same with a child who might ask too many questions, make too many requests, fail to follow the rules and regulations of the classroom. We could do the same for a child who was a year or two behind in his work, a child who had problems with 'b's' and 'd's,' a child who preferred to stay at home rather than going to school, a child who cried more than other children, a child who laughed more than other children, a child who was too quick, or too slow, or too average. The possibilities are endless. All we have to do is to determine what inside explanations we will use. We will need some new names, some new diseases," the educator said as he sat down.

"You'll find them," Clarity stated, supportively.

"Thank you, Dr. Clarity."

Clarity was about to continue his lecture when a second hand was raised from the audience. Clarity urged the young woman to ask whatever she desired. She stood, and all eyes turned toward her. There was an audible murmuring throughout the remainder of the group. It was atypically strange that a woman would stand and make a comment. The males in the audience recognized this difference, but kept their interpretations to themselves. They expected that her comments would be unusual, her gestures would be unusual, and she probably would have a runny nose. For the moment, they paid little attention to what she had to say. Clarity, however, was diplomatic. He listened. He knew he could always rely on the leeching, cupping, and fumigation if her ideas went a little too far.

"Dr. Clarity, would you please explain to me how you can be so certain that a germ is present after just looking at a person's actions?"

"An excellent question," Clarity said. "We know that a germ is present *because* the behavior is present. It is as simple as that."

"But you don't really see the germ?" the woman said, now staring at the seated educator.

"That was *not* a good question!" Clarity retorted. "Of course you don't see the germ. You don't have to. You just know it must be there." His pleasant tone had now totally disappeared. The audience felt the change. They became very still. They listened very carefully.

"If you do not see it, how do you know that it is there?" the woman persisted.

"Why is that so important," Clarity asked, attempting to change the tide.

"Because, if you say it is present, and it is not, you have made a serious mistake."

"Try to understand what I am about to say," Clarity urged sarcastically. "What other reason could there be for an unexpected, unacceptable behavior other than an inside germ? The fact that we don't see the germ is inconsequential. We know it is present by looking at the pop-out."

"That is not true!" the woman answered back. "All you know is the behavior is present. You know nothing more than that." She turned toward the educator who was busy taking notes. "If a child's handwriting is less than you expect, that does not mean that there is anything wrong with the child. If the same child asks questions, makes requests, refuses to stay in his seat, has difficulty with reading, writing, arithmetic, or finds school something less than fulfilling, that does not mean that there is something wrong with the child. There may be several explanations for such behaviors and none of them have to suggest that the child is the one with the problem." The educator squirmed, but said nothing. "Don't you see what you are doing?"

she asked the gentleman. "You are using the child's behavior as a means to determine that *something* might be wrong . That is likely true, but you may be looking at the wrong *something.* You are not looking at the total picture. You are neglecting something that could be crucial. If you totally accept the balloon theory; if you believe that the outside behavior tells you that there is an inside problem, you will not look at anything else. And, there is something else to look at!"

"Ma'am," Clarity broke in. "Let me remind you of where you are . . . of who you are. *Your* behavior is beginning to let *us* know that you are suffering from some serious problem. If you persist any longer, you will have to suffer the obvious consequences."

"I will persist!" the woman stated sharply. "I'm not afraid of your leeches, or your threats of cupping, fumigation, or any other such thing. Shortly, in the very near future, you will see me, or *someone* just like me, again. We will force you to look at the alternatives. You will have no other choice but to do so! The children will demand it!"

* * * * *

A Few Explorers and Their Unique Discoveries

> Unfortunately in the field of mental health there have been relatively few practitioners who wish to put their heads on the chopping block by challenging orthodoxy. Some of these, while repeating the catechism of accepted credos for the benefit of their associates, do admit in off-the-record comments a disagreement with original doctrines. But we are confronted too frequently with the frightening spectacle of men so committed to their beliefs that they refuse to relinquish them even when evidence proves that they are wrong.[25]
>
> — Lewis R. Wolberg, M.D.
> Psychiatrist

The future, the woman in the audience was referring to, was not ready to show itself. As a result, the "Clarities" persisted and the new dragons began to find themselves in professional offices and the laypublic's living room. Some unsuspecting "patients" suffered little from them. The little beasts served as objects of discussion over coffee or bridge.

Some "patients," however, were not so fortunate. They believed they were infected by the germs and they spent months, years, attempting to rid themselves of something they likely didn't even have. We'll take a look at a few of the "demons" of the new technology.

Our first explorer is one you are probably familiar with. His dragons were among the most colorful. He was probably the most influential of all the early explorers. He showed us, among other things, that what we say is *not* really what we said, that what we dream is *not* really what we dreamed, and what we do really means something entirely different than what we did — colorful as well as enlightening. I am speaking, of course, of Sigmund Freud.

As to his own dragons, Dr. Freud once said something that implied rather strongly that he was not totally convinced that his explanations were completely valid —

> One might ask me whether and how far I am convinced of the correctness of the assumptions here developed. My answer would read that I am neither myself convinced nor do I ask that others shall believe them; or better said, I don't know how far I believe them.[26]

An honest statement, to say the very least. That was to be expected for Freud was a scientist, as well as being a physician. He understood the importance of credibility. He was, however, faced with "unusual" behaviors that were manifested by some of his patients, and as an authority, he was obliged to explain them.

Sex, the Un-Conscious, the Oedipal complex, and the conflicts they purportedly brought on were among Freud's major dragons. He, or perhaps more accurately, his followers, believed that these dragons explained why various people behaved as they did. For example, A. Salter, while skeptically reviewing some of Freud's tenets pointed out that according to the Freudian technology, sex underlied most everything —

> Mr. Jones wrote a story for his high school magazine only because he was sexually frustrated. Now, Mr. Jones collects stamps and is trying to build up his savings account only because of his poor toilet training as a child.[13]

I've got to believe that there is a little girl, sitting in an office, who is about to say, "I don't buy it!"

Mr. Jones was also bothered by something else. According to Salter, Mr. Jones wasn't fond of standing on the top of a forty-story building and looking down to the street. You'd think there would be a simple explanation for such a *rational* fear. Such is not the case.

> Mr. Jones is afraid of leaning out of tall buildings not because he gets dizzy and is afraid of falling, but because he once surprised his mother in the shower.[13]

(Frankly, I have no idea what the dragon means. One can only guess at what might have happened to Mr. Jones if he had accidentally discovered both his mother and father in the shower, at the same time.)

Toilet training and surprising Mom in the shower weren't the only "germs" responsible for the serious behaviors of stamp collection, fear of heights, and the like. Another major dragon was the Oedipal complex. Dr. Freud considered this complex and resulting conflict to be the nucleus for the disease known as "neurosis."[27] As you remember, it was also responsible for roller skating wrecks.

If you are not familiar with the complex you should be, for you went through it. Don't be alarmed, however, for it was one of those experiences that you experienced that you didn't know you were experiencing.

The complex represents a wish for sexual relationships with a parent of the opposite sex — the little boy "wants" Mommy and the little girl "wants" Daddy. Unfortunately, that's not all that happens. Guilt happens. That in itself is intriguing. How is it possible to feel guilty about something when you didn't have the slightest idea that the something happened? The pat answer from the past is that the guilt, like the complex, is Un-Conscious. What that means is that no one really knows that it happens.

Pursuing this complex complex just a drop further, a little girl in a family observes that she doesn't have what her little brother has and she wants one — according to the theory. A little boy, on the other hand, sees that he has one, but that his sister doesn't. Now the dragon becomes really complicated. The little boy gets scared that he will lose what he has. He suffers from something called "castration fear," which is no laughing matter! The little girl can't suffer from castration fear for obvious reasons, right? Wrong!! There is something called an "inverted Oedipus."[5] When you are inventing dragons, it pays to cover all the loopholes. After all, it certainly seems plausible that a little girl might prefer to be intimate with Momma. If such a "strange" thing happened, it might mean that the little girl was experiencing an overwhelming fear that she might get what her little brother has. That must really be frightening. If one assumes that most little girls don't suffer from that castration problem, they obviously must be made to suffer from something else. The new technology guaranteed that. So . . . the little girl falls victim to "penis envy." Disgusting!

All of this supposedly takes place between two and six years of age. Of course, no one ever sees it happening, but the technology says it does. One can choose to believe it or not. What appears real, however, is that children during Freud's time were observed to do things, say things, or feel things that were not easily explainable. Someone, an authority, had to come up with some explanation. Ignorance, of the honest kind, was not an acceptable alternative.

Not all of the explorers agreed with Dr. Freud's ideas. They had some of their own ideas which they did not hesitate to use to explain unusual occurrences. Alfred Adler, for example, parted company with Freud's dragons. He didn't seem to be overly concerned with a child's supposed fear of having his or her genitals changed. Instead, "In the early phase of his thought he accounted for whatever the quality of an individual's adjustment — whether apparently normal, neurotic, or superior — as the result of organic inferiority."[108] That was a pretty safe dragon, so it persisted for a time. Later, Adler indicated that man's energy was spent moving away from what he later called "social inferiority." He liked that idea so much that he ultimately used it as an explanation for the serious disease called "neurosis." He felt that was a better dragon than Freud's "Oedipal."

Erik Erikson, another explorer, decided on a compromise between Freud and Adler. He liked the idea that toilet training was very important but he also liked the inferiority business as well. Most important, however, was Erikson's opinion of what might happen to a youngster during what was called the "standing stage." You might not have thought much about the trauma of standing for the first time, but Erikson did.

> In becoming upright, the child experiences in a new way his sense of smallness. When he looks forward, he sees the eyes of others examining him. Feeling small, he may not be ready for that exposure . . .

(I'm not sure how much sense all of that makes. My assumption is that a child, prior to standing, has been looked at before. Why would that be any different now that he is standing? In fact, he might even sense how *big* he has become. After all, when he stands, the tables, chairs, and pets don't get any bigger. The child might even notice that for the first time, he is looking down on them and feel pretty good about that! I could be wrong, though.)

Since the child is now standing . . .

> . . . The child cannot see his own buttocks, but others can. A

> feeling develops that others can dominate the backside, even invade and lay low one's autonomy. Paranoid fears of unseen and hostile people can come into being.[29]

I'm sure it must be very comforting for young parents to learn that their little youngster may be experiencing paranoid fears due, in part, to the fact that he "cannot see his own buttocks." All this time they probably thought that standing tall was a magical, memorable event.

Carl Jung was another of the major explorers. One of the most interesting things he discovered was an "unconscious" underneath the previously discovered "unconscious." In this new basement, called the "Collective Unconscious," Dr. Jung found representations of the "collective wisdom of man's remote past, in which the individual could learn to draw with profit."[28] After some additional exploration, Carl found that this collective Un-Conscious carried the "heritage of the ages impressed upon the structure of the more primitive part of the nervous system."[28] (Despite scientific rejection of these discoveries, Carl hung onto his dragons for many years.)

One last thing Carl found. It was called "The Shadow." It was a pretty depressing discovery but a profitable one for some early radio program promoter. "It represented the evil that is instinctive in many . . . the whole ugly burden of world evil . . . ."[28] Of course, only the *Shadow* knows whether Jung's discovery was factual or artifactual.

Despite the vigor and seeming thoroughness shown by the early explorers, one particular area of dragons went uninvestigated for quite some time. It took someone who was "explicitly . . . anti-scientific in his approach"[27] to discover the missing area. As a result of his discovery, the explorer received the following accolade from Dr. Freud himself. "It is the most important progress since the discovery of psychoanalysis."[24] As sometimes happens, however, the accolade was later withdrawn after the discoverer discovered that his discovery wasn't all that sound. What was the "most" important progress?

Otto Rank, the explorer, suggested that you and I are forever seeking to return and re-enter the blissfulness of intra-uterine life. Translated, that means we want to go back to the womb because we remember it to be peaceful and quite. Otto further suggested —

> . . . that pathological states result from the fear of the womb and the wish to return to it. The female womb represents the locale of the young boy's first horrifying experience . . . the child attempts to overcome the trauma of birth by attempting to rid himself of his fear of the mother's genitals by wishing to penetrate it. This fails because the child is unequipped physi-

> cally to reenter his mother and because the anxiety of birth . . . prevents a sustained effort in this endeavor.[24]

Thank goodness for the absence of the necessary equipment and the acquisition of a short-attention-span.

I think the basis for Otto's dragon was the assumption that intra-uterine life was blissful. While I can't recall what my feelings were about being inside, I would hesitate to use the word "blissful" to describe what I think the experience must have been. There you are, surrounded by a little bag of fluid. The temperature never varies. You've got this "rope" attached to your stomach, and if it starts to itch, there is no way you can scratch. You have no freedom, no privacy. Everyone knows where you are all the time. You have no choice as to what you want to eat. The food you do receive from the person you're hanging around with probably tastes the same day after day. You are poked around without being able to poke back. You are listened to without being able to tell the listener to bug off. Every once in awhile, someone sticks a finger into your whatever, and as hard as you try, there is no way you can bite it. All sorts of people — some who you don't even know — place their unwashed hands near you, then they squeal with delight after you try to kick their hands away. Everytime your "partner" plays bridge, you are banged up against the bridge table. Toward the end of the whole deal, you're used . . . *used* as a table to support plates and coffee cups. Bliss? come on, Otto.

Next, Melanie Klein, a "famous" child analyst. Ms. Klein was an interesting lady. She "found" some dragons that no one had ever dreamed of. Some *authorities* have been pretty sorry about what she found and what she did. I am introducing Ms. Klein to you hesitantly. It is very difficult to have fun with what she said. She did slip every so often and come up with a comment that one can chuckle at —

> She considered that the child had knowledge of his parents' sexual relationship. To her, for instance, the child who bumped two play cars together was expressing symbolically his unconscious knowledge of parental sexual intercourse, even though he had never witnessed the primal scene.[24]

That's harmless, even humorous. What will follow is *not*! It is taken from a book entitled *The Psycho-Analysis of Children.* The revised edition was published by Dell Publishing Company, 1975 A.D.[30] I won't make any comments about what she said. All I ask you to do is to realize that we are talking about children. Real children. Young children. Children with parents. Nonskeptical parents. I do not mean to misrepresent the following quotes in any way. I am simply going to pull out various thoughts and words Ms. Klein produced. I have included the page numbers in Klein's book.

Rita. (About TWO years old.)

. . . Another symptom — an obsession — which Rita developed at the age of two was a bed-time ritual which took up a lot of time. The main point of it was that she had to be tightly tucked up in the bedclothes . . . her doll had to be tucked up too, and this double ceremonial became more and more elaborate and long-drawn out. . . . On one occasion during her analytic session she put a toy elephant into her doll's bed so as to prevent it from getting up and going into her parents' bedroom and 'doing something to them or taking something away from them.' The elephant was taking over the role of her internalized parents whose prohibiting influence she felt ever since, between the ages of one year and three months and two years, she had wished to take her mother's place with her father, rob her of the child inside her, and injure and castrate both parents . . . . (p.6)
. . . Early analysis of children has shown . . . how many different meanings a single toy or a single bit of play can have . . . . Rita's doll, for instance, would sometimes stand for a penis, sometimes a child she had stolen from her mother, and sometimes her own self . . . . (p.8)

Peter. (About FOUR years old.)

. . . One day . . . when one of the toy men happened to fall over, Peter flew into a rage. Immediately afterwards he asked me how a toy motor-car was made and 'why it could stand up.' He next showed me a tiny toy deer falling over, and then said he wanted to urinate.[1]
. . .When he was back in the room again he took a toy man, whom he called a boy, who was sitting in a little house, which he called the lavatory, and stood him in such a way that a dog which he placed beside him 'shouldn't see him and bite him.' But he placed a toy woman so that she could see him, and said: 'only his Daddy musn't see him.'. . . He again turned to the motor-car, admired it and began to alternate incessantly between admiration and rage at its continual movement. . . . In the . . . session just described, Peter had been depicting the following

[1]. . .if a very small patient wants to go to the lavatory, and is still unused to doing so alone at home, it is my practice to go with him. But I do the least possible for him and thus remove from such assistance the character of an act of love which the unconscious of the child desires . . . . (p. 18)

things: the toy man, the deer, etc., which kept falling down, represented his own penis and its inferiority in comparison to his father's erect member . . . The motor-car which would not stop moving and which aroused both his admiration and anger was his father's penis that was performing coitus all the time . . . .

. . . Once, when he had put the motor cars, which symbolized his father's penis, in a row side by side and had made them run along, he lost his temper and threw them all about the room, saying: 'We always smash our Christmas presents . . . .; we don't want any.' Smashing his toys thus stood in his unconscious for smashing his father's genitals . . . .

. . . In uncovering bit by bit the primal scene I was able to gain access to Peter's very strong passive homosexual attitude. After depicting his parents' coitus he had phantasies of coitus between three people. They aroused severe anxiety in him and were followed by other phantasies in which he was being copulated with by his father . . . .

. . . When he was four years and four months old, he brought forward a long dream, rich in associative-material, from which the following is an extract. 'Two pigs were in a pig-sty and in my bed. They eat together in the pig-sty' . . . . Most of the associations I got from this dream were verbal ones. They showed that the pigs represented himself and his brother and that their eating meant mutual fellatio. But they also stood for his parents copulating together . . . . (p. 16-23)

Ruth. (About FOUR years old.)

. . . Thereupon she began to suck her fingers. She was still very pale and her eyes were shut, but she was visibly calmer and had stopped crying. Meanwhile I went on playing with the dolls, repeating her game of the session before. As I was putting a wet sponge beside one of them, as she had done, she burst out crying again and screamed, 'No, she mustn't have the *big* sponge, that's not for children, that's for grown-ups!' . . . I now interpreted this material in connection with her protest against the big sponge which represented her father's penis. I showed her in every detail how she envied and hated her mother because the latter had incorporated her father's penis during coitus, and how she wanted to steal his penis and the children out of her mother's insides and kill her mother . . . . (p. 28)

* * * * *

These and other early explorers, with the possible exception of Ms. Klein, served their purpose. They offered explanations that accounted for differences. They momentarily ended some concerned parents' ignorance. They gave answers to the question "Why?" Unfortunately, their explanations and answers weren't capable of being scientifically refuted. Thus, under the stress of "having to know why," parents and teachers alike were inclined to believe what was said. The dragons began to be used as answers to all sorts of everyday occurrences — occurrences such as building model airplanes, little boys playing with other little boys rather than with little girls, and little girls playing with girls rather than boys. For some professionals, these occurrences weren't given too much thought. They realized these behaviors weren't so terribly out of the ordinary. That fact, however, did not dissuade some authorities from *explaining* their presence. Two such authorities, physicians, wrote a book entitled *Emotional Problems of Living - Avoiding the Neurotic Pattern.* Their names are O.S. English and G.H.J. Pearson. Doctors English and Pearson obviously believed that the above mentioned occurrences were serious and warranted some authoritative explanation.

> . . . We knew one child of four whose entire interests centered around the construction of model airplanes. He could build complicated models suitable usually for a much older child, and he did the work in the most exact and meticulous manner. He had little time or interest in playing with children his own age and he was not interested in their usual games and pursuits. This constriction of the usual activities and interests of his age was his attempt to avoid the pain of his unsolved anal and oedipal conflicts.[16]

(Maybe he was just a gifted little kid who one day will design a complicated space ship. That might be an alternative explanation for such an "unusual occurrence." Maybe not, though. Maybe the authorities were right. Maybe it is seriously pathological for a four-year-old to do something better than other four-year-olds. Maybe it was sick that he preferred to play with children older than himself. After all, it would be heresy to assume that four-year-olds could possibly be different from one another.)

How about why little boys prefer to play with little boys, and little girls with little girls? There should be a simple explanation for such a serious circumstance —

> This tendency in the development of the human being for boys to seek the company of boys and girls to seek the company of

> girls is referred to as a 'natural homosexual period.' The fears of castration during the genital period cause the boy to be afraid of and therefore dislike girls. The humiliation of the girl when she observes her penisless state during the same period causes her to dislike boys.[16]

There is one special thing about some of those dragons that appears slightly unfair. I think the girls are catching the brunt of much of what has been said so far. Some of the early authorities believed, according to their opinions at least, that a penis is the absolute greatest thing in the world. Not to have one apparently causes all sorts of difficulties. Little girls suffer seriously because they don't have one. Little boys suffer seriously because they are afraid to lose what they already have. It is almost as if without a penis, a little kid wouldn't know who or *what* he or she was —

> If her castration problem was not solved during the genital period, the girl continues to be distressed because she
> does not
> have
> a
> male
> genital
> organ.
> She may maintain the belief until puberty that she is neither woman exactly, nor a castrated individual. However, the true nature of her anatomy becomes more definite with the onset of menstruation . . . .[16]

Thank goodness for puberty and menstruation . . . !

Education's Dysentery: Dyslexia, Dysgraphia, Dyscalculia

The transition from the "3 R's" to the "3 D's" was guaranteed because of the success the early explorers had when explaining the behavioral differences of the people of their time. It was inevitable that the dragons would soon find themselves seated in the hard wooden desks that were among the mainstays of the educational environment. Educators watched with envy the ease with which the physicians and psychologists explained the unexplainable. They saw immediately the convenience of the balloon theory, the idea of inside "causes" for everyday behaviors, and the advantages of hypothesizing safe, irrefutable answers for the problems that differences promised.

The educators were impressed with the over-all neatness and efficiency of the explanations that continually pointed the finger of fault at the child. It was the child who had the problem, the explanations said, and alternatives to that assertion required little consideration. It was the child who needed the major focus of treatment. Those "others" who were significantly involved in the child's life were only given perfunctory glances. It was the child who was diseased, disabled, and derelict. The previous authoritative answers made that quite clear. The educators realized that anything so clear, so simple, had to be right. All that was necessary was to name the names, label the labels, and box the children who were different into convenient categories. Once placed in the categories, the question "Why?" would be answered, the ignorance would be appeased, and what was needed to be known, would be known. How easy it all appeared to be.

The End of Conformance, The Death of Silence

The appearance, however, was deceiving. What was predicted to be easy turned out to be anything but easy. Oh, the names were named and the labels were labeled. That part was easy. The categories were formulated and the children who were different were moved from point A to point B with little resistance from anyone. For a time, those people who were most affected were silent. They accepted the validity of the authority. They had little reason to be suspicious. They had less reason to challenge. What was being done, they were told, was being done for the children.

After awhile, however, a few began to recognize the similarity between the "modern-day" logic that was being used to determine the existence of the dragons and the logic that had been used so many thousands of years earlier. A few began to ask questions about alternative explanations for the children's behaviors. A few began to realize that differences among children was something to be expected, to be worked with, rather than feared and avoided. A few began to argue that a "disease" explanation served only the purpose of removing responsibility of helping from those professionals who had pledged to offer that which they were now relinquishing. A few began to notice what the disease-names and labels were doing to the children. In the beginning, there was mostly silence. In the beginning, there were only a few who let their voices be heard . . . .

The silence was everywhere . . .

The warm, fine-grained sand that had baked all day under the Nevada sun lay quiet. The moonless black sky dotted with millions of flickering fires hung overhead, seemingly satisfied to be seen and not heard. The wind had come and gone. It took with it the welcomed gentle rustling of the few parched scrubs that existed despite the absence of Nature's rain. The amphitheater-shaped sand dune that jutted a hundred feet above the glass-like lake was smooth, unmoving, undisturbed. Its steepness dared the climber. It teased him. It beckoned him to try. It smiled confidently, knowing all along that its flat pinnacle was safe.

But it was there, and notwithstanding the oppressive silence, it had to be tried. Nothing less would have satisfied the eight youthful eyes that stared, hoped, and reminded the one who cared that other youthful eyes were also staring, and hoping.

The lone climber braced himself for what was ahead. His thighs tightened. His lungs opened wide, sucking in the sustaining air that would soon be gasped for with whatever strength remained. His first step against the dune was small, delicate. His bare foot did not break the thin crust of sand and his weight was supported. Confidently, he took a second step. It, too, failed to penetrate the porous sandy body. Carefully, he leaned forward, plumbing himself with the floor of the beach. Four quick steps followed. Reacting against the rapid intrusion, the dune opened and the climber's right foot sunk up to his knee. A hurried retraction sent the left foot deep. Its toes clutched onto the cool sand that had not been touched by the blazing sun. Reflexively, the right leg was lifted; its movement straightened the back of the climber. His arms desperately reached for the support that was not there. A suddenly appearing moon watched as the full body of the man fell backwards to the eight eyes that had not blinked. Disappointedly, he picked himself up and turned to look at the dune's wall. Its surface was once again smooth. No signs of tracks. No signs of effort.

"It's important, you know," someone quietly said from a distance. "It's worth the effort. They aren't old enough to help themselves. They will bear the consequences if you do not try. They will have no choice. Someone must say something," the voice added, as it drifted into the darkness.

He understood.

He pulled his head back as if to indicate that he had regained his determination. He closed his eyes for a moment. There in the depths of his mind he saw the picture of the owl. Its wings were spread. Its eyes were opened to their limits. Sharp claws protruded, glared menacingly. It hovered a fraction of an inch above the frail, naked mouse. The mouse was standing its ground. His little head was held high despite the hot breath of the preying bird. His small chest remained motionless and his tail calm. An imperceptible smile came to his narrow lips. He waited. He watched. Then when a tip of one of the outstretched claws grazed his unperturbed forehead, he calmly, without fanfare, lifted his right hand into the face of the screeching owl and politely shot him a most pronounced *bird.* Not believing what he saw, the owl blinked his eyes. The finger was there. No doubt about it. The meaning of the finger was also there. No doubt about that either. The shock was too great. Immediately the owl dissolved into a gentle puff of helpless feathers and glided the remaining two inches to the ground. He looked once more at the mouse, then he rolled over and fainted. The little mouse took a natural breath, turned his back to the unconscious owl, and went on his merry way.

The climber opened his eyes and smiled. He had been refreshed. He briskly turned toward the dune. It was then that he saw the bleachers in the upper left side of the sandy amphitheater. He nodded as he saw that they were there — the eight eyes, his four children. Next to them were countless other children, all shapes, sizes, and colors. All different. All silent, all staring. The moon had positioned itself above the heads of the children. Its light was just enough to let the climber know that the children were real, were warm. They were no longer someone else's children. They were no longer a safe distance away. They were no longer a name on a form, a number on a file. What was done to them, and what was said about them, would now have to be faced by whoever did the doing and saying. He smiled in their direction. As he did, he reached down to his side and found a sleek silver sword tied to his thin waist. His pulse quickened. Intense energy flowed throughout his body. He stepped back from the center-most, steepest part of the dune. The children watched. The moon shifted its position. Its light provided a bright narrow path that ran from the bottom to the top of the now ice covered precipitous mountain.

"You don't frighten me!" the climber shouted to the face of the mountain. "Your smug omnipotent veneer can't hide the uncertainty that has plagued you all these years. You are afraid that you are wrong, but too cowardly to admit it. Now you will have to admit it, for they will demand it," he stated, as he pointed to all the different eyes that were watching. "They see the truth. They know it."

The mountain said nothing. It did not waver. It had been challenged before by weapons more powerful than swords. He held the glistening saber high above his head. The moon quickly shot a stream of light to the broad side of the silver blade. Instantly, the words that were engraved deep within the steel reflected onto the black fireless sky and the eyes of the children read Hippocrates' challenge —

". . .TO KNOW IS SCIENCE;
TO BELIEVE ONE KNOWS IS IGNORANCE."

The words burned themselves into the sky and remained. The oldest child, now almost a man, stood from his hardwood, backless seat. His intense brown eyes scanned the vastness of the arena. He watched as the empty bleachers began to fill. The other eyes also watched as figures from the past and present silently took their places. Each figure, as he sat, glanced toward the children. Their glance was momentary, for they did not like what they saw within the children's eyes. The oldest child sensed the discomfort of his brothers and sisters. He protectively turned toward them and held out his strong hands. His brown-eyed sister arose and stood between her younger brother and sister. She took one hand from each. The hazel and blue eyes moved close to her, knowing the safety of her touch. The oldest child motioned for them to follow. Together, they silently walked down the seventy rows of seats until they reached the climber who enfolded them within his arms. The youngest child, the hazel eyes, whimpered. He knew he was the most susceptible. The sound of his small voice ran with the speed of light up the narrow aisle. Its honesty caused the heads of the figures to lift and their eyes to fixate on him. Each raised head and forward stare was accompanied by the abrupt lifting of dated placards that read from the very front row, 5000 B.C., to the very back row, 2000 A.D. The placards were neither held by human hands nor were they fixed to the rising floor of the arena. They stood motionless, suspended in air, proud, as if to indicate that each passing year was a little better, a little more enlightening than the previous one. With the same speed of the small voice, the oldest child ran to his brother and stood in front of him, preventing the fixated stares from touching or harming. The other children, in the bleachers, also stood, symbolically lending their support. There was no fear within them.

The climber looked toward the hazel eyes. When he was certain that the child was safe, he pointed his sword in the direction of the moon. Instantly the sphere split into hundreds of illuminating pieces. The mountain was engulfed in light and the darkness disappeared. Satisfied that nothing could be hidden any longer, the climber pointed his sword at the first row. He slowly raised it as if preparing an orchestra for their performance. As the nose of the lance passed by each row, most of the figures, who had been sitting, stood. Those who stood were holding in their hands a flag pole. In place of national emblems and flowing colors, the faces of the flags proclaimed the names of the honored, idolatrized answers. They were there, all there. The climber pointed his sword to the children who were standing in the upper part of the ampitheater. Immediately the flags were turned toward the children for their viewing and inspection. Their eyes carefully read each proclamation, each explanation. A controlled sliver of cold wind brushed along side the back of each flag, causing it to wave for a brief moment.

It was Yjerkie's mind doctor's flag that waved first. "Unwanted, Evil, Defiling Spirits," the flag said. Its holder, an aged man in a white robe, stood silently until his flag went limp. Then he whispered, "If I would have known what this was to lead to, I would have admitted my ignorance. I never meant to cause you harm," he said, looking at the children. The children nodded, knowing that he was being honest. In rapid succession the flags of "Demons," "Witches," and "Devils" waved. Then "Black Bile," "Diseased Blood," "Clogged Blood," "Decaying Matter in the Nervous Tissue," waved. More of them felt the cold sliver of wind. More of them waved. "Phrenitis" and "Mania" and the "Wandering Uterus." "Small Genitals," "Castration," and "Masturbation," had their moments. "Penis Envy," "Have Sex With Mom," and "Kill Dad," followed shortly thereafter. "Oedipal Complex," "Insecurity," "Organ Inferiority," "Standing Stage," and "Can't See My Buttski," came next. "Birth Trauma," "Unsolved Anal Conflict," were displayed as the centuries flew by. As the motion of each flag died, the bearer turned toward the climber and the four children who stood behind him.

When all of the flag wavers were seated, the attention of all the children focused on the very top row of the arena. The seats were empty. Although flags were present, they were blank. For a brief moment, everyone in the arena joined the children as all eyes looked at the row that was partially within the 20th century and partially outside of it. It was as if everyone was trying to determine what would be coming next.

The climber did not look. He already knew. He waited for the assemblage to turn toward him. When they did, he raised his sword that had suddenly turned into the shape of a "Y." "You haven't changed much," he shouted. "None of you!" he said to the entire audience. "From you, 5000 B.C.," he stated as he pointed to Yjerkie's mind doctor, "to you, 2000 A.D.," he continued, as he raised the Y shaped sword to the upper levels of the arena. "You have all persisted in the notion that we are sick; that they are sick!" he exclaimed, looking up toward the children. "You have used the identical approach for 7000 years to reach a conclusion that defies scientific validation or refutation. Oh . . . there has been some progress. You have been kind enough to change the names of your dragons. You have been thoughtful enough to invent new ones. But you are still so afraid of differences that you have allowed your fear to govern your thoughts. To you . . . all of you, difference is still synonymous with abnormality, with disease.

"I had hoped," the climber continued, "that you would grow tired of your imposed sicknesses. I thought that you would finally give up the idea of your devils, demons, and dragons. That you would see a child as a child. That you would not put the child down, but raise him up. That you would tell him that it is okay not to be like everyone else. That you would tell him that whatever he is, is of value to himself and to others. I had hoped that you would deflate the pressure cooker; that you would realize that time and illness do little more than maintain your power, your authority. I had hoped . . . but I should have known better." His face reddened and his tone was sharper, cutting. "You're never going to change, are you?" he asked rhetorically. "As long as one person will listen, that will be sufficient audience for you." The grip around his sword tightened. He made sure the eight eyes were close to him. "Now you are going after the young ones. You have decided to invade a new world of theirs. A world that should be enjoyable and stimulating. A world that should be free of sameness. A world that should emphasize differences. You're not about to let that happen, are you? You are going to tell us that differences are dangerous; that differences are going to be indicative of pathology. You are going to shift the focus of responsibility off of the shoulders where it belongs and onto the Un-Seen, Un-Necessary dragons that you say exist."

As he spoke, "authorities" began to appear in the empty seats at the top most row. Hands automatically grabbed flag poles and letters began to fill the blank spaces of the flags. The audience turned toward their new colleagues. For some reason, many of the children turned away and closed their eyes. Some began to tremble. The older ones, the ones who had made it through, germ free, tried to comfort the little ones. "Don't be afraid," the climber urged the children. "Your parents and many professionals are going to do something about it. They will no longer remain silent. They will challenge. They will demand."

"They must," the oldest child with the brown eyes whispered.

"They will," the older sister agreed, as she placed the hazel and blue eyes behind her.

The climber turned toward the little children. "It's okay," he quietly told them. "The *new dragons* won't touch you. I promise!"

The words "new dragons" reverberated throughout the amphitheater. They touched the ears of all who were willing to listen. They found their way to the upper right hand section of the arena where a new group of people had suddenly appeared. For a brief second, everyone in the arena disappeared with the exception of the children on the left hand side and their parents on the opposite side. Equally as suddenly, an aged man in a white robe stood in the front row. The light of the moon shone upon him.

"What new dragons?" he asked. Silence. He looked toward the children, toward their parents, toward the climber. "Did you hear me!!" he shouted. "WHAT NEW DRAGONS! I had a hand in starting this. I want to know. I must know. Part of this was my fault. I could have been stronger . . . been stronger." His voice grew weak. He fought the lump that had swelled in his throat. But he stood. With all his strength, he stood.

"Do you all want to know?" the climber asked the audience who had returned. The back row didn't answer. "Are you afraid to tell them?" the climber asked the back row. Silence. He took a step toward the iced stairway. The moon's light showed him the way. The mountain braced itself. The children and their parents remained motionless. The brown-eyed children held tightly to the hazel and blue. The climber took another step. Then another and another. His barefeet were unaffected by the slippery surface. He climbed to the seventieth row. "Tell them!" he demanded.

> In less than a decade, the ailment spread from virtual obscurity to something well beyond epidemic proportions. It has no single name, no universally accepted symptoms, and no discernible anatomical or biochemical characteristics which can be diagnosed in a clinic or a laboratory, yet it is said to afflict as many as 40 percent of all American children, to reflect an organic or chemical dysfunction of the brain or nervous system and to be the cause of most, if not all, pediatric problems in learning and behavior . . . . Before 1965 almost no one had heard of it, but by the beginning of the seventies it was commanding the attention of an armada of pediatricians, neurologists and educational psychologists, and by mid-decade, pedagogical theory, medical speculation, psychological need, drug company promotion and political expediency had been fused with an evangelical fervor to produce what is undoubtedly the most powerful movement in — and

beyond — contemporary education . . . . [8]

The printed words on the flags were now clear. One read "Learning Disabilities." A second proclaimed "Minimal Brain Dysfunction." Others had their turn. "Hyperactive," "Perceptual-Communicative Disorders," "Neurologically Impaired," "Emotional Disturbance," "Over Achiever," "Under Achiever," "Slow Learner," "Mentally Retarded," and "Dyslexia," "Dysgraphia," "Dyscalculia."

"Are those the new germs, the new diseases?" Yjerkie's doctor asked, hesitantly.

"They are."

"They infect mostly children?"

"Mostly children between the ages of three and eighteen," the climber answered.

"Isn't that the time when kids go to school?"

"It is."

"How do the 'authorities' know the kids have the diseases," the aged man asked.

"How did you know that Yjerkie was infected by an evil spirit?"

"I didn't know. I looked at what Yjerkie was doing — then I guessed," he answered, lowering his head.

"Although I know it won't be of any comfort to you, we are still guessing today. The behaviors we use to help us make our guesses are somewhat different than tantrums, but the approach we are using is the same as the one you used."

"Are the authorities still assuming that if a child doesn't do what someone says he is supposed to be doing, that the child is the one with the problem?" the mind doctor asked.

"They are."

"Why? Haven't they learned that there are alternative explanations that do not suggest that the problem exists within the child?"

Before the climber could answer, the flag wavers in the last row stood. They joined hands and spoke in unison. "Most of the general public likes the idea of inside sicknesses. It makes them feel comfortable. They know that as a result of the inside problem they are not responsible for what the child is doing. School teachers like it too. It is easier for them to simply say that a child has a learning disability or suffers from emotional disturbance. That way, they don't have to look at themselves."

"I don't buy that!" the climber interrupted. "Parents and

teachers do not like that at all. They are willing to accept responsibility. They are willing to look at themselves. You and your ideas just make it difficult for them to do so. They are not sure quite what to believe after you bring in your irrefutable dragons."

"You can scream all you want," the back row said. "You're not going to change anything. The public is not going to challenge. They might think about it for a moment, but their attention span is too short. They have other things to worry about."

"You are wrong," the climber said, as he thrashed his sword against the sky. "You'll see. The kids will be safe from you."

The back row just laughed. Calmly, the closest one to the climber placed his hand on the climber's chest. Before he pushed him, he said, "Nice try."

The children screamed as the climber desperately fought to maintain his balance. His right foot slipped. The eight eyes opened wide. Their arms went out as if to brace their father against the inevitable fall. The figures in the audience stood, breath taken away. They watched helplessly. Some sad. Some not caring. The climber fell to the icy floor. His sword went tumbling down the slick stairway. He grabbed for something to hold onto. But there was nothing. His prone body began to slip past the placards, past the dated cards. His eyes, saddened, distressed, watched as he fell back through time. Faster and faster he went. The faces from the back row, smiling, became smaller. He watched as they raised their flags higher in the sky. So high, that the flags covered Hippocrates' message. He felt the children's tears, but was helpless to stop them. The moon was once again a total body. It was shining its light on a distant, almost imperceivable table, that rested at the end of a dark tunnel. The climber's body had turned and he was now sliding headlong toward the light, toward the tunnel. He saw the eight eyes. They were not distressed. They were not frightened. Even the hazel eyes seemed comfortable, confident. He saw their hands reaching out to him. He felt their warm fingers as they touched his shoulders, held his arms. He, himself, inexplicably felt comfortable as the children led him to the spot where the light was the brightest. He saw the table. It was round, sturdy, strong. As he approached with his children, the men and women, seated around the table, stood. They were bedecked in colorful flowing capes. Each had an emblem that rested against their proud chests. Each held a sword in his gloved hand. Each reflected the determination to do right, to protect, to serve. He felt nervous in their presence, but they beckoned him to approach the empty, high-backed chair that matched the strength of the round table. As he touched the chair, a lone figure, tall, secure, approached him. The others watched intently. They watched the majestic, regal figure as he placed his hand on the shoulder of the climber. With his other hand, he gestured for the children to come closer. As they did, the men and women around the table produced their swords that were gleaming from the moon's light. The figure removed his mighty hand from the shoulder of the climber and reached down to his own side. Smoothly, he pulled his sword from its holder. He raised it to the sky. He slowly brought it down and rested it on the shoulder of the climber. He said a few silent words. Then he looked into the eyes of the climber and said, "You may have mine." The climber took the King's sword. "Together," the regal figure said, "we will protect the children from the dragons."

"We must," the climber whispered as he looked at the brown, the hazel, the blue.

* * * * *

Educational Diseases of School Children

Despite "King Arthur's" avowal, the dragons came and inflicted themselves on countless numbers of unsuspecting children. No matter how noble in intent was his pledge, he overlooked several variables that were bound to dull his blade.

First, and foremost, were the observed differences amongst the children. Some of the children had no difficulty with what was asked of them. They caused no problems while in the classroom. Academically, they excelled. Socially, they cooperated. Some of the children experienced some difficulty both socially and academically, but their manifested differences were benign and either overlooked or tolerated. Some of the children, however, were too different. They neither did what was asked nor showed any interest in doing what the teacher expected. They saw no reason to cooperate, to be like the others, so they didn't and they weren't. Some of these children didn't learn as fast as the others, some required additional time, material, and support. Some of these children did not receive that which they required. Some of them saw no reason to keep trying. Their effort was simply not enough. At times, the adaptive indifference of this group began to affect some of the other children. When that happened, tolerance dissipated and the decision was made that something had to be done before the entire class went amiss. That decision lead to the second variable the "King" had overlooked. Influenced by the logic of the past, the educational authorities began to investigate *why* the children were not all alike. They knew that something had to be wrong with the children; the past had told them that. They knew further that admitting their ignorance as to the "cause" of the observed differences was not a viable alternative. That admission, they believed, would be of no help to either the parent who wanted to know "Why?", or to the teacher who believed that knowing the answer to the question would automatically bring about the solution. The need for the answer set the stage for the third variable. The authorities set about discovering which dragons might be appropriate for the social and academic dissimilarities. Again, they were guided by the principles of the past. Their dragons would be irrefutable, safe, circular, and sick. Kings and noble climbers aside, the authorities had to do what was best for the children. They had to be able to tell everyone why some children were different. The infectious dragons had to be identified and then slain. Order and *homogeneity* had to be restored. Those who were *too* different would have to be relocated and placed together. That way, their differences would blend and not be as noticeable. That way, they wouldn't bother the others. That way, the educators wouldn't have to spend their time with the deviations; they could exercise their expertise with the means.* For awhile, that's how things went.

Exceptionality. Whereas the educators once used the term "exceptional" to denote those children who were superior at some activity, they decided that the term would be best used to describe all children who deviated from some determined norm, or from some professional's own personal opinion as to what should be and what shouldn't be. Thus the "gifted" child along with the "retarded" child were considered exceptional. They both were different from the "ordinary," therefore, both were exceptional.

Likewise, the deaf child, the blind child, and the cerebral palsied child were considered exceptional for, again, they were not ordinary. Soon the child who was academically *too* slow, or academically *too* quick was considered exceptional. Before long, the child who was socially *too* shy or *too* loud or *too* aggressive or *too* passive or *too* indifferent or *too* interested was viewed as exceptional, as different. Categories of exceptionality began to be formulated and agreed-upon signs and signals of the excep-

* The term "mean" is synonymous with the term "average."

tionality began to be listed and etched. If a child failed to read as well, write as well, solve math problems as well as the ordinary, the signs were observed and the question, "Why is the child different?" was asked. If a child failed to play like the ordinary played, smile like the ordinary smiled, socialize like the ordinary socialized, the signs were observed and the same question was asked. The lists of exceptionalities grew and the signs and signals of the differences began to multiply. In the fervor of the names and labels and the signs and signals, some of the children began to lose their identity. Some were no longer little kids with different hair colors and different eye colors and different skin colors. Some were no longer little people who came from different places, who had different parents, or had different priorities. It was homogeneity at all costs and the different ones became categories.

Parents of the little kids began to hear of the insidious danger of being different. It started with the one child on the block whose parents were informed that he was "too" this and "too" that. Before, the children were children and their differences were noticed, but there was little fear attached to that which was expected. But no more. "Don't you be different," the parent told the child before the school bus came. "Be like the teacher wants you to be. Do what the teacher wants you to do. Behave like the other children behave. Write as well as the others. Read as well as the others. Raise your hand. Drink your milk. Ask the question. Answer the question. Listen to the question. Understand the question. Don't ask to have the question repeated."

"I don't want any demerits from the teacher, or sad faces from the teacher, or letters from the teacher, or phone calls from the teacher, or warnings from the teacher. Be a member of the homogenous group," the parent said to the bewildered child.

It couldn't be done! Some child had to be different. Statistically, it was guaranteed. In fact, a lot of little kids had to be different. Only so many children can be average. Only so many children can be placed on the center-most point of the "normal" curve.

When a parent was informed of the difference that existed, there was only one thing that the parent could do. The past assured that. Ignorance was still far from a state of bliss —

Behavior

1. Being Different

Soon sincerely concerned educators were deluged by parents who wanted to know why their child was different. An answer was demanded and the authorities found themselves in the same pressure cooker that had produced the evil spirits and the wandering uterus. There was little time for controlled, well-thought out scientific experiments. Expediency overtook credibility. Answers were needed, and were needed now. The parent, sitting across from the principal, was not in a mood to wait. The child was different and somebody wanted to know why. The teacher was in no better position. He, too, felt the parents' urgency. An explanation was wanted, was ordered. Right or wrong, some authority had to say something. Under the pressure, the authority spoke out. Unfortunately, the authority didn't listen too carefully to his own words. Had he, he would have realized that what he was saying was very similar to what had been continuously said for the past seven thousand years. Had he looked at the logic he used to determine his answers, he would have seen that it, too, had not changed despite the passage of so much time. But he neither listened nor looked, and the result was a proliferation of the most ill-defined, confusing, and professionally frustrating list of descriptions and explanations.

The Answers For the Differences

Before beginning what I hope will be a very frustrating few pages for you, a reminder of our purpose is in order.

The overall goal of this book was to put you in the position to both demand accountability and be accountable. Its intent was to show you the logic that has been used to conclude that the child is the one with the problem. The purpose was not to deny that there are special children. There are many very special children who require very special patience and expertise. At the same time, the book's purpose was to suggest that the concepts of "Special," "Exceptional," "Different," "Handicapped," have been blown way out of proportion. In our zealousness to explain differences, a concept that really doesn't require much explanation, we have created exceptionality where it *doesn't* exist. Our zealousness has produced inflated numbers of exceptionality and the result is that we have spread ourselves and our resources so thin that those children who are truly special, *not just different*, can't always receive the very expensive help they need. That is not a tolerable situation!

There are things that can be done to alter that position. The question is, are we willing to consider them? We need to step back and look at what our logic has created. We need to reevaluate the concept of differences. We need to reconsider what the etched signs and signals are indicative of. We need to recognize that an educational system which operates on the values of sameness and homogeneity, on blanket comparisons and unchecked expectations, produces the deviations that set the stage for the new dragons. We can look at what we are doing, or we can do nothing and let the new dragons have their day.

* * * * *

Thanks to the effort of Robert M. Smith and John T. Neisworth who have written a book entitled "The Exceptional Child, A Functional Approach,"[31] I am able to provide you with the following overwhelming list of "new" answers to the question "Why?" After doing so, I will tell you of an assignment I asked some of my graduate students to complete regarding the new answers. Then I will share with you their reaction to the assignment. Almost without exception, the students have been in the classroom with many different children. Almost without exception, the students, as professionals, have been called upon to answer the question "Why?" I believe you will find their remarks interesting. After presenting those remarks, I will select two of the "new" answers and look at them carefully.

The List

> A number of disciplines and professions outside education have wielded great influence on the nomenclature used to identify and classify children with special educational needs; among these have been medicine and psychiatry, developmental psychology, psychometrics, sociology, and law. All such groups, of course, have their own foundations and interest; accordingly, each views and labels children from its own perspective . . . .
>
> Basic labels have been further subdivided by various professions to suit their own needs, and the literature abounds in a multitude of names for children. The resulting terminological confusion has generated much fruitless controversy and debate. The following is a partial list of labels drawn from articles published during the last five years in several special education journals, e.g.,[31]
>
> *Exceptional Children, Journal of Special Education, American Journal of Mental Deficiency, Journal of Learning Disabilities and Academic Therapy.*

1. Academically handicapped
2. Acting out
3. Adjunctive
4. Aggressive
5. Antisocial
6. Aphasia
7. Autistic
8. Behavior-disordered
9. Below-average learner
10. Brain-damaged

11. Cerebral dysfunction
12. Child with educational problems
13. Child with failure sets
14. Culturally deprived
15. Delinquent
16. Educable mentally retarded
17. Educationally disabled
18. Ego-development deficiency
19. Emotionally disturbed
20. Emotionally handicapped
21. Emotionally maladjusted
22. Exceptional
23. Genotypically retarded
24. Hyperactive
25. Hyperkinetic
26. Impulse-ridden
27. Latent development
28. Learning-disabled
29. Low cognitive capacity
30. Low IQ
31. Mentally defective
32. Mentally handicapped
33. Minimal brain dysfunction
34. Neglected
35. Neurotic
36. Overgratified
37. Overstimulated
38. Perceptually handicapped
39. Physically handicapped
40. Primitive
41. Psycholinguistically disabled
42. Psychopathic
43. Psychotic
44. Retarded development
45. Schizophrenic
46. Slow learner
47. Socially defective
48. " deprived
49. " disruptive
50. " handicapped
51. " impaired
52. " maladjusted
53. " rejected
54. Speech and language latency
55. Symbiotic disorder
56. Trainable
57. Withdrawn

As the authors indicated, the above list is only a partial one. There are, perhaps, three or four times the number of descriptive and explanatory terms that have been used to classify and categorize. What the total number of terms might be is irrelevant. If the terms were clear, objective, self-defining, and used correctly, there would be little problem. Everyone would know what everyone else was talking about, and valuable information could be communicated. But in the authors' view —

> An examination of the preceding 'classificatory' labels strongly suggests that there really is no classification system within special education. What might appear to be a system is, in reality, an unsystematic crazy quilt of labels. The categories and labels do not constitute a scientific classification system. First, there is no common logic, criteria, or order within the scheme. Second, the various classificatory labels come from different disciplines, reflect different perspectives, and serve no single purpose. The crucial and fundamental inadequacy of current special education classification is simply that the scheme does not serve educational purposes.[31]

The Assignment

Because the terms are used as frequently as they are, I asked a group of my university graduate students to spend three days searching every possible authoritative source (e.g., books, journals, professional articles) in order to come up with an acceptable operational* definition for twelve chosen terms. The justification for the assignment was the importance of knowing precisely what the terms represent. Without that knowledge, two professionals might use the same term, but not mean the same thing. Two children could be described by the same term, but the intent of the description might not be the same. A set of signals might be *explained* by the same term, yet the explanation might not have any meaning.

The following were the terms that were chosen:

1. Hyperactive
2. Learning Disabled
3. Dyslexia
4. Perceptual-Communicative Disorder
5. Minimal Brain Dysfunction
6. Emotional Disturbance
7. Short-attention Span
8. Mental Retardation
9. Gifted
10. School Phobia
11. Neurologically Impaired
12. Brain Damaged

My Students' Reactions

The following comments were not solicited. The assignment did not

---

* There are several ways to operationally define a label. One way deals with numbers from a test score. A second deals with frequencies of particular behaviors. "Creativity" for example can be operationally defined by a test score on an instrument that purportedly measures creativity. Thus if a child scores higher than another child on the test, the first child might be viewed as being more creative. The test score is said to define the label. (That method isn't very good if the test doesn't measure what it says it is going to measure.) The second method uses the child's actual behavior to gain access to the meaning of the label. A "hyperactive" child is said to *do* various things more frequently, or less frequently, than a child who is said not to be "hyperactive." The second method is mainly concerned with the frequency with which the child does something. This was the method my students were asked to use. The assignment required that I be told specifically what a child would have to do before being labeled "hyperactive." With this information (and only with this information), the term "hyperactive" would have meaning. Without the information, the term is practically useless.

require any editorializing. The date of the class was July, 1979. The words are the students' words. I suspect they were somewhat influenced by my numerous harangues.

> I came into this class with very little knowledge of the exceptional child. My background is in teaching secondary English, and, more recently, gifted classes.
>
> I cannot say that I enjoyed doing this assignment. It was frustrating and often impossible to try to find definitions and then to try to choose those that were operational, concise and clear. It made me realize that many of these terms have multiple definitions, many of which are fuzzy and ambiguous. Some terms such as learning disability, emotionally disturbed, minimal brain dysfunction, mentally retarded and psychoses seem to be catch-all categories with interchangeable, unmeasurable symptoms. This confusion arises when we try to come up with answers in spite of an absence of measurable data.
>
> A.C.D.
>
> This assignment was a particularly frustrating one to complete. The reason being, that in the course of finding definitions for these terms, one comes to the conclusion that there are not any really good operational definitions. The definitions are filled with vague, imprecise, and biased words. Consequently, any particular definition could mean one thing to one person and an entirely different thing to someone else. In completing this assignment, I was thus impressed with the need for people to explain these definitions and terms whenever they are used. This would hold true during staffings or informal meetings with specialists.
>
> G.W.M.
>
> Note: Operational definitions don't seem to exist for many of these terms. Also, in many cases, one label could be exchanged for another with no effect on the existing definition, measurement, and treatment.
>
> S.P.
>
> Operational definitions are virtually non-existent in the sources. Except for the possibility of *brain damage* as defined medically in hospitals through an EEG, not a source, not one single term on the list had an operational definition, and only a couple of terms had measurement devices listed through the source.

The few measurement devices applicable at all to these 'conditions' come from teachers and therapists who examine children, and the particular measurement devices used vary as frequently as do the number of teachers and therapists in the school and medical systems.

B.W.

This assignment was more difficult than I ever anticipated. My search for books to adequately meet the requirements proved futile. I for one have been successfully brainwashed by your lectures and attempts to frustrate me.

V.R.

When you first gave us this assignment I thought it was going to be simple busy work. Boy! Did I have a rude, but a necessary awakening! . . . . I have grown.

S.J.

The one really valuable bit of information which resulted from this assignment was that there are no good, objective numerically definable definitions in any of the resources I was able to locate. All of them were definitions based upon the qualitative judgment of the authority or person who made the diagnostic test.

M.A.N.

And finally —

In attempting to find operational definitions for the labels, it did not take much time to find out that operational definitions are non-existent. The attached list of definitions were the best I could compile from the sources I used. None of them say much, but they say it in intellectual terms!

J.T.

* * * * *

A Closer Look

The listed terms attempt to describe and/or account for differences that are observed in classrooms. In actual practice, they fail to accomplish that goal. More often than not, they close educational doors, pigeon-hole children, and offer authorities a false sense of security. They imply that we know why children are different, why children behave as they do. The false security, along with the latter implication, accounts, more than anything else, for the epidemic-like rise in the numbers of children who are said to be educationally diseased. The terms are the easy way out for the authority who is pressured into providing something that will appease the fear of ignorance. Most of the "conditions" have about as much descriptive and explanatory credibility as did the wandering uterus.

It would seem appropriate to look closely at the two "diseases" that have increased so much during the past few years — "learning disabilities" and "emotional disturbance." After doing so, you should be able to make a clear judgment as to whether they are real.

Learning Disabilities

The disease of learning disabilities: First, what is it? First, before anything else, *it is not an it!* It is not something with identifiable physical parameters. You can't take a picture of it. You can't see it running through an elementary school hallway. Neither can you see it sitting in a hard-wood desk. It is not something that can be attacked with either a fly swatter or a large vial of medication. It is a term that is used to describe and, *incorrectly, explain why* some children aren't doing what someone is expecting them to be able to do. It is a term, used to answer the question "Why?", that carries the characteristics of being safe, circular, irrefutable, and sick.

It is used only after differences and deviations from expectations have been observed. Its presence is based on pure inference, for it is not something that can be directly observed. It is a term that clearly tells a parent and a teacher that a child's inadequate performance is due to a problem that exists within the child. It clearly states that the child suffers from some neurological impairment.

Quickly, I hear one of you saying, "I have heard that there are tests that are used to diagnose the presence of a learning disability. An authority doesn't just look at what a child is doing. He has an instrument that helps determine the presence of the cerebral injury." In one respect, you are right. There are tests that are used to attempt to measure the existence of this purported phenomenon. But do the tests measure what they claim to measure?

An article was written recently (August, 1978) that looked at the typical learning disability test battery. The article was published in a highly respected journal — *Harvard Educational Review*. It was written by Gerald S. Coles, from Rutgers Medical School. I would like to share some of Coles' remarks with you.

He, too, had some thoughts about our apparent epidemic —

> Efforts to solve the problems of learning disabilities have experienced a period of growth unparalleled by almost any other specialized field. Although the subject of learning disabilities was virtually unheard of ten or fifteen years ago, today education, psychology, and medicine are all contributing to its growing body of literature, with which one can barely keep abreast .... Learning disabilities ... has become a fertile field of specialization for students seeking a marketable degree and for industries seeking new markets.[32]

Coles then shifted his attention to the question of diagnosis —

> The special knowledge of learning-disabilities specialists, and, indeed, the special knowledge on which the entire field rests, is the ability to diagnose the presence of learning disabilities ....
>
> Using a medical model and equipped with their own black bag of diagnostic instruments, the learning disabilities specialists ... examine child patients. If they think there are learning disabilities, they write authoritative diagnoses stating that, based on the results of certain tests, it has been determined that the children have neurological problems that impede learning. Parents and teachers will be likely to accept these findings as true. Because the children have been given a set of seemingly scientific and valid tests, the conclusions must also be valid. The children, now proclaimed to be learning disabled, begin the remedial path toward cognitive competence.[32]

Coles then provided his readers with the names of the ten "most frequently" recommended tests and evaluations suggested for a learning disabilities test battery. Then, he carefully reviewed the research literature that has evaluated the effectiveness of the tests and evaluation methods. (The tests and evaluative methods were: the Illinois Test of Psycholinguistic Abilities, the Bender Visual-Motor Gestalt Test, the Frostig Developmental Test of Visual Perception, the Wepman Auditory Discrimination Test, the Lincoln-Oseretsky Motor Development Scale, the Graham-Kendall Memory for Designs Test, the Purdue Perceptual-Motor Survey, the Wechsler Intelligence Scale for Children, a neurological evaluation by a neurologist, and an electroencephalogram (EEG).)

As to the usefulness of the tests and evaluation methods, Coles stated —

> Taken as a whole, the tests used in a representative learning-disabilities battery fail to demonstrate that children categorized as learning disabled are neurologically impaired.
>
> The evidence from studies using formal neurological examinations of learning-disabled children is especially damaging to the neurological impairment explanation. Surely, if the neurological thesis were to find support anywhere, it would find it in the techniques and science available to neurologists. Unfortunately for those who have held this thesis, studies of border-line symptoms, soft signs, have uniformly failed to contribute to the diagnosis of academic underachievement.
>
> The evidence appears . . . to point to the conclusion that the tests do not measure neurological dysfunctions in learning-disabled children, but that methodological inadequacies [of the tests] prevent us from drawing this conclusion with certainty. These same methodological problems do, however, provide support for the position that we do not know what these tests measure . . . .[32]

Finally, Coles offered a summary opinion —

> There is little question that eventually the tests reviewed here will be discarded; the evidence against them is mounting. The central question is really whether recognition of the invalidity of these tests will result in abandonment of an untenable professional dogma, or whether it will merely result in the test battery being replaced by other equally questionable instruments . . . . The future of the learning-disabilities test battery will depend upon how we answer the following question: How catastrophic . . . will it be for dependent industries, institutions, and professionals to acknowledge that, so far as we can tell, Johnny's neural connections are intact? If we do not 'blame the victim,' where then does the blame lie?[32]

A possible answer?

> . . . Specialists in the field have resorted to biological explanations for institutional failures, focusing our attention, concern, and attempts at remediation on the child rather than on the social context in which that child must perform.[32]

* * * * *

Definition

The National Advisory Committee on Handicapped Children in 1968 gave us the following definition of learning disabilities —

> Children with special learning disabilities exhibit a disorder in one or more of the basic psychological processes involved in understanding or using spoken or written language. These may be manifested in disorders of listening, thinking, talking, reading, writing, spelling, or arithmetic. They include conditions which have been referred to as perceptual handicaps, brain injury, minimal brain dysfunction, dyslexia, developmental aphasia, etc. They *do not** include learning problems which are due primarily to visual, hearing, or motor handicaps, to mental retardation, emotional disturbance, or to environmental disadvantage.

The committee practically guaranteed that specialists in the field of education would use "neurological impairment" as the dragon to explain the differences among children. It practically guaranteed that the number of children who would eventually be medicated for their differences would reach overwhelming figures. (Ritalin is one, and only one, of the major cerebral stimulants used to treat learning-disabled children. Coles, in his article, reported the following numbers of prescriptions dispensed by physicians for Ritalin. In 1972, approximately 396,000 prescriptions were written for young patients. In 1974, the numbers increased to 480,760. In 1975, 608,660. For the first ten months in 1977, the figure was 1,463,000. It was projected by the end of that year, the total number would be 1,800,000. In about five years, the number of prescriptions *increased* by 1,400,000. See page 333 of Coles' article.)

The committee, without intending it, guaranteed confusion among dedicated educators, for its definition was replete with terms that were next to impossible to define, and "exclusion conditions" i.e., emotional disturbance and environmental disadvantages, that were next to impossible to measure. It guaranteed circular and irrefutable conclusions by telling the specialists to —

1. First, look at the child's behavior

Behavior

1. Disorders in Listening
Thinking

---

* Emphasis mine. The terms after the asterisk are called "exclusion factors." They would take precedence over the label "learning disabled."

Talking
Reading
Writing
Spelling
Arithmetic

2. Second, compare the child's performance with other children.
3. Third, evaluate the child's intellectual potential to see if it is "normal" — a feat that is next to impossible given what "intelligence" tests do and don't do —

   Conventional intelligence tests: CANNOT reveal the capacity or potential of a student.

   Conventional intelligence tests: CAN provide fair predictions of school success, assuming we do nothing exceptional to help or hinder certain students and thus destroy the prediction.[33]

4. Look at the exclusion factors.
5. Then, if no other explanation is possible (given the alternatives that were within the committee's consideration), conclude that the child's problem rests inside of his or her neurological make-up.

Behavior	**Why?**
1. Differences	Learning Disabled a. Perceptual Handicaps b. Brain Injury c. Minimal Brain Dysfunction d. Etc.

Since the answer to the question "Why?" sets the stage for remediation, there is little wonder why so many youngsters have been placed on medication. If by chance, medication, or change in educational remediation, the child begins to appear more similar to his classmates, the conclusion, inevitably, is that the medication worked wonders. That conclusion undoubtedly produced some rewards for an authoritative decision and, equally undoubtedly, increased the chances that another child would also be medicated.

Behavior	**Why?**	**Treatment**	**Outcome**	**Conclusion**
1. Being Different	Neurological Impairment	Ritalin	More Like the Other Kids	Medication Worked Wonders, Neurological Impairment Affected

You probably can discern some serious methodological problems with the above logic. First, the neurological impairment is a guessed-at answer. Second, the fact that the child began to look like the other children does not automatically mean that the medication had a therapeutic effect on the disordered brain. No more so than the fumigation resulted in the return of the uterus. It is just as likely that the medication influenced the teacher! It is just as likely that the medication created a major change in the child's educational program!

Finally, there is one more thing the committee's definition accidentally accomplished. It decreased the chances that an alternative answer to the question "Why?" would be considered. The committee ruled out differences due to visual and hearing problems. It ruled out differences due to "organic" mental retardation — although the term "organic" was not included. But it did not rule out everything. In fact, it missed a few "minor" variables that should have been considered.

I will reword the very last sentence of the committee's definition that specified the exclusion factors that had priority over the diagnosis of "learning-disability." I will include what I believe are obvious omissions to the committee's definition. Why the committee members left them out, I do not know. Perhaps it had something to do with the logic the committee used to define and identify its dragon.

> . . . They do not include learning problems which are due primarily to visual, hearing, or motor handicaps, to mental retardation, emotional disturbance, or to environmental disadvantage . . .
>
> **. . . or to children whose teachers ask them to perform some task for which they are not totally prepared . . .**
>
> **. . . or to children whose teachers ask them to perform some task that has already been accomplished many times before . . .**
>
> **. . . or to children whose teachers ask them to do something that the children do not value . . .**
>
> **. . . or to children who find themselves with a teacher who has little or no interest in the children . . .**
>
> **. . . or to children who find themselves with a teacher who is ill-prepared to individualize the curriculum . . .**
>
> **. . . or to children who find themselves in overcrowded, understaffed classrooms. . .**
>
> **. . . or to children whose parents neither reinforce nor support**

their children's academic efforts or their children's teachers' efforts. . .

. . . They do not include learning problems that are due to unknown cultural differences that have influenced the child and have made the child different than his classmates . . .

. . . They do not include problems that are due primarily to the uniquenesses of the child where the uniqueness and the necessary adaptive remediation have been overlooked . . .

. . . They do not include problems that are due to unknown factors; problems and factors that defy immediate explanations . . . .

Emotional Disturbance

The advisory committee indicated that a learning disability might not be present if the child in question was suffering from "emotional disturbance." That is a convenient exclusion, but it doesn't help very much. You see, no one knows what "it" is. The reason is that "emotional disturbance" is not an *it*. Rather, it is one of those terms that is used when no other term seems to fit. Yet, it has no universally accepted definition.[34] It has no universally accepted set of signals. It is not something that can be seen or measured. It is a safe and irrefutable answer. When used to explain why children are different, it is totally circular, and it definitely states that the pathology exists within the child.

The term is used only after a child has manifested certain behaviors for a certain period of time. It is used only after a child has been compared with other children who are believed to be similar in age, environmental experiences, and endowments. It is used only after existing alternative explanations have been considered and dismissed. When it is used, certain assumptions are made:

1. The behavior, in its context, is "abnormal" and "inappropriate."
2. Most children with "similar" backgrounds etc., don't do whatever it was that was done.
3. *All* possible alternative explanations for the child's behaviors have been carefully examined.

For these assumptions to be valid, the following is necessary:

1. Knowledge of what is "normal" and what is not.

2. Precise knowledge of the child's background, experiences, and endowments, along with the comparative group's background, experiences, and endowments.
3. Knowledge of what variables might have influenced the behaviors in question.

Validating the above assumptions will not be an easy task. The entire notion of "normality," as it relates to children's behavior, might be best discussed in a college dormitory over a six-pack of beer. Determining what is normal and what is not is similar to determining whether a chicken or an egg started the entire chain of *Kentucky Fried Chicken* stores. Yet, without some definitive statement as to what is normal, the term "emotional disturbance" is useless. That dragon is used only after someone has determined that a particular set of behaviors are not within an acceptable — normal — range. No authority, in his own right scientific mind, would ever suggest that "between-meal-nibbling" was a sign of "emotional disturbance" unless that authority had some inside information that indicated that eating between meals was an abnormal behavior. The obvious question: "Where does an authority obtain such information?"

The first way is the statistical way. The statistical method states that if most people don't do it, it must not be right. The implication is that "what is common is normal."[35] This method implies that what is statistically infrequent (deviating from the average) is also unhealthy.[35]

> Take the case of a very creative youngster. On the basis of the normal curve, his creative performance may be statistically infrequent and therefore deviate markedly from the average. Are we to say that this youngster is abnormal . . .?[35]

This method also implies that we have carefully obtained data on all the behaviors that an authority would use as an indication of "emotional disturbance." For example, from *Square Pegs, Round Holes*, by Harold Levy, M.D., we find out that emotional instability or "emotional disturbance" is exemplified by a "child who cries more readily than other children." That is a nice authoritative statement. It is also a statement that states that some comparisons have been made between one child and other children. For the statement to have any value, we would have to know how readily *most* children cry. Without that information, we wouldn't have any grounds for a statistical comparison. Even if we had that type of data, which we don't, we still wouldn't have any grounds (other than personal opinion) to explain the "more readily" with the term "emotional disturbance." That would just be a safe, circular conclusion.

A second method for determining whether a behavior is within "normal" limits is to adopt a cultural-norm-reference approach. This approach declares that societal norms determine what is normal and thus, what is acceptable. If a youngster fails to conform to a known or unknown societal guideline, it is the youngster who is assumed to be at fault.

Although this approach doesn't say much for individuality, if there were only one culture, one set of societal norms, perhaps it would have some utility. However, this approach fails to take into account the total number of cultures that are present in the world, much less the child's own neighborhood. It talks about cultures as if there were only a few — the Black, the White, the Red, the Brown, the Catholic, the European, etc. It fails to recognize that within the above exists an infinite number of other cultures. These other cultures are more than "sub-cultures." They are unique and different in the same way that two families, of the same color, same religion, same socio-economic stratum, who live on the same block, are different.

In one house (culture), children are to be seen and not heard. They are to be compliant. They are not to ask questions. They are to go to school and be very quiet. In school, they are seen as "too" quiet, according to the culture of the teacher. Their "extreme" quietness is viewed as excessive "shyness." They are seen as less than normal. They are judged to be disturbed — to be having some problem. In a second house, the children are expected to speak their mind. They are to assert themselves. They are to use the necessary means to gain the teacher's attention. They are to demand. Next to the quiet children, they appear overly aggressive. Their aggressiveness is seen as hostility. They are judged to be disturbed.

Both children are referred to a psychologist who has his or her own set of cultural preferences. The psychologist knows very little about the subtle cultures of the children. The psychologist may see that both of the children are fine, neither are fine, or one is fine while the other is "emotionally disturbed." Almost without exception, the authoritative determinations are made on the basis of opinion, not scientific evidence.

I have met an authority who uses this cultural-norm-reference approach to an extreme. She said to me on one occasion, "If I am asked to judge whether a child's behavior is normal or abnormal, I look at what the child is doing. Then I think back to when *my* children were that child's age. If my children did what the child in question is presently doing, I conclude that the child's behavior is normal. If my children did *not* do what the present child is doing, I conclude that the child's behavior is abnormal, and the child is disturbed."

It is that type of logic that has produced the belief that "between-meal-nibbling," and "sucking one's thumb," are abnormal behaviors. It is that type of logic that has produced so many of the dragons that have plagued us for thousands of years.

There are growing numbers of professionals who are fully aware of the absurdities associated with such terms as "learning disabilities" and "emotionally disturbed." Until recently, the number of alternative means to discuss children who were behaving differently than someone said they should, were limited. Those who suggested alternatives weren't always listened to. It was easier for many professionals to stay with the logic of the past; to stay with the mysterious terms that did little more than confuse and frighten. It was easier to avoid the real question: "What can be done?"

Hopefully, you are ready to look at alternatives to the irrefutable dragons, the questionable categories, and the technically sounding adjectives that describe very little. If you are ready, there is an excellent chance you will be able to help a child, and his parents, avoid an "unfortunate mistake" —

> The child who unpredictably explodes in violent behavior, who screams, tantrums, who is taken to an authority. The authority finds no physiological etiology. The choice is made to rely on the mystical terms. The choice is made to conclude the presence of an irrefutable dragon. The child is said to be "retarded," with "minimal brain injury." From the "authority's" point of view, the matter is settled. The names have been named; the "etiology" has been determined.
>
> The parents are skeptical. They recognize that the answers are safe, circular, irrefutable, and devoid of any information that might be helpful to them, or to their child. They decide not to accept what little has been provided.
>
> A second professional is asked to become involved. The professional is not afraid to admit his ignorance. The authority is willing to look at alternatives that can be tested.
>
> One is found. The child suffers from a unique allergy to the very air that is breathed. The child is *not* "retarded." In place of worthless description, comes prescription. The child and his parents survive the "unfortunate mistake."[36]

ALTERNATIVES

The Complexity of Causes

There is little chance of dislodging the notion that a singular "cause" might be capable of producing a complex set of "effects," or behaviors. Too many professionals in education and psychology make their living hypothesizing simplistic causes. This occurs despite repeated statements that such an approach does more harm than good. Over twenty-five years ago, we were told that —

> The terms 'cause' and 'effect' are no longer widely used in science. They have been associated with so many theories of the structure and operation of the universe that they mean more than scientists want to say . . . .[37]

Today, the warning continues with the hope that those individuals, who are in the position to suggest a possible answer to the question "Why?", will at least be aware of the dangers in hypothesizing causality —

> Educational researchers are constantly cautioned about the *problems in inferring causality* . . . Such cautions are necessary in that they remind both researchers and consumers of research of the importance of maintaining an open mind and of constantly considering other explanations of research findings.[38]

We have been told that not only must we be careful of assuming "causality" in general, we must recognize that thinking in terms of some singular "cause" for the subject areas we deal with, approaches folly —

> Most educators and researchers would agree that it is impossible, even erroneous, to assign a single cause to effects as complex as increases in academic achievement or reductions in juvenile delinquency . . . .[38]

It should be equally erroneous to assume a single cause for academic "failure" or social behaviors that are said to be maladjusted. Yet we continue to attempt to do so and our efforts have been duly characterized —

> A 'Rumpelstiltskin fixation' . . . [a term coined by Dr. Alan

Ross]. . . characterizes the preoccupation of some psychologists with whether a given child who manifests a learning disability is or is not brain-damaged. That question and related questions of etiology and classification often dominate psychological evaluations and staff conferences as if everything depended on that one answer. In a well-known fairy tale the chance for the princess to live her life happily ever after depends on her discovering the name of an ill-tempered dwarf. As a result she goes to great lengths to learn his name, and upon doing so, earns her salvation. Many clinicians and educators seem to engage in similar fairy-tale behavior. They act as if, could they but give the condition a name, the child would be saved. It is time that psychology and education lead the way in calling a halt to this labeling so that sooner or later, parents may follow. We must rid ourselves at long last of the mistaken notion that one of our tasks is diagnosis, 'identifying a disease from its signs and symptoms.' We should instead get on with the job of training, teaching, and rehabilitating the children . . . .[31]

The Alternative Explanations

The content over the next few pages provides examples of explanations from various professional fields (e.g., Psychology, Physical Medicine, Education) that are used to explain differences in children's behavior. I will characterize the explanations in terms of whether they are safe, irrefutable, etc., and whether they state that a problem exists within a child. I will estimate the value the explanations have for the parent and teacher. It is hoped that this information will provide the impetus to seek alternative explanations for observed behaviors when alternative explanations would seem justified.

Number One: PSYCHOLOGICAL —

Inside, Safe, Irrefutable, Circular

Explanations from this category include emotional disturbance, insecurity, mental retardation, ego-disturbances, immaturity, as examples. When these "conditions" are used to explain undesired or unacceptable behaviors, no one can be certain whether the explanations are right or wrong. The "conditions" are not directly testable. They exist on the basis of inference, not direct observation. As answers to the question "Why?", their value is extremely limited.

These explanations do not tell us what a child does or does not do. There are no universally accepted signs for the above "conditions." Thus when one of them is used to explain a behavioral deviation, we must 1) have a clear definition of the "condition," 2) know what signs are being used to suggest the presence of the "condition," and 3) consider the possibility that something else is responsible for the behavioral difficulty that has been observed. Let me give you an example of numbers 2 and 3 above.

Several years ago, some of my former students asked if I would be willing to have a debate with a professor who taught a course in "Abnormal Psychology." After discussing the proposal with the instructor, I agreed. The format was simple. The instructor would present a case, interpret the case, and suggest a possible "cause" for the presented problem. I would have the opportunity to agree with the instructor's opinion or offer my own.

The case involved a 35-year-old woman who had come to the instructor for psychological help. The patient had been married and divorced twice, and was contemplating a third marriage. Believing that something was wrong with her, and thus something within her was responsible for the two divorces, the woman sought the professional counseling in the hopes of avoiding another "failure." After several interviews and tests, the psychologist-instructor suggested that the woman not get married at this time. The psychologist indicated to the woman that she was a "latent homosexual" and that condition was responsible for her marital difficulties.

Behavior	**Why?**
1. Twice Married	Latent Homosexual
2. Twice Divorced	

The instructor, who was a very qualified clinical psychologist, suggested that psychotherapy was indicated and that after the "problem" had been resolved, perhaps marriage could be considered.

When she concluded her presentation, I walked to the front of the classroom that was composed of sixty or seventy students. I was about to offer an alternative view of the situation when a hand was raised by a young man seated toward the back of the room. I acknowledged his hand

and he said the following. "Perhaps I am wrong, but isn't it possible that the woman had *two lousy husbands?*" The class laughed, I smiled, and the instructor-psychologist agreed that it was possible. There was little else she could do, at least, in front of the class. Since I didn't believe I could have said anything more astute, I sat down and the debate ended.

Quite obviously, the "disease" of "two lousy husbands" would be almost as difficult to substantiate as "latent homosexuality." At least, an alternative view was offered and that, I felt, was the major purpose for my presence. It was comforting to note that a "naive" sophomore had the gumption to question the authority.

Number Two:
PHYSICAL —

Inside, Safe, Irrefutable, Circular

As with category number one, these explanations may be right or wrong. The proposed answers for the deviations are not directly testable. They indicate that something is wrong *inside* the physical make-up of the child.

Examples would be congested or clogged blood, as well as the wandering uterus. Today, those answers are no problem. Other examples, however, such as minimal brain dysfunction, hyperactivity, perceptual disorders (not visual or auditory acuity problems), organic as versus functional mental retardation, visual-motor-integration problems, dyslexia, learning disabilities, are believable. They are not, however, directly observable. They are said to exist only after a wide variety of behaviors have been observed. When the observed behaviors are explained through the use of the above constructs, the authority has spoken in circles. The terms are not acceptable when answering the question "Why?", unless there is unequivocal evidence to support their presence. If the evidence can be provided, the explanations will not come from this second category.

Frankly, in education, the above explanations have become waste baskets. They are used when no other explanation seems to fit. They do not help, though, because they fail to tell anyone what needs to be done. Thus, our task is to determine what behavioral differences are being used as a sign of the presence of the above "conditions." We need to consider the possibility that other explanations might be more accurate. We might also need to consider that no explanation is possible. Under the latter circumstance, we need to spend our energy exploring what can be done.

Number Three: PHYSICAL —

Not Safe, Refutable, Testable, Inside

This is one of the most difficult categories to make decisions about. These conditions are testable and capable of being confirmed. The problem is that while being confirmable, they may not be the "cause" of a behavior that is being looked at closely.

Examples would be vision and hearing acuity problems, allergic reactions to chemicals, or foods, cerebral palsy, Down's syndrome, San Felipo's syndrome, *confirmed* brain injury, *confirmed* neurological impairment, and epilepsy.

Let me show you some of the difficulties with this category. Suppose it has been confirmed that a child suffers from epilepsy. Seizures have been observed and EEG readings are positive. With medication, the seizure activity is controlled. Suppose the child manifests certain learning problems along with some social-behavioral problems. He doesn't appear to be interested in reading and he often has tantrums. Once his teachers are informed that he has seizure activity, it becomes very easy to attribute his learning and behavioral difficulties to the epilepsy. Although one cannot deny that such a relationship is possible, it is equally possible that no such relationship exists. It is equally possible that the learning and behavioral difficulties are related to any number of other factors that might influence the child. The notion of "cause" and "effect," when considering the learning and behavioral differences is, in this instance, incorrect. There are many youngsters who have epilepsy who are excellent, cooperative students. The point is that we have to be very careful about the conclusions that are reached once a physiological condition has been confirmed. It is easy to attribute any undesired deviation to that condition.

While a graduate student at Arizona State University, I was fortunate to have worked in a laboratory setting similar to the school that I presently consult for. The laboratory setting was part of an inpatient facility that housed some 150 children ranging in ages from several days old to 13 or 14 years of age. Several of the young children (five and six years old) were confirmed Down's Syndrome children. Being an inpatient facility, these children spent their days and evenings under the guidance of the staff that was responsible for their welfare. As with some state facilities, there were relatively few numbers of staff personnel assigned to each ward. On the particular ward where these children were located, there were two adults responsible for fifteen youngsters. This was a difficult situation for the two staff members.

They simply did not have enough time to work with each and every child. As a result, many of the children were tied to chairs — to prevent them from running off — or maintained in their crib-like beds for a large percentage of the daylight hours. In every instance, the children in the chairs were ambulatory. They could walk. However, several of the Down's Syndrome children who were maintained in their cribs were not ambulatory. They did not walk. When the staff members were asked why the children were kept in their cribs, their answer was a disheartening one. It depicted the reality of the situation. The two women admitted they were not sufficiently equipped to handle all of the children. It was, as they indicated, easier for them if some of the children stayed in their beds.

When asked *why* the cribbed children were not walking, their answer was more than disheartening. It was highly disturbing. Without hesitation, the staff personnel indicated that the children were unable to walk *because they were Down's Syndrome.*

Several of the graduate students, myself included, asked the staff if we could work with the children. Our intent was to teach them to walk, if at all possible.

With considerable skill and patience, the students, under the supervision of several psychologists, did teach several of the children to walk. It was a thrill for me, as a student, to see these little kids walk and play outside. It was also a very critical lesson for me. How easy it would have been (in fact, it had been done) to simply conclude that the condition of the Down's Syndrome, which had been confirmed, was somehow responsible for the non-ambulatory condition. Fortunately for the children, the graduate students were not convinced that confirmation and causality were necessarily one and the same.

The lesson we all need to learn regarding this category of explanations is, if a confirmed physiological condition exists, it is necessary to be extremely cautious about attributing behavioral deviations to the physiological problem. There are a lot of children today who have proved the authorities wrong. Many of them are doing things that someone said would never be done.

Number Four: SOCIAL-PSYCHOLOGICAL —

Outside, Usually Observable, Difficult to test

The explanations in this category generally do not say that anything is wrong with the child. Rather, they suggest that the child is reacting adversely to some observable, *outside* event that the youngster has experienced. The amount of influence these explanations are said to have on the child's behavior is often difficult to determine.

Divorce of the child's parents would be an example. Loss of a loved one, birth of a sibling, Christmas vacation, moving to a new home, would be other examples.

Most of these events have a negative valence. Most are emotionally laden. Authorities often assume that there are expected, "typical" reactions to such situations. They often assume that if the "typical" reactions do not occur, something is wrong.

There is little reason to expect that all children will react in the same manner to these events. It may happen that a child is relieved that a mother or father is no longer around, given the tenseness that accompanied a poor marriage. It is equally plausible to suggest that there will be differential reactions to the loss of a loved one or to Christmas vacations.

The basic issue is not whether the child is involved in the event. There is a good chance that he or she will be. The issue is whether the event can be considered a "cause" for any change in the child's behavior. The fact that two events (the outside incident and the child's home/school behavior) occur within a short period of time from one another, does not allow one to assume causality. It is rarely that simple. There is likely a relationship between the two events, but a relationship does not mean that one "caused" the other. An authority might incorrectly use the assumed relationship to account for changes in the child's actions and *continue* to use the relationship to explain various observations of unacceptable behavior long after the event has transpired.

One of the difficulties in validating these types of explanations is that we rarely have the opportunity to alter the event that is said to be the responsible variable. It is not likely that we could ask estranged parents to put it all back together so we could test out our hypothesis that a divorce "caused" a child to suddenly misbehave. On the other hand, there are occasions when we can test out some of our ideas. A good example of this occurred quite recently. One of the children in the deaf/blind classroom at "my" special school was observed to be having severe tantrums that had not been observed before with any great frequency or intensity. This took place during a brief period when the child's regular teacher was ill and forced to miss over a week of school. During that time a teacher, unfamiliar with the child and a person the child was unfamiliar with, initiated, quite by accident, a major change in the child's routine. When I was called in to observe the situation, I was unable to discern anything unusual. The substitute teacher was pleasant, warm, and noticeably caring. Yet the tantrums were occurring and something had to be done for the sake of the child, the teacher, and the other children. One of the instructional assistants, who knew the child and the regular teacher quite well, suggested that the tantrums were due, in part, to the change in routine. That was her hypothesis and, in this case, it was testable. A quick, but thorough, review of what the child was being asked to do disclosed what the assistant had suspected. Although the regular teacher had left a clearly spelled-out schedule for the child, it was not being followed to the letter. With some children, this probably would have made little difference. For the deaf/blind child, however, the routine might have been very important. The hypothesis was checked out. Once the regular teacher's schedule was reinstituted, the tantrums stopped almost immediately. Although no "cause" and "effect" conclusions were drawn, there did appear to be a relationship between the child's expectations of her routine and her accompanying behavior.

Inside the physical parameters of the school, such hypotheses are sometimes testable. Outside, however, it is very difficult to know whether a particular situation is influencing the child's actions. The danger in accepting and believing these types of explanations without some means of verification should be obvious. It is important, therefore, that you once again consider alternative explanations to the ones that are offered from this category unless some validation is possible.

Number Five: HONEST ADMISSION OF IGNORANCE — "I JUST DON'T KNOW WHY!"

Perhaps the most difficult answer *both* to offer and to accept! The difficulty results from the notion we have held for so many years that without knowing the "Why," we can't do anything about what we are observing. Quite simply, that is false. Today, we still do not know why cancer occurs. We have ideas that are in the process of being tested. But we do not know precisely what causes this dreaded disease. Yet, we are capable of doing a great deal about the outcomes of cancer. One day, the cause or causes will be found. At that time, we will be able to answer the question "Why?"

The idea of singular or multiple causality in education, psychology, and early medicine has produced many of the erroneous dragons that we have looked at throughout this book. If we desire, we can continue to perpetuate the idea of the existence of *the thing* which somehow is responsible for the problems that youngsters manifest. Or, when faced with a complicated situation, we can simply admit our ignorance and do the very best we can.

One of my colleagues once accused me of not being interested in the "causes" of various behaviors. That assumption was made after she observed that on occasion, I admitted my ignorance when asked the question "Why?", and didn't appear to be overly upset about doing so. Well, my colleague was wrong. I am most interested in what might be responsible for various behaviors. But in the absence of knowing an answer to a complex situation, I am not compelled to invent one simply to satisfy the orthodoxy of the past. The invented, unconfirmable answer will undoubtedly close some important doors. I do not have to do that.

Number Six:
FUTURE FINDINGS AND ANSWERS —

Not Safe, Refutable

One can only guess what the future will bring. The hope is that it will bring a lot. Not only do we want to know why birth defects occur, we want to know how to prevent them. Mental and behavioral retardation is maddening. It is purposeless. We want to know "Why?", and how to prevent it. Physical, neurological, developmental, educational dysfunctions are not needed. We can do beautifully without them.

The reality is that they are here. No sincere wishing will remove them. Science, its methods and dedicated personnel, will remove them, if they are removable.

What is equally unneeded are new answers that are no better than the old ones. New ones that are safe, irrefutable, circular and sick. We must watch for them. It is our fear of ignorance, our impatience, and our unwillingness to admit both, that breeds them.

Number Seven:
THE EDUCATIONAL ENVIRONMENT: ANOTHER CHOICE

As we approach the end of our journey, there is one additional alternative category that has to be looked at. It is the most complex of all. It includes explanations that are sometimes testable, sometimes not. It includes answers that are sometimes refutable, sometimes totally safe. Some of the answers suggest that the problem lies within the child. Others, however, place responsibility for the child's difficulties on the shoulders of the teaching environment.

This alternative looks at the child, but it looks at the child from a standpoint somewhat different from the other alternatives. It conceives of the child as being a highly unique individual with equally unique experiences and endowments. These experiences and endowments interact not only with each other, but they interact with the *present* academic and home environment in which the child finds himself or herself. It further conceives the child to be educationally and psychologically *healthy*, not sick. It views the child's behavior to be adaptive, appropriate, although not necessarily desirable from the standpoint of those authorities who are responsible for deciding whether the child should be behaving as he is. It contends that the child should not be compared with any other child for purposes of determining which one is better, healthier, brighter, etc. Its rationale for such a contention is that no two children are the same; that the concept of "peers" is inadequate, for no two children have had, nor presently have, the same experiences or endowments. It assumes a "zero-reject" or "zero-failure" attitude. If the child fails to accomplish that which someone expects, the failure is assumed to rest on the shoulders of the authority who has been given the responsibility for helping the youngster to accomplish the task at hand. It neither needs, desires, nor accepts the concept of psychological or educational diseases that are said to exist within the child. On the other hand, it fully accepts the reality of physiological and environmentally produced difficulties, but it holds with the notion that while the physiological disability may be of an irreversible nature, the environmentally produced ones are not. Even with the acceptance of a physiological disability, it does *not* concede that nothing can be done. It always assumes that compensatory skills can be acquired if the authority is skilled and the resources are available.

It is a reality based alternative. It recognizes the present limitations of technology available to the authority. It recognizes that not everything, which is desired for the child, can be accomplished today by any singular authority. It is not interested in the constructs of "fault" or "guilt." Instead, it is interested in what can be done, given the present conditions the child *and* the authority find themselves in.

It *is* interested in "causes." It is interested in hypotheses. It is interested in looking at all possible alternatives so long as the "causes," the hypotheses, and the alternatives are testable and subject to careful scientific scrutiny.

It is interested in both the child and the child's educational environment. It recognizes that without the former, the latter is unnecessary. It recognizes that without the latter, the former will not receive his due.

It is deeply interested in the child's academic growth, but more deeply interested in how the child feels about his experiences, his growth, and himself. It recognizes that the "3 R's," are only part of the child. It recognizes that the school-aged child has lived only a very small portion of his total life and while happiness may be related to a degree of proficiency with the "3 R's," his happiness is not totally dependent upon them.

It recognizes differences and welcomes them.

It is an optimistic alternative. If a remediation approach fails to live up to its predictions, another remediation approach is available.

It knows that time is *not* the key issue. It knows that what is not accomplished today, always has the promise of the tomorrows. It understands that not all children learn at the same rate, nor that all children are interested in learning the same thing at the same time. It recognizes emphatically that homogeneity, and all its pressures, is a convenience for the educational system and only rarely is a benefit for the child!

It recognizes that parents exist. It recognizes the complexity and the emotion that is involved in parenting. It recognizes that parents need support, that parents need to know what can be done, and what *they* can do.

It recognizes that the artifactual diseases we have been talking about occur almost exclusively between the ages of three-and-a-half and eighteen. It recognizes that these ages and these diseases correlate very highly with the years the child is enrolled in school. It recognizes that man's inability to admit his ignorance along with man's inability to find alternative explanations for the differences that exist amongst children have produced both the need and the names of the diseases.

This last alternative has the warm sound that rings of idealism. That is as it should be. It is idealism that leads a teacher to believe that he or she has something very special to offer each child. It is the idealism that allows the teacher to believe that all children can be reached, that all children can be offered successful experiences, regardless of how they compare with other children. It is the idealism that offers parents hope, usually when they need it the most.

The final alternative, however, is useless unless the teacher gives its biases an opportunity. It is not required. It is just an alternative. If it is rejected, the diseases and their reification will persist. Given that possibility, a few more items need our attention.

In a moment, I will present you with an awesome looking flow chart. It looks worse than it is. The chart will depict how a typical child might earn a disease-sounding label. The chart, and the accompanying discussion, will demonstrate the difficulty inherent in using differences in behavior as a sign that an "inside" problem exists. It will clearly state that differences, rather than being signs of an educational/psychological problem, should be signs that a change is needed in some authority's method of operation. It will further state that as a result of an overwhelming number of unknown factors that help to make a child what he or she is, differences should not be something that frightens. Differences, instead, *must be something that is expected . . . and accepted.*

Flow Chart Overview

Before we look at each item of the chart, let me outline its basic message.

1. When a child enters school, the first crucial thing that happens is that he is greeted by a teacher. Both the child and the teacher will be unique individuals, each with his or her own special characteristics, endowments, and experiences. (Steps 1, 2, and 3)
2. At some point, the child will be asked to accomplish a task. (Step 4)
3. Once the task is completed, to whatever degree of proficiency occurs, the child's "end product" will be evaluated. (Step 5)
4. Based on the authority's evaluation, there are two options. The first indicates that the child's work was satisfactory. If this option is selected, the child is given more work and the sequence continues indefinitely or until some deviation is observed in the child's work. The second option indicates that some deviation was observed immediately. (Steps 6-A, 6-B)
5. If the second option is chosen (Step 6-B), the question "Why?" is raised. (Step 7)
6. An answer to the question "Why?" once again produces a juncture. Typically, there are two possible answers. The first answer suggests that the problem, the deviation is due to some dysfunction within the child. That is the "disease" model. The second answer suggests that the deviation is due to an educational methodological error. (Steps 8-A, 8-B)
7. Depending upon whether 8-A or 8-B is selected, some treatment is invoked. (Step 9-A, 9-B)
8. The treatment brings about a new end product (Step 4) and the sequence starts again either from there, or from step 2.

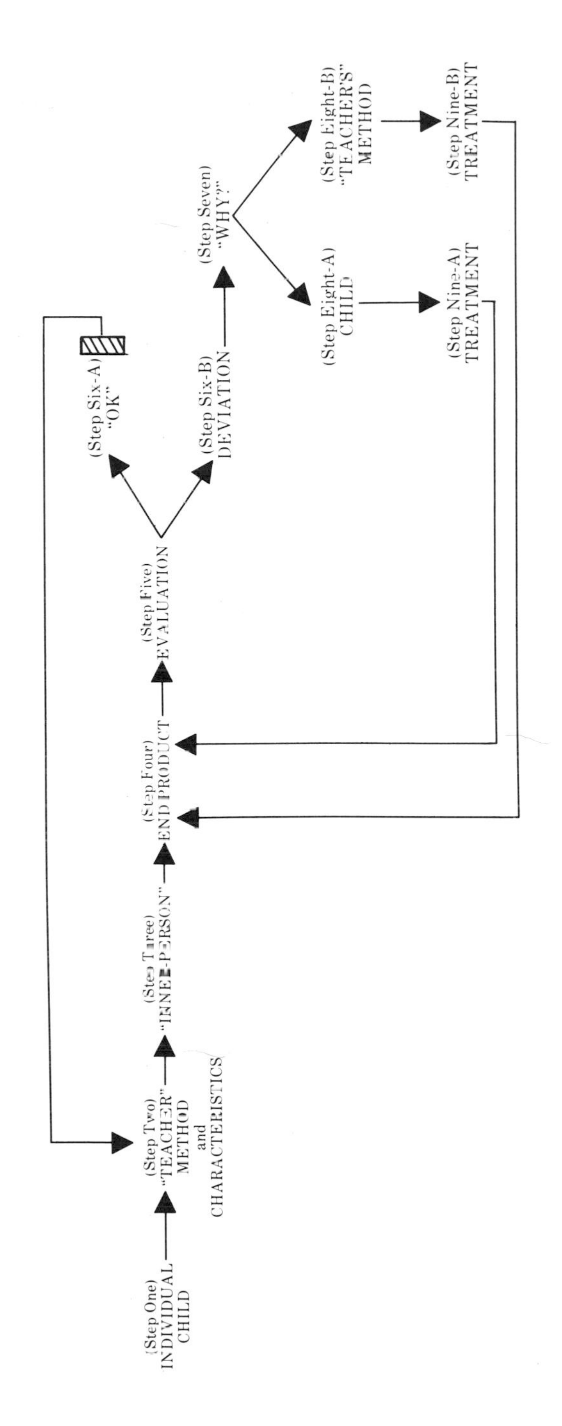
(Step One)
INDIVIDUAL
CHILD
(Step Two)
"TEACHER"
METHOD
and
CHARACTERISTICS
(Step Three)
"INNER-PERSON"
(Step Four)
END PRODUCT
(Step Five)
EVALUATION
(Step Six-A)
"OK"
(Step Six-B)
DEVIATION
(Step Seven)
"WHY?"
(Step Eight-A)
CHILD
(Step Eight-B)
"TEACHER'S"
METHOD
(Step Nine-A)
TREATMENT
(Step Nine-B)
TREATMENT

The chart does not depict the option of a "combined" responsibility of teacher and pupil (a combination of steps 8-A and 8-B) for the child's observed deviation. This omission is not to suggest that the two presented options are mutually exclusive, for they are not. Attempting, however, to determine who is "more responsible," teacher or student, is probably an unanswerable "chicken" and "egg" scenario. If such a debate is undertaken, it is likely the teacher will come out the "rose," while the child will likely be more an "onion." This may sound harsh, but there are grounds for my offered opinion. If you remember, we talked a little about the test batteries, reviewed by Coles, that are often used to determine the presence of a "learning disability." Dr. Coles suggested that the test battery had some inherently serious problems that made it difficult for him to evaluate the tests. One of these problems, or as Dr. Coles calls them "methodological deficien[cies]", is a most interesting one. Dr. Coles comments —

> Another methodological deficiency — and one which is extraordinary in view of the large number of studies that have been done — is that apparently no study examines the teaching and school environment of learning-disabled children to see how the quality of their education might have contributed to, if not actually created, the difficulties they encounter in acquiring basic skills. Despite the literature critical of teaching and its effect on children participating in learning-disabilities studies, the quality of the instruction these children receive is always assumed to be adequate — as well it must be if it is to accord with the definition of learning disabilities . . . .[32]

* * * * *

Now that we have looked at the basic thought represented in the chart, we need to look at each item separately. Frankly, the discussion is going to be a little "dry." It is, however, crucial. The problem with the concept of differences being synonymous with sickness should become very evident.

Step One: The Individual Child

Think, for a moment, of *all* the things that might go into making one child different from a second child. Knowing completely what makes up a child is one of those unanswerable, unending questions, for a child is never a static creature. Indeed, the challenge, the enigmatic charisma of the child is his constant, often unpredictable change from day to day.

Yet the continual changing, along with the enormous number of differences that exist among children, are rarely given the attention they deserve. The result is that "knowing" the child is often reduced to a few basic variables that are easily documented (age, sex, "I.Q.") and easily printed on a general information form. From these *known* variables, predictions are made about what a particular child *should* be able to do . . . is *expected* to do.

As we all know, a child is much more than what is known, what is written on a convenient form. A child is a composite of many things, most of which will *never be known.* It is the unknowable, more than anything else, that helps make the child different from any other child.

I will list a few of the important variables that go into producing differences among children. There are many factors that could be included within the list. Each additional factor that you might wish to include will result in making an individual youngster even more different than any other youngster. One last thing. As you look at the entries I have provided, consider how much the authority can know about each variable. Remember the *less* the authority knows about the child, the more *unknown* the child will be to all of us. Finally, the less we know about the youngster, the more cautious we must be about our comparisons and expectations.

1. *Genetic Predispositions.* If there is one general category that guarantees differences among children, it must be the genetic make-up of the child. While the field of "behavioral genetics" is still in relative infancy, one of the key words within the field is "variability."

> The concepts of genetics leads us to *expect* individual differences in behavior, because the mechanisms of hereditary transmission ensure that individuals are biologically unique prior to the onset of differentiating experiences.[39]

Science has yet to determine the full influence that our genetic system has on our behaviors — both social and intellectual. It is appropriate, however, to say that the influence is there and that differences are guaranteed. It is also correct to conclude that relatively few authorities know anything about the precise influence the genes have on an individual child's school behavior. From a genetic standpoint, at least, the child is a puzzle whose total composition is presently *unknown.*

2. *Physiological Parameters.* This category includes factors that are both known and unknown. Some of the obvious variables relate to hearing, vision, fine and gross motor skills, smell, touch, and the like. Variations within any of the above will produce variability within a youngster's behavior. Other variables include a child's metabolic system, his hormonal system, and his neurological system. Uniquenesses within these systems will also produce variability in behavior.

   A child's intellectual differences are also related to the category of physiological parameters. Presently, physiological intellectual differences are an *unknown* quantity. Intelligence tests do not tell us anything about a youngster's true intellectual capacity. While a child's school performance might give us an opportunity to speculate about his speed of learning, his ability to maintain information, and his skills in problem-solving activities, the physiological correlates to these activities are unknown. In fact, the vast majority of the subtle physiological influences that affect children are, for the most part, *unknown.*

3. *Interests and Values.* Different interests and values will help produce different actions and reactions from school children. You will be hard pressed to find any authority who would say that children of the same age will have the same interests or value the same things. While it is possible to determine some of a child's interests, the determination will require effort and time on the part of the authority. If the time and energy are not spent, a child's value system will, again, be an *unknown* quantity.

4. *Experiences.* While not diluting the importance of the above categories, this one is the most influential of all. Regardless of the importance of genetic predispositions, physiological parameters, and sets of interests and values, experience has the ability to magnify the differences they might produce. The term "experience" represents a process whereby events, occurrences, and reactions touch an individual and influence him in varying degrees. The degree to which these planned or chance encounters influence the individual is

unknown. These encounters begin at birth, and possibly before. A child is capable of being influenced by the encounters at that early time. The total number of potential experiential influences is enormous. The child is not capable of recounting all of the encounters. His parents, or significant others, can't do it either. The full impact of the few encounters that can be recalled are rarely capable of being remembered or described in complete detail. The quality of the encounters is very difficult to communicate, for our words rarely do the quality justice. What all of this means is that we are, in effect, mysteries to ourselves and to others.

From the standpoint of the individual child, his experienced success or failure with varying activities teaches him something about teachers, schooling, subject areas, and, again, himself. His parents, relatives, siblings, and "peers" teach him something about support, encouragement, love, patience, understanding and himself. And all, or part, or none, guarantee above anything else, differences — the etiology of which is rarely known, or, today, capable of being known.

Step Two: The Individual Teacher

Our unique youngster is now in school. He meets, for the first time, an equally unique adult, known as a teacher. The teacher is at least as unique as the child and probably two to five times more unique, for the teacher has undergone the effects of two to five times more experiences.

Among other things, our teacher teaches. Information is disseminated. Lessons are required. Workbooks are completed. Reading, math, spelling, social studies, etc., are practiced, printed, and handed in.

The child, being the student, is subjected to the teacher's method — the way the teacher talks, explains, understands, considers, and listens. The teacher is unlike any other teacher. The teacher and the teacher's method are different. Even if the child has had many teachers before, this one is new. This teacher, like the others, may have as many as thirty other unique children to work with. The teacher's method may be aimed at all children. The method may have been adapted to meet all the individual differences of the unique youngsters. The method may have been aimed at those children who are most responsive, most interested in what the teacher is interested in. The method may be the same for all the children regardless of the known and unknown differences. The attitude of the method may reflect the attitude of the teacher. It may be exciting, stimulating, motivating, or stifling. The specifics of the teacher's method may be unknown to everyone, even to the teacher. The method may be good or it may stink! One thing for sure: The teacher will be different; the teacher's method will be different.

Step Three: The "Inner-Person"

Teachers interact with children. Children interact with teachers. At this point the differences between the two major characters — the teacher, the student — come into sharp focus. In the process of teaching and learning, our characters' physiology comes together. Their genetics come together. Their expectations, prejudices, interests, values, and experiences come together. The "inner-person" represents the store house of all the uniquenesses and differences. As the child listens to what is said, all that may have transpired in the past may influence what he hears. When he is asked to perform some task, all that has happened and all that he is, will influence what he accomplishes and what he gives to the teacher. His interests, values, and perceptions will influence what he does and what he wants to do. His interests, values, and perceptions may be quite different from what the teacher *expects* or *predicts* they will be. The child's previously imprinted remembrance of his successes and failures will influence what he does and what he wants to do. His teacher will not know of most of those successes and failures. His physiology will influence him regardless of his motivation. His motivation will influence him as much, if not more, than the teacher's method. It is not likely that the teacher will know much about the child's subtle physiology or the factors that have helped to produce his state of motivation.

Young David was asked to write his name. The teacher expected him to do so. She also predicted, based on his *age*, what he should be capable of doing. She knew nothing of his physiology. Nothing of his present state of interest. She failed to determine, and thus knew nothing of his state of readiness, his developmental level, his prerequisite skills. She forgot for the moment that he was an individually unique child. She perceived him to be a member of a homogeneous group, with homogeneous characteristics, interests, and skills. She did not know that name writing was not top priority for the unique youngster. She did not know that "*R2-D2*" and "*Star Wars*" had earned that lofty position. The child did not share his "inner-person" with his teacher. That was not his responsibility to do so. The teacher did not share her "inner-person" with him, nor did she attempt to find out about his. There was not a great deal of similarity between the child and his teacher.

Step Four: End Product

As inevitable as the rising sun, an end product is produced. In schools, that's a guarantee. Not much need be said about this step. The end product may be verbal or nonverbal. It may be something written, said, or acted out. It may have something to do with math, reading, balancing on a beam, throwing a ball, or socializing with classmates.

It is usually something observable. Something measurable. Something capable of being graded. Something that lends itself to comparisons with others' end products. It may be the best the child can do. It may be all the child wishes to do at the moment. It may be something the teacher believes to be very important. It may be something the child could care little about. It may be something the child has experienced before. It may be something totally foreign. It may be something someone says has to be accomplished today. It may be something that could just as easily be accomplished tomorrow. It may be something that has been associated with success. It may be something that has brought only failure.

Step Five: Evaluation

Despite the unknown, the differences, the uniquenesses, the end product is evaluated. This becomes a most crucial step in our flow chart for part of the child is put on the line. What happens as a result of the evaluation can be critical, not only for the child, but for all of the people who are concerned about his welfare. The purpose of the evaluation becomes the key issue. It can be used in any one of the following ways —

1. To suggest that the child's work *and the child* are fine. This will occur when the child's work falls within the teacher's expectations of what the child should be able to do.
2. To suggest that the child's work *and the child* are not fine. This will occur when the child's work falls outside the teacher's expectations of what the child should be able to do, and outside the teacher's defined area of successful performance.
3. To suggest that the teacher's *method* is in need of some assistance. This will occur when the child's work is seen as being below expectations and when the teacher believes that his or her method may have influenced the degree of success

the child has manifested. This will occur when the teacher assumes the responsibility for the child's work.

4. To suggest that the child is *diseased* and belongs in a special category. This will occur when the teacher *assumes* that his or her teaching approach is sufficiently adequate to produce the desired successful performance and believes that assumption to be true, despite the child's performance.

In educational circles, more times than not, one child's work is compared with another child's work. Such methodology serves the educator's need to sort out children into categories of those who have it, those who don't, those who can, and those who can't. Group comparisons and comparisons with standardized norms accomplish that very successfully.

> . . . Standardized tests appear to be one of the more powerful and efficient sorting mechanisms available in modern societies. . . .[40]

Interestingly, the children who are being compared with one another are all unique, all *different!*

Evaluation of end products is a critical part of teaching. It can shine some light on the effectiveness of the teacher's method. But evaluation that reaffirms what is already known — namely that differences exist —is another issue. Evaluation of a child's progress as it is measured against *his own performance* is again a critical part of teaching. It might help an authority to determine that a particular approach needs to be altered to fit the child's style of learning. But evaluation that pits one child against another, when the two rarely start at the same point, rarely have experienced the same teaching methods, rarely have the same physiology, interest, or experience, can do little more than guarantee that one child will do better and be advanced in Step Six-A, the "OK" category, while a second child will not do as well and be "advanced" to Step Six-B, the deviation category.

Step Six-A: The "OK" Category

If a child's work is graded as acceptable, the child returns to Step Two, or Step Four. He is introduced to new subject matter and new educational experiences. He will once again face the teacher's method and uniquenesses. End products will come about, evaluations will be repeated, and the degree of success will be determined. The process will continue and will stop only when the child's work is viewed as being unacceptable or until he graduates.

Step Six-B: The Deviation Category

Now begins the road that will have a definite impact on the child's educational, psychological, and social future.

A deviation in the child's work has been noted. For whatever reasons, the child is not the same as some of the other children. To the surprise of everyone, the child is different. To the consternation of everyone, the difference should not exist. The assumption was made that the child was similar to the other children, so his work should be similar. But, things didn't turn out that way. The difference, the deviation is there and the inevitable, that has taken place for thousands of years, predictably occurs.

Step Seven: "Why?"

Somebody asks the question "*Why?*" It's a legitimate question, an important question. It sets the stage for an answer, an answer that is believed to be necessary. An answer that will tell everyone what the problem is and provide the hint as to what should be done.

Now, if you will, sit back for a moment. Recall what we have been talking about over the last few pages.

First: There are extensive numbers of factors that go into making the child what he or she is. Most of these factors are *unknown*. Our present technology is simply not sensitive enough to be able to catalog *all* that has transpired and *all* that has been given to the child that potentially influences what he does and what he is.

Second: There are extensive numbers of factors that go into making teachers what they are. Most of these factors are also *unknown*. The teachers, like the child, are different and unique. Their methods, perceptions, and motivations are different.

Third: The interactive factors between the child's and teacher's "inner-persons" that represent their histories, values, interests, prejudices, and experiences are both complex and, for the most part, a mystery. Any number of factors might interact with any number of other factors, and some "effect" *might* take place.

Think about these things and perhaps you will understand why the title of this chapter was, "The Complexity of Causes." The most astute conclusion that one should reach after reviewing all the factors, all the unknowns, is that the idea of a singular cause, *a singular answer* for educational or psychological difficulties, is, at best, highly questionable and likely ludicrous.

In education and psychology, we are not talking about *a* single cell that has gone haywire. We aren't talking about *a* vital organ that has weakened and can no longer do its part. We aren't talking about *a* potent virus, that on its own or in combination with other physical difficulties, has produced a debilitating effect.

We are talking about an unbelievably complex and unique *whole* youngster who has special endowments that we know very little about and has special experiences that we are equally unaware of. Then we take this youngster and place him in an educational setting whose important subtleties are as foreign to him as they are to those of us who think we know what's happening. From this complicated, intricate, predictably overwhelming state of affairs, we expect to find *the* cause, *the* simple, singular answer? Wow!

Even the idea that a singular or multiple answer is findable, much more answerable, should be sufficient to boggle the clearest mind. Yet we talk as if the answer is not only findable, but indeed has been found for the millions of children who are different than what someone expects them to be. Labels such as "learning disabled" and "emotionally disturbed" and "dyslexic" and "minimally brain injured" imply that the cause has been located. They imply that now that we know "why," we can get to the business at hand. No doubt our past has played a part in the belief that if you name what you believe the problem to be, you somehow can solve it. This was the logic used to invent the evil spirits, the body humidity, and the rest of the safe, circular, irrefutable dragons we looked at earlier. Our past has convinced those of us in the present that the "it" exists, and the "it" needs to be treated. Our past taught us the advantages of trephining and swirling people in chairs, and it sets the stage for us to pulse great quantities of electricity through people's brains and flood bloodstreams of young children with countless medicines in order to make them less different and more like "us."

The past has taught us to fear our ignorance and to do whatever might be necessary to eliminate it.

The "Why?" *is* an important question if it is used to stimulate alternative solutions to the complex problems that are observed while authorities attempt to educate young people. It, however, has outlived its usefulness if its intent is to produce a safe, circular, sick answer that leads the authority to believe that the "it" has been found. In education and psychology, there is *no* "it," and there aren't any diseases. What we have are children who differ from one another, who need special help from highly trained authorities who are no longer mesmerized by the fancy names and intellectual phrases. What we have are children, all children, who at some time in their educational experience will require that special something that teachers are supposed to provide. To accomplish that, we must give up our love affair with the simple and the artifactual. When we ultimately do that, we can then face the complexity of what really is and try to do something about it.

Step Eight-A & Step Eight-B: The Child, The Teacher

The two offered alternative explanations for the observed differences and deviations in the student's end-product *are obsolete*! To be accurate, the flow chart needs to be altered to include a group of factors that will likely never be known. The chart needs to look like this,

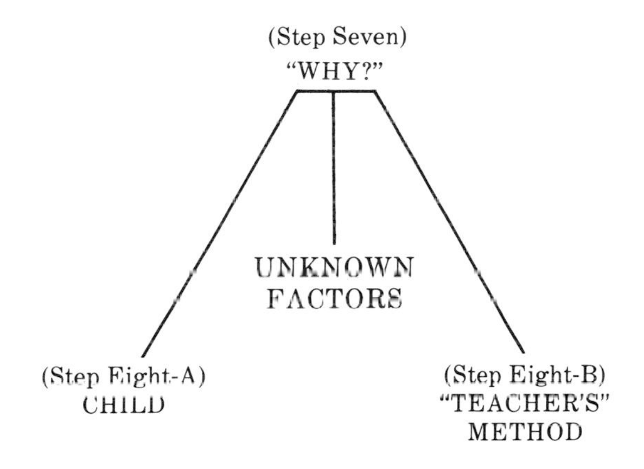

for the responsibility for a youngster's behavioral difficulties can neither be solely the child's, solely the teacher's, nor solely a combination of the two. It can neither be solely the physiology, the endowments, or the experiences. It can neither be solely the interests, values, perceptions, or prejudices of either party. It can't be solely the parents or their absence. It can be a combination of all of the above and of a lot more that is never given consideration.

Despite my assertion that it can't be any singular variable, the everyday educational, psychological, and medical worlds say I am wrong. The authorities continue to talk about children as if they have some inside, medically-sounding disease. They continue to use the pseudo-scientific labels to describe the children despite repeated pleas to stop it and repeated attempts to show that it serves no useful purpose for either the child or the child's teacher.

> Relatively little educationally pertinent information is conveyed by . . . categorical descriptions. Calling a child 'emotionally disburbed,' for instance, does not provide the special educator with any specifics regarding the child's instructional needs. Does he read, write, use language . . . pay attention, dress himself, follow instructions, adhere to safety regulations, move about competently, get along with others, and learn and remember information . . .? Does he show any significant physical deviation? These and more questions must be asked about any child who bears a categorical label. If the child did not carry the label 'emotionally-disabled' but instead carried the label 'learning-disabled,' the teacher would still be without the specific information mentioned. Thus, categorical labels based on the origin of a disability or the general 'condition' of a child have been found to be of little assistance to educators.[31]

The finger of responsibility cannot be pointed at any singular person, nor any singular thing — not if we are talking about educational and psychological "diseases." They do not exist and neither does the singular cause.

But the flow chart does offer us the phrase "Teacher's Method." It is the method that must become our major target for consideration. *Not* in the sense of a "cause," but rather something that can be altered and adapted to the child's deviation.

By looking at the method, we do not have to conclude that anything is wrong with either the child or the teacher. Rather, we can begin looking at the mechanics of the educational environment. We can look at the actual and intended operations that are going on within the classroom. We can begin to accept the attitude that differences amongst children exist; that differences are not synonymous with illness; that differences and individuality require different and individual programs and techniques. We can meet the needs of the child without ever having to suggest that the child is plagued by some invented "condition" that takes us away from what we really have to do — teach!

> When will we start working with . . . individual differences as we find them in our classrooms? When will we start to tailor an educational program to the needs of each child? If we are to give more than just lip service to the sacred dictum of the teaching profession, i.e., that we are to 'teach children,' then surely we will take our cues from the children we have and move in the direction of changing classroom management techniques and altering methods for building effective levels of performance.[41]

Step Nine-A & Step Nine-B: Treatment

The term "treatment," with all its disease connotations — "the systematic effort to cure illness and relieve symptoms . . . ."[1] needs to be replaced by the term "method." The simple change of the terms can be the beginning of a critical change in the professional's consideration.

When the *method* is considered, something very exciting begins to happen. First, questions are asked by dedicated, interested educators. "How can I help the child?" "What changes need to be made?" "What can I do to help him learn, understand, grow?" "What part of the puzzle is missing?" "What have I left out?" "What have I failed to consider?" "What could I do differently?" "How can *I* help the child!"

Second, enormous energy, cooperative energy, is spent looking for alternative ways to teach. Problem-solving, the kind that is mentally exhausting, begins to build. Ideas from other professionals are listened to, even tested out. Little things, that may have been overlooked, come into focus. Little things are tried.

Third, attitudes change. There is *no* failure *within* the child. There is only an inadequate method that needs more refining, more changes, more individualization. The pressure of time is ignored. The pressure of illness is not even considered.

Fourth, an end product is produced. Fingers are probably crossed, for everyone realizes that the term "authority" has been overused, that flying by the seat of one's pants is an occupational hazard, and that there are few, if any, guaranteed technologies. But the doers aren't upset with the absence of guarantees. They know that if the end product is less than what was hoped for, the drawing board is still there. New things can be tried. There's frustration, but not closed-door-pessimism.

Fifth, when progress occurs (it will, even though it may be small), there is a felt sense of satisfaction that is immeasurable. There's a teacher who feels awfully good about his or her efforts, and there's a child who is stronger and more ready for what is to come next.

The method is the solution. If a finger needs to be pointed, that should be its direction. It can take into consideration all the differences that exist. It can be adapted. It is the logical choice from Step Seven — the "Why?" Pointing to the child denies the reality of the differences that are there. It tells the child he is to be like everyone else. It tells the child that something is wrong with him. It answers the question raised by Albert Cullum in his "The Geranium On The Window Sill Just Died But Teacher You Went Right On"[42] —

> Don't you see my rainbow, teacher?
> Don't you see all the colors?
> I know that you're mad at me.
> I know that you said to color the cherries
> red and the leaves green.
> I guess I shouldn't have done it backwards.
> But, teacher, don't you see my rainbow?
> Don't you see all the colors?
> *Don't you see me?*

The Method: The Tool for the Non-Categorical Approach

The realization that there aren't any clearly discernible educational/psychological "diseases," has led to a movement away from categorical labeling and classification, toward a different scheme for providing services for large numbers of youngsters who have experienced mild or severe difficulties with school activities. While this task has not been an easy one, due in part to state and federal guidelines for purposes of funding, progress has been made. The state of California, for example, combined several categories that were once perceived as separate, exclusive conditions thought to warrant separate, exclusive treatment methodologies. Massachusetts went a step further. In that state, traditional categories of "diseases" were almost totally eliminated and the state provided aid "based on the type of services required to meet individual needs."[43] The state of Colorado has begun to consider an additional step. Presently, the state is conceptualizing a noncategorical certification approach for its special education teachers. Rather than teachers being certified in "mental retardation" or "emotionally disturbed," certification would be based on the severity of involvement on the part of children and on the type of services needed to meet the needs of those children. The Colorado concept paper was founded on the fact that "it was recognized that the present approach to the delivery of services to handicapped students was based on the fallacious assumption that the disability defined the *type of program* as well as the *competencies* of the *teachers* to provide the services. What was discovered was that special education children did not fall into neat categories simply because of their handicapping conditions. Rather, their educational needs overlapped several defined categories. The end product was to have many programs based on categories but no assurance that the handicapped were receiving appropriate educational services." The Colorado concept paper went further and indicated that . . . "school systems . . . are moving to a practice of grouping handicapped children according to the intensity of their educational needs rather than their handicapping conditions. Such grouping is especially true for children who are mildly/or moderately handicapped where handicapping conditions often create educational needs that are more similar than dissimilar."

The three states, progressive in their thoughts and actions, discovered, independently, that categorical placements on the basis of a supposed "educational disease" simply did not provide for the children what the states desired. They further discovered that no discreet, clearly discernible parameters separated one condition from another. Most importantly, they discovered that special strategies thought to be necessary for specialized handicapping conditions were strategies that were necessary for *all* children, whether the children were classified as special or not. They discovered that the irrefutable dragons of the past and present simply had no place in today's classrooms.

Programming for Differences

Implicit within these new conceptualizations is the fact that differences amongst children's behaviors will require differences in academic programming. Heterogeneity will be expected and accepted. The classroom teacher's methodology will have to be equally heterogeneous. Where a child may start on any academic task will have to be accommodated, for not all the children will start at the same level of difficulty. Neither will all the children be able to complete the same amount of work in the same amount of time. Goals will have to be accommodated to fit the differences in speed and ability to complete the expected work. The types of materials used in the classroom will also have to vary. Some children will benefit more from materials that have strong visual properties; while others will benefit from materials that are more tactual and concrete. The language the teacher uses within the classroom setting will also have to vary. Some children will simply not be able to understand some of the teacher's directions because the children will not be familiar with the words the teacher employs to get the message across.

The required list of methodological adaptations could go on for several additional pages. Regardless of their numbers, the major point would be the same: Children who are different will require different strategies. Since almost every child is different from one another, slight or even major alterations within programs will have to occur.

Frankly, it would be a whole lot easier to keep all the teachers' methodologies the same. It would be a lot easier to simpy conclude that if a child were unable to benefit from the "same" methodology, the child would be the one with the problem. It would be so much simpler to separate out the heterogeneity and to classify those children who didn't make it as handicapped.

Equally frank, no one would benefit from going back to where we have been. Certainly not the children. Not the children's parents either. So, we are faced with the decision of how to implement the different methodologies that will accommodate the differences within the children. To some degree, the accommodation has been put into effect with successful results. The importance of age has been diluted, for it has been recognized that age in itself guarantees little. The predictions of what a student should be able to do, on the basis of his present grade level, has also been diluted, for it has also been recognized that not all third graders either know the same or are capable of doing the same. Individualized approaches have been put into effect. If a child fails to be like everyone else of the same age, within the same grade, so be it. No one becomes overly alarmed. That which is observed is accepted, and the teacher's methodology moves from there. It is the child's individual needs, not his evil spirits, that receives the bulk of the educators attention.

Partnership for Success

It is a wise teacher who accepts help from anyone willing to learn what needs to be done and willing to do it. Few teachers can afford to go it on their own. The profession is too difficult. Parents are in an excellent position to support a teacher's efforts, but often times parents are uncertain about the potential they have for helping their youngster. Part of their uncertainty stems from an unfamiliarity with the methods used in the classroom. Over the next few pages, I will mention some of the components that should be a part of a teacher's approach. Most teachers are very familiar with these components. As a parent, it would be helpful to be equally aware of them, particularly when parent-teacher meetings are held. With this information, the question "Why?" will occur less frequently. The question, "What can we do" will take precedence. When both teacher and parent speak, and understand, the same language, both can help each other help the child.

Goals

Early in a school year, a teacher begins to establish a clear set of goals for each student within the classroom. Once established, the goals represent behaviors that are directly observable by the teacher, the student, and the parent. They are expressed so that each party knows 1) what the goals represent, 2) what is needed to be done in order to accomplish them, and 3) when they have been accomplished. They need to be as unambiguous as possible.

The purpose for this desired precision is to enhance the teacher's accountability. The precision aids the teacher in determining the effectiveness of the methodology. If the goal is not accomplished, or progress toward the goal is not attained, the teacher looks carefully at the procedures being used and makes the necessary modifications.

Math, reading, spelling, and name writing lend themselves to precisely stated goals. The correct solution of 80% of single digit addition problems with sums no greater than ten, on a fifty item exercise, is a clearly stated goal. It may not be a very romantic or exciting goal, but it is a precise one. But math, reading, spelling and writing are not the only areas where growth is desired. There are areas that are more romantic and equally fundamental. Problem solving, inquiry training, creativity, comprehension, hypotheses testing, imagination, invention, and good old understanding are examples of these other areas. Teachers, who help children experience success in these areas, still maintain the needed precision when describing what they would like the youngsters to accomplish. The problem with these areas should be apparent. Different students and teachers might interpret them to have different, necessary operations. While on the surface that might appear to present insurmountable difficulties in terms of precision, such does not have to be the case. What will be necessary is for the teacher and student to agree on the specifics of the operations as they see them. The teacher needs to determine the answer to the following question: "What does the student have to do in order for me to know that the student is demonstrating problem-solving, creative, or inventive behavior?" The emphasis must be on the word "doing." That is the word that reflects the operations desired on the part of the student. Once the operations have been clearly defined, the teacher, parent, and student will know what is expected in order to accomplish the goal.

Present Performance and Developmental Levels

Precise goals are important, but they will have little immediate utility if they are neither relevant nor appropriate for the child. A goal must take into consideration a student's skills and prior experiences. Teaching a child long division may satisfy a teacher's or parent's needs, but it won't be of much benefit to the child if he has yet to fully understand that the number five represents a specific number of objects.

Perhaps the most crucial measurement or form of evaluation a teacher obtains is a measure of a child's Present Performance Level (PPL).[44] It is absolutely essential to carefully find out what abilities each child has acquired either through his or her own unique experiences or through his or her physical maturation. Age will not tell us what those abilities are; nor will the child's present grade level. Nothing so simple will be sufficient. Rather we must measure, with great care, the precise skills the child has in math, reading, writing, concept formation, receptive and expressive language, and the like. We must know what the child has going for him, rather than what we believe he has going for him. By failing to find out what he has, we may assume he has *more* than he does, or *less* than he does.

When I was a senior in college, the very last class I had to take was entitled, "Beginning Conversational Spanish." Frankly, I had heard it was one of those "cribs," where a grade of "B" was assured if one showed up to class fifty percent of the time. I will tell you ahead of time, that information was false! The first day of class, a very attractive Señorita introduced herself to the approximately thirty students who had enrolled. From the first moment of the first day, she *never once* spoke a word of English! It was "Hello," in Spanish, "What is your name?" in Spanish, and "This class will be enjoyable" — in Spanish! The "Hello" was no problem. The name was no problem. Beyond that, everything else was. There was no question that graduation was important enough to motivate us to learn enough to either answer her back or ask her six times to repeat whatever it was that she had said. In truth, the class was a bust. We learned a thimble full, where we should have learned a whole barrel full. Part of that was our fault, I'm sure. I think. But given our youth, our absence of wisdom, and our inability to predict the future, Spanish, at that time, did not have a great deal of relevancy. Who would have ever thought, that some twenty years later, it would have been absolutely necessary to tell a cab driver, driving very fast through some hills in Mexico, to slow down. He spoke no English. I spoke no Spanish. At eighty mph, at midnight, it was not chummy.

All the Spanish professor needed to do was walk into the class, say hello to us in either English or Spanish, tell us in English what she had in mind, and find out how much Spanish we knew. As it turned out, some of the students were fluent. For them, it was a crib. They could have helped us. In fact, some of them did. But she didn't. We would have at least learned something from her had she started us at a level we could have understood. Instead, she started us at *her* desired level, rather than *our* actual one. She got paid for what she did, and we passed. I can't conceive that any of us benefited much from the experience.

The above story is not too far-fetched from what often happens in today's classrooms. Teachers ask children to perform tasks for which they do not have the necessary prerequisite skills. By doing so, they speak to the students in a language that is next to impossible to comprehend. The teacher then becomes upset with the students. The students become upset with the teacher, and we are back, into the bust.

The avoidance of such a situation is possible. It does, however, require effort, a lot of effort. It requires an individual examination of all children, for every subject area undertaken by the teacher. It might take a week or two weeks during the first month of school. In addition, the "test" will have to be administered each time a new "academic" subject is introduced. Because it is a very time consuming activity, some will not attempt it. For them, it is a lot easier to expect all students to speak the same level of Spanish. If we choose not to determine a child's present level of proficiency, we are inviting a dragon to step inside.

Let me show you what the PPL can do —

1. The PPL will show where the individual child is in reference to the goal the teacher hopes to accomplish. It will let the teacher know whether the youngster has already attained the goal, whether he is close to it, or whether he is simply nowhere near it.
2. It will tell the teacher where to begin his teaching or remediation program.
3. It can tell the teacher that a program's methodology is not suitable for a given child at this point in time.
4. It will give a teacher an accurate way of avoiding comparing child A with child B. It will tell the teacher where each individual child stands, and what strengths each individual child has.

By taking the measure, the teacher will be able to determine the logic, or cognitive approach, the child is using. The teacher will be able to sit with an individual child and determine what he was thinking about when he gave his answer. The teacher will discover that the correctness of the student's answer is not as important as the approach he used to devise his answer. The teacher will have a better handle on what types of words and concepts the youngster is having difficulty with and what types of words and concepts will be needed to help him. The teacher will literally be able to prepare a program tailor-made for the student.

Academic PPL's

Academic PPL's are are best determined by the use of an examination that directly tests the skills that are necessary to accomplish a particular goal. The examination can either be oral, written, or motoric. Teacher made tests are very suitable so long as they measure the criteria that will be used to determine the accomplishment of the goal. The examinations are not graded. Rather, they are analyzed in terms of the following:

1. At what point do the correct answers cease to occur reliably.
2. What skills are missing that would have enabled the student to produce further correct answers.
3. Is there a consistent pattern in the incorrect answers.
4. What cognitive steps did the child use to produce his answer.

The examinations are designed to determine the child's ability to handle a variety of tasks. Simple addition problems, sounding out words, drawing a straight line, writing a book report, are examples. There are very few limitations. What is necessary is to determine what the child is expected to do and what the child is presently able to do.

Language PPL's

It is really unfortunate that this discussion is even necessary. Its point is very obvious.

In the present context, the term "Language" is being used to represent the words that are used by a teacher to ask questions, convey ideas, make requests, describe directions, and provide feedback to a student. The term is also being used to represent those words that a student will find on assignment sheets that are meant to tell the student what to do.

The English language may be English to those of us who understand it, but it may be Greek to a student. All that is necessary is to use a word that the child is unfamiliar with and whatever is being said rapidly approaches worthlessness. Most teachers do not have a very good idea of a particular child's "useable language" — the words and conceptualizations that are viable and meaningful. Assumptions are made as to what a child *should* know, based on the child's age or grade level, but rarely are the assumptions checked out. The result may be that a child is asked to do something, he may be able to do it, but he doesn't quite know what he is being asked to accomplish.

A PPL measure of a child's language ability is certainly as important as the measurement taken to determine the child's prerequisite skills in math or reading. It is easy to obtain. All it requires is that a teacher double check that what is being said is being interpreted correctly. The teacher's question, "Do you understand what I mean?" is rarely sufficient. Too often it is followed by an affirmative nod that guarantees little more than that the youngster has some control over the muscles in his neck. When the teacher has the slightest suspicion that the student does not understand, the child should be asked, prior to doing the assignment, to show the teacher what was requested.

The experiential differences of children guarantee language differences. If we fail to find out the useable language of a particular child, we may set him back to a point where progress will be very difficult. If that happens, it may appear as if the child is having a problem. In truth, however, it is our problem.

Interest/Values PPL's

The more information we are able to obtain about what a youngster values and what areas hold the most interest for him, the better we will be able to develop a unique curriculum program that will turn him on. This speaks about the issue of the child's motivation, or specifically what the child is motivated by. By taking several hours during the first few weeks of school to sit down with the children and explore what they value, we'll gain information that might help us make curriculum compatible with their present interests.

The issue is more than simply making curriculum palatable. The more exciting it is to the student, the greater the chance he will want to invest himself into it. Without the interest or investment, his performance might be reduced appreciably. The absence of a desired or expected behavior can be used as a barometer to suggest that a child is incapable of completing some task. The absence may not be directly related to his incapacity, but to his view that the task is not worth his effort. It is critical that we discriminate between an absence of *ability* and an absence of *motivation.*

Sequential Learning

Frankly, a machine can set forth goals and measure, to some degree of efficiency, various PPL's. To my knowledge, however, no machine can adequately present the subtle material necessary to help the child grow from his PPL to his goal.

The most exciting part of teaching is the careful analysis and delivery of experiences and materials that help students acquire skills that teachers believe are necessary for a student's independent functioning.

It is the most difficult part of teaching, for it requires something beyond text books and materials. It requires that a teacher have an innovative and constantly turned-on educational mind. It requires a controlled sense of gambling, a willingness to take a chance.

Once a goal has been determined and the PPL measured, the teacher asks the question, "How do I help the child move from where he is, to where I would like him to be?" It is a "brain-storming" exercise that is exciting . . . never ending . . . not always successful . . . sometimes very frustrating, but it continues for as long as the individual child is enrolled in the class. It is a question that attempts to determine what the child needs to experience in order to move from point A to point B. It asks, "What part of the puzzle is missing?" It seeks to find that part and help the child discover its educational value.

Sequential learning looks at the problem a child is having with some piece of curriculum. It seeks out the steps that will help the child solve that problem. It takes the problem and breaks it down into its component parts. It continues to break it down until the point at which the child can succeed. It takes the letter "b," if the letter "b" is a problem, and separates it into its line and curve. If that is not sufficient, it breaks the line and curve into small dots. If that is still insufficient, it takes the child's hand, places it within the teacher's hand and together, they find a way. It does not wait for a dragon to show its face. It aggressively attacks the confusion and the absence of understanding manifested by the child. It looks at where the child is coming from and what skills the child has going for him. It works directly on the deficiency.

Trials to Success

In selected cases, this final point may be the most important one requiring investigation on the part of both parents and teachers. It speaks to the issue of how long it takes a child to learn a particular concept, or how many presentations of a piece of material are needed before a child masters that which was presented. The findings of such an investigation will help educators determine the type of setting that would be most beneficial to the youngster.

If the trend continues, as it is predicted to do, students will be grouped and serviced on the basis of specific needs rather than disease categories. Knowing how many trials it takes in order for a youngster to achieve success will be a critical component of the needs assessment. A child, for example, who appears to be a "one-trial-learner" (who learns the material the first time it is presented to him) will likely require less individual time from a teacher than a youngster who is, let's say, a "ten-trial-learner." While both of the above children might find themselves in the same classroom, a child who is a "fifty-trial-learner" might be better off if he or she were in a classroom with fewer numbers of other students — at least during times of academic learning.

How much teacher-time a child will require at a particular point in time is a very important question. The determination of a child's "trials to success" will tell us more about the child than any "intelligence" test could ever tell. We need to know if the amount of time the child will require is beyond that which a teacher, with thirty students, can provide. If that is the case, for the child's sake, we have to face it. If sufficient support services are available to the child, thus making it feasible for the child to remain in a large classroom, then fine. If not, then a smaller class, where a teacher will have more time for the child, must be considered.

Overview

The above speaks to the issue of individual needs. It speaks to the assertion that all children, regardless of whether they are labeled anything else but children, need individualization. If it is believed that individualization is too time consuming and cannot be accomplished given the present school system's limitations, then let's finally concede that the schools are not doing all that they could do. Let's do it, be done with it, and cross our fingers hoping *most* children make it through, educationally and psychologically unscathed. At that same time, let's not blame the kids for our failure to do what is necessary!

It is easier to "blanket" curriculum and methodologies. It is easier to treat each child as if he should be like everyone else. It is easier to ignore the fact that all children are different. It is easier to assume that a child who is different is also diseased. It is easier to do the above, little question of that. But if we take the easy way, we will perpetuate the existence of the irrefutable dragons. That's a guarantee.

Individualization will not eliminate the dragons. Some children do have legitimate difficulties that make growth and success more difficult for them. But individualization will make it easier for us to determine which dragons are legitimate, which dragons are a result of our inadequate methods, and which ones are born out of ignorance and our fear of ignorance. The latter ones are safe, and help no one.

The Pin the Tail on the Donkey Game

As a little kid, at a birthday party or two, I played a game called "Pin the Tail on the Donkey." Maybe, you too. As I remember, it was a fun game, although it was difficult to accomplish the main objective. It wasn't until recently, while I watched my daughter Kim and her friends play the game, that I realized why it was so difficult. The pregame preparations made it almost impossible to find what one is hoping to find.

The purpose of the game is to stick a pin, with its accompanying tail, on the rear end of a two dimensional donkey. Before making that attempt, however, the following takes place. The player, with pin in hand, is blindfolded. Great care is taken to assure that the individual cannot see what she is doing. If that would not be enough to insure that an occasional pin would find the poor donkey's ear, the player is spun around several times, inducing a confusing state of disequilibrium. The result of that maneuver is the erasing of whatever directionality the player has tried to hold on to, to help her on her way. Then, because of the humanity that exists in all of us, someone positions the player in the general direction of where the donkey is attached to a wall, and with an affectionate pat on the back, the humanitarian whispers, "Lots of luck!"

It's a kids' game. It is obviously a lot of fun for the participants. It is apparent, however, that kids aren't the only ones who indulge themselves in the activity. The logic and history that we have looked at strongly suggests that trained, dedicated professional adults have been playing the same game as the kids. They, too, with "pin" in hand, have attempted to place the pin's point in the anatomical area they have believed to be correct. However, while the children have hoped to find the donkey's derrière, the professionals have hoped to find the explanation for school aged children's unacceptable and unpredicted differences in behavior and performance. In my judgment, the birthday child's efforts have met with more success. Every once in awhile, she has found the sought after rump. For the professional, no such piece of anatomy exists.

It can be argued that the adult's blind stabbing, no matter how noble in intent, has resulted in the loss of critically needed information. We have been so occupied with the "Why's?" of the unaccepted, that we have nearly neglected the more important "What To Do's." Every day, in almost every classroom, teachers (and ultimately parents at home) are faced with the task of determining how to help one, or several, youngsters. As a once trained "ghost hunter," but now as a professional "brain stormer," I, too, am faced with the "What in the world do I do to help that child?" While I can run to literally hordes of books that will theorize the "Why's?", I am left with only a few whose brave authors have taken a chance at a "cookbook" format. As a practitioner, I have found the few to be considerably more valuable than the horde.

My hope is that I have convinced you that we no longer need names, labels, or categories that give the false impression that differences of children can be packaged in neat, easily differentiated boxes. Such differentiation is simply not possible, given the present state of our knowledge. My additional hope is that you now realize that what we need is an enormous growth in the types of methodologies that can be used with all children.

For those of you who have yet to be convinced, those who still believe that the "Why's?" are more important than the "What To Do's," allow me to suggest that you need not search for the answer to the "Why's?" any longer. The answer has been determined. Indeed, it has been known for thousands of years. It hasn't changed, despite the passage of all that time. It has been ignored. It has been repudiated. But it has withstood the epithets thrown by those who have tried to deny it.

The Absence of Behavior and the Question "Why?"

If I were to tell you that we now have absolute, unequivocal, undeniable evidence that the *moon* is responsible for the differences and deviations that are observed amongst school children, what would be your reaction? Probably, despite the "undeniable evidence," you would deny it. I'm sure the same reaction occurred when the first scientist proclaimed that the moon was responsible for the changing tides of the great oceans. The moon? Too far-fetched. Too far away, for that matter.

Well, the other day in one of my graduate classes, I asked my students, "What would you do if it were shown that the moon was the correct etiological explanation for school children's deviations?" After they uttered a few phrases that implied that I had lost my sanity, they sat quietly. I did the same. Finally, one of the braver ones spoke.

"You'd have to accept it, I guess," she said. "Not a whole lot we can do with the moon."

"Like the tides," another student ventured, "we could predict that the deviations would occur. In time, we would probably know how many serious deviations we could expect each year."

"With luck, if we could determine that the moon's influence occurred primarily during conception, we might ask prospective parents to plan more carefully when conception would take place," a third student offered.

"Do you think you could convince parents to do that?" I asked.

"Probably not all of them, I'm sure," the student responded.

"And the outcome of that?" I persisted.

"We would have a certain number of deviations," the student said.

"Okay, you have the deviations. They are predictable. Now, what are you going to do?" I asked.

"The only thing I can think of," the first student said, "is that you would have to *work with the children, whatever they were like.*"

"Would you forget the etiology?"

"No, but in the case of the moon, there is not much I can do about it," she replied.

The class did not end on a pessimistic note. Rather, on a realistic one. It also did not end with the belief that the moon was responsible. Yet no student was able to refute the possibility of such.

Before the students left the class, I asked them to provide to me, on the following day, an alternative to the idea of the moon as an explanation. I knew what I was looking for and I hoped that one of them would discover it. As it turned out, one did.

"It is the absence of the expected behavior that places us in the position of seeking out the etiology," she began. "When a student does everything that is expected of him, the question of 'cause' is never broached. It is only when he is different that the search begins.

"Yet being different is something that most students have to be," she continued. "It is not difficult to know *why* that has to be the case. While the answer to the question 'Why?' is not the moon, it is, nevertheless, something like the moon in respect that there is *not* a lot we can do about it. We can definitely help the student, but we can't influence, to any degree, that which is responsible for the differences that exist amongst the students."

She stopped talking for a moment and walked to the front of the room. After erasing the chalkboard, she wrote the following.

"WHY?"

1. Endowments
2. Experiences

> Both Unknown Quantities

"For the individual child, there's your etiology," she said. "There's the Why! It is really quite simple. Obvious! It is also unbelievably complicated. With only the most extreme exceptions, the degree of their influence is unknown. Assertions as to what part each play in the behavior of children is neither completely verifiable, nor refutable. Yet, there's your etiology.

"The intellectual argument should not be whether it is a nature or nurture, endowments or experiences, question. It can't be an either/or proposition. It has to be both, for it is impossible to conceive that one can work independently of the other.

"From the practical standpoint, the argument approaches foolishness. By the time a child sets foot into a classroom, the question of etiology is moot. So much has happened to the child, so much that we can know so little about, that we are left simply with the child — what he has, what he has been given, what he has experienced. Like the moon, his endowments and experiences from the past are situations that we can do very little about. We are left with the pressing responsibility of providing for the child all that our time and resources avail.

"The answer to the question 'Why?' is as known as it can be — at least today. The answer may not be very satisfying, nor popular, but our ignorance prevents us from knowing more. All the invented shots in the dark will not change that. Our knowing what to do in behalf of each child is limited only by the time we spend on matters that do not relate to the direct question of the child's presented deficiencies and needs. The drawing board, upon which inventive ideas will be proposed as to 'What To Do' is available to all who accept the responsibility for the child. That is where our genius is needed now."

* * * * *

When the day finally arrives when we will reluctantly, or gladly, admit that the likely etiology of children's differences is buried in the unknown complexities of the children's own physical and experiential uniquenesses, we will no longer need the categorical-labeling approach. We will no longer become frightened of the unknown or unpredicted. No longer will the absence of expected, hoped for behavior send us scurrying into the comfort of our intellectual caves where pin-tailing can occur without being confronted. Rather, we will admit that the absence of the expected will be used as a sign that a problem exists, that it will serve as a catalyst for our energies. It will be the flare that tells us that we must look at what *we*, and the educational system, are doing. What fault exists, lies within our absence of methodologies. It does not lie within the child.

We do not need the irrefutable dragons. There are alternative paths which we can take, and none of the alternatives have to suggest that there is something wrong with the child.

Footnoted Bibliography

1. Urdang, L. (Ed) *The Random House Dictionary of the English Language.* New York: Random House, 1968.
2. Haring, N.G. (Ed) *Behavior of Exceptional Children.* Columbus, Ohio: Charles E. Merrill Publishing Company, 1974.
3. *Readings in Special Education.* Guilford, Conn: Special Learning Corporation, 78/79 Edition, 1978.
4. *College Catalog.* Guilford, Conn: Special Learning Corporation, 1979.
5. English, H.B. & English, A.C. *A Comprehensive Dictionary of Psychological and Psychoanalytical Terms.* New York: David McKay Company, 1958.
6. McCall's, Vol. *CVI,* No. 4, January, 1979.
7. Suran, B.G. & Rizzo, J.V. *Special Children: An Integrative Approach.* Glenview, Ill.: Scott, Foresman & Company, 1979.
8. Schrag, P. & Divoky, D. *The Myth of the Hyperactive Child and Other Means of Child Control.* New York: Dell Publishing Company, 1975.
9. Gardner, W.I. *Learning and Behavior Characteristics of Exceptional Children.* Boston: Allyn and Bacon, 1977.
10. Hammil, D.D. & Bartel, N.R. *Teaching Children with Learning and Behavior Problems.* Boston: Allyn and Bacon, 1975.
11. Thorpe, L.P., Katz, B., & Lewis, R.T. *The Psychology of Abnormal Behavior.* New York: The Ronald Press, 1961.
12. Tift, K.F. The disturbed child in the classroom, *NEA Journal, 57,* 1968, 12-14.
13. Salter, A. *The Case Against Psychoanalysis.* New York: The Citadel Press, 1952.
14. Stuart, R.A. *Trick or Treatment: How and When Psychotherapy Fails.* Champaign, Ill.: Research Press, 1970.
15. Withington, E.T. *Medical History from the Earliest Times.* London: The Holland Press, 1964.
16. English, O.S., & Pearson, G.H.J. *Emotional Problems of Living -Avoiding the Neurotic Pattern.* New York: W.W. Norton & Company, Inc., 1963.
17. Schierbeek, A. *Measuring the Invisible World.* London: Abelard-Schuman, 1959.
18. Thompson, C.J.S. *Magic and Healing.* London: Rider and Co., 1946.
19. Ordronaux, J. *Regimen Sanitatis Salernitanum.* Philadelphia, 1871.

20. Haggard, H.W. *Mystery, Magic, and Medicine.* Garden City, New York: Doubleday, Doran & Company, Inc., 1963
21. Schachner, N. *The Mediaeval Universities.* New York: A.S. Barnes and Company, 1962.
22. Szasz, T. The myth of mental illness, *American Psychologist*, 15, *2*, 1960, 113-118.
23. Ackerknecht, E.H. *A Short History of Psychiatry.* New York: Hafner Publishing Company, 1968.
24. Alexander, F.G. & Selesnick, S.T. *The History of Psychiatry: An Evaluation of Psychiatric Thought and Practice from Prehistoric Times to the Present.* New York: Harper & Row Publishers, 1966.
25. Jurjevich, R.M. *The Hoax of Freudism.* Philadelphia: Dorrance and Company, 1974.
26. Freud, S. *Beyond the Pleasure Principle.* London: The Hogarth Press, 1948.
27. Ford, D.H. & Urban, H.B. *Systems of Psychotherapy.* New York: John Wiley & Sons, Inc., 1963.
28. Woodworth, R.S. & Sheehan, M.R. *Contemporary Schools of Psychology.* New York: The Ronald Press Company, 1964.
29. Freedman, A.M., Kaplan, H.I., & Sadock, B. *Modern Synopsis of Psychiatry.* Baltimore: The Williams & Wilkins Company, 1972.
30. Klein, M. *The Psycho-Analysis of Children.* New York: Dell Publishing Company, 1975.
31. Smith, R.M. & Neisworth, J.T. *The Exceptional Child: A Functional Approach.* New York: McGraw-Hill, Inc., 1975.
32. Coles, G.S. The learning-disabilities test battery: empirical and social issues, *Harvard Educational Review*, Vol. 48, *3*, August, 1978, p. 313-340.
33. Smith, R.M. *Teacher Diagnosis of Educational Difficulties.* Columbus, Ohio: Charles E. Merrill, 1969.
34. Reinert, H.R. *Children in Conflict.* St. Louis: The C.V. Mosby Company, 1972.
35. Clarizio, H.F. & McCoy, G.F. *Behavior Disorders in School-Aged Children.* Scranton: Chandler Publishing Company, 1970.
36. Bell, J.N. Nobody can help your child, *McCall's*, Vol. CVI, *No. 1*, October, 1978, p. 118.
37. Skinner, B.F. *Science and Human Behavior.* New York: Free Press, 1953.
38. Dyer, J.R. *Understanding and Evaluating Educational Research.* Reading, Mass.: Addison-Wesley Publishing Company, 1979.

39. Dushkin, D.A. (Publisher) *Psychology Today: An Introduction.* Del Mar, Calif.: CRM Books, 1970.
40. Orasanu, J., McDermott, R.P., Boykin, A., & The Laboratory of Comparative Human Cognition. A critique of test standardization, *Social Policy,* September, 1977.
41. Harshman, H.W. Toward a differential treatment of curriculum, *Journal of Special Education, 3,* 1969, 358.
42. Cullum, A. *The Geranium On The Window Sill Just Died But Teacher You Went Right On.* Holland: Harlin Quist, Inc., 1971.
43. Lilly, M.S. *Children With Exceptional Needs.* New York: Holt, Rinehart, Winston, 1979.
44. Macht, J.E. *Teacher/Teachim: The Toughest Game In Town.* New York: John Wiley & Sons, 1975.

Author/Subject Index

Ackerknecht, E.H., 95, 97, 103
Adler, A., 119
Age
- as a barometer, 10, 12, 21
- importance of, 21, 165-166, 174, 185, 187, 189

Alexander, F.G., 100, 101, 102, 103, 104, 105, 120, 121
Alternatives
- in the absence of, 15, 20, 53, 71, 73, 96
- need for, 6, 12
- physical 160-162
- psychological 158-159
- social psychological 162-164

Authoritative validity
- explanation of, 73

Bartel, N.R., 29
Bell, J.N., 154

Causes
- complexity of, 157-182

Circular answers
- logic of, 33, 53
- meaning of, 20, 34
- results of, 36, 69, 151-152

Clarizio, H.F., 152
Coles, G.S. 146, 147, 169, 170
Comparisons
- and conclusions, 14
- in education, 136-154
- use of, 13, 20-22

Cullum, A., 182

Differences
- acceptance of, 20, 22, 165-182
- and sickness, 12, 14-15, 21-22, 28, 70, 96-97, 131-132
- and the individual child, 170-173
- and their meaning, 13-14, 17, 19-20, 22, 35
- concept of, 11, 13, 15
- in education, 136-154
- programming for, 184-185

Divoky, D., 27, 28, 133, 134
Dragons
- accurate/testable, 66-68
- definition/explanation of, 65-66
- inside psychological, 105-125
- irrefutable, 46, 64, 66-72

Dragons
- accurate/testable, 66-68
- definition/explanation of, 65-66
- inside psychological, 105-125
- irrefutable, 46, 64, 66-72

Dushkin, D.A., 171
Dyer, J.R., 157
Dyslexia
- as a label, 142, 178
- definition of, 26
- prevalence of, 25
- treatment of, 26

Educational methods
- and non-categorical placement 183-197
- need for, 181-182

Educational/Psychological problems
- from within, 21-29, 34, 60, 64, 71, 105-154
- from without 26-27, 29, 165-197

Education's germs
- and differences, 138-154
- and diseases, 136-154
- and dragons, 132-136
- and exceptionality, 137-139
- explanation/examples of, 126-154

Emotional Disturbance
- as a label, 142, 178, 183
- as an explanation, 19-20
- circularity of, 34
- prevalence of, 24-26

English, A.C., 26, 97, 100
English, H.B., 26, 97, 100
English, O.S., 78, 79, 80, 124, 125
Erikson, E., 119, 120
Etiology
- definition of, 4

importance of, 4-5, 193-197
in education 177-179, 193-197
Evaluation
purpose of, 175-176
Exceptionality
explanation of, 137-139
Expectations
concept of, 13-22
results of, 14-15, 20-21, 174

Ford, D.H., 118, 120
Freedman, A.M., 120
Freud, S. 117

Gardner, W.I., 28
Goals
importance of, 185-186

Haggard, H.W., 85
Hammil, D.D., 29
Haring, N.G., 24
Harshman, H.W., 181
Hippocrates, 84, 129, 135

Iatrogenic disorders
explanation of, 70-71
Irrefutable answers
meaning of, 20
problems with, 46, 53, 67-68, 71 72, 80 81, 93, 104, 151, 193-197
results of, 34, 36, 42, 93, 126

Jung, C., 120
Jurjevich, R.M., 116

Kaplan, H.I., 120
Katz, B., 31
Klein, M., 121, 122, 123, 124

Labels
as adjectives, 32-35
as nouns, 32-35
examples of, 140-141
in the absence of, 165-197
the use of, 126-155
Learning disabilities
and the test battery, 146-147, 169-170
as a label, 142, 178
definition of, 148
effects of, 27
explanation of, 145-151
prevalence of, 24, 27
treatment of, 27

Levy, H., 152
Lewis, R.T., 31
Lilly, M.S., 183

Macht, J.E., 187
Masinter, I., 23
McCoy, G.F., 152
Medicine's "Germs"
and early dentistry, 85-86
and the "germ theory" 87-88
and the microscope, 86-87, 94
explanation/examples of, 83-93
prediction of, 88-93

Neisworth, J.T., 140, 141, 180

Operational definitions
explanations of, 142
Oracanu, J., 174
Ordronaux, J., 84

Pearson, G.H.J., 78, 79, 80, 124, 125
Peers
definition of 20-21
inadequacy of 166
Present performance level
academic, 189
explanation of, 186-190
interest/values 190
language, 189-190
Psychology's "germs"
and the balloon theory, 109-116
and their influence, 114-116
explanation/examples of, 94-125
irrefutable. 94-125, 104
that exist within us, 105-125
the logic of, 96-97

Rank, O. 120, 121
Reinert, H.R., 151
Rizzo, J.V., 26, 71
Ross, A., 157, 158

Sadock, B., 120
Safe answers
meaning of, 20, 34
results of, 33, 36, 80-81, 104, 126, 151
Salter, A., 61, 62, 63, 117, 118
Schachner, N., 86
Schierbeek, A., 83
Schrag, P., 27, 28, 133, 134

Selesnick, S.T., 100, 101, 103, 104, 105, 120, 121
Sequential learning
importance of, 190, 191
Sheehan, M.R., 190, 191
Sickness
educational/psychological, 20, 22, 35-36
examples of, 35, 140-141
diseases of children 136-154
prevalence of 23-29
Skinner, B.F., 157
Smith, R.M., 140, 141, 149, 180
Stuart, R.A., 71
Suran, B.G., 26, 71
Szasz, T., 94

Thompson, C.J.S., 84
Thorpe, L.P., 31
Tift, K.F., 31
Trials to success
explanation of, 191-192

Urban, H.B., 118, 120

Withington, E.T., 73, 84, 90
Woodworth, R.S., 119, 120